NORTHERN KWAKIUTL

BELLA COOLA

SOUTHERN KWAKIUTL

COAST MOUNTAINS

SQUAMISH

North Vancou

Vanc

SALISH

Strait of Georgia

Victoria

WASHINGTON

S

Kingcome

Mimkwamlis

Guyasdoms

Kalokwis

Alert Bay

Salmon R.

Johnstone Strait

VANCOUVER ISLAND

Quatsino

Nootka Sound

Hitats'uu

Ucluelet

CANADA
U.S.A.

NOOTKA
(NUU'CHAH'NULTH)

Hecate Strait

Cumshewa

Skedans

Tanu

Ninstints

Skidegate

HAIDA

QUEEN CHARLOTTE
ISLANDS

Pacific Ocean

0 Miles   50   100   150

0 Kilometers   150

© 2003 Jeffrey L. Ward

The Forest Lover

The
Forest Lover

Susan Vreeland

VIKING
CANADA

VIKING CANADA

Penguin Group (Canada), a division of Pearson Penguin Canada Inc., 10 Alcorn
Avenue, Toronto, Ontario M4V 3B2

Penguin Group (U.K.), 80 Strand, London WC2R ORL, England
Penguin Group (U.S.), 375 Hudson Street, New York, New York 10014, U.S.A.
Penguin Group (Australia) Inc., 250 Camberwell Road, Camberwell, Victoria 3124,
Australia
Penguin Group (Ireland), 25 St. Stephen's Green, Dublin 2, Ireland
Penguin Books India (P) Ltd, 11, Community Centre, Panchsheel Park,
New Delhi – 110 017, India
Penguin Group (New Zealand), cnr Rosedale and Airborne Roads, Albany,
Auckland 1310, New Zealand
Penguin Books (South Africa) (Pty) Ltd, 24 Sturdee Avenue, Rosebank 2196,
South Africa

Penguin Group, Registered Offices: 80 Strand, London WC2R ORL, England

First published 2003

10 9 8 7 6 5 4 3 2 1

Manufactured in the United States of America.

NATIONAL LIBRARY OF CANADA CATALOGUING IN PUBLICATION
Vreeland, Susan
The forest lover / Susan Vreeland.
ISBN 0-670-04481-4
1. Carr, Emily, 1871–1945—Fiction. I. Title.
PS3572.R43F67 2004   813'.54   C2003-905205-2

American Library of Congress Cataloging in Publication data available

Visit the Penguin Group (Canada) website at **www.penguin.ca**

For

C. JERRY HANNAH

who makes strong talk

There is something bigger than fact: the underlying spirit, all it stands for, the mood, the vastness, the Western breath of go-to-the-devil-if-you-don't like it, the eternal big spaceness of it. Oh the West! I'm of it and I love it.

—Emily Carr
Hundreds and Thousands, 1966

This is the forest primeval.
The murmuring pines and the hemlocks,
Bearded with moss, and in garments green
Indistinct in the twilight
Stand like Druids of eld,
With voices sad and prophetic.

—Henry Wadsworth Longfellow
Evangeline, 1847

Acknowledgments

A person can understand so much more with help. I thank the many people who have contributed to my understanding of Emily Carr. In particular, I am grateful for Paula Blanchard's *The Life of Emily Carr*; Susan Crean's *The Laughing One: A Journey to Emily Carr*; Gerta Moray's *Northwest Coast Native Culture and the Early Indian Paintings of Emily Carr, 1899–1913*; Doris Shadbolt's *Emily Carr* and *The Art of Emily Carr*; Maria Tippett's *Emily Carr: A Biography*; and Sharyn Udall's *Carr, O'Keeffe, Kahlo: Places of Their Own*. In addition, I wish to acknowledge the works of Amanda Hale, Edith Hembroff, Robin Laurence, and Stephanie Kirkwood Walker, each of whom provided a different angle from which to see.

Stepping into the experience of another consciousness can be daunting, but Carr left volumes of journals and narrative sketches which made this a joy. *Klee Wyck; Hundreds and Thousands, The Journals of Emily Carr*; and *Growing Pains, The Autobiography of Emily Carr*, all published by Clarke, Irwin, and Company, and her correspondence, *Dear Nan*, edited by Doreen Walker, published by University of British Columbia Press, gave me her characteristic phrases, which, like her trees, "go whiz bang and whoop it up."

I wish to thank my dear friends of the Asilomar Writers' Consortium for their continued literary guidance during the seventeen years which spanned the writing of this book; the Provincial Archives of British Columbia for making available Carr's unpublished papers; writer Bill Kittredge for his encouragement and reading of early drafts, and for telling me it's not a foot race; Steve Brown, former curator of Northwest Coast Indian Art at the Seattle Art Museum; Flora Sewid of Campbell River, British Columbia, whose recollections of Emily Carr provided information unavailable in printed material; actress and writer Helena Hale for sharing Emily's spirit; librarian Ross Parker for always coming back with an answer; Jan Ross, resident curator of The Emily Carr House in Victoria, BC, for her delight in the project; John Baker for his good-spirited sharing of ideas and sound advice; curator Sharyn Udall, for her scholarship in conceiving and executing the highly informative landmark exhibition *Carr, O'Keeffe, Kahlo: Places of Their Own*, and writing its accompanying catalog, and who, in the vein of Emily's own self-mythologizing, encouraged me to imagine; and my husband, Kip Gray, who, in countless ways has walked with me the pathways of this book.

I am profoundly grateful to Ron Hamilton (Wuuyaakiihtuu) of the Nuu'chah'nulth People, for his generous and knowledgeable help on First Nations cultures, native art, and natural history of British Columbia, gently delivered. I hereby give him a new name to add to his many other honors: Chamaḵtl, Having a Full Heart.

And always, love and deep gratitude to my trinity of mentors, as solid as great cedars: C. Jerry Hannah, Barbara Braun, and Jane von Mehren, for their counsel, insight, and belief in me.

May all of you find a moment in the book, personal to you, which recompenses in some small way what you have given me.

Contents

The Forest Lover

Part I

1: Salmonberry, 1906

Letting her cape snap in the wind, Emily gripped her carpetbag and wicker food hamper, and hiked up the beach, feasting her eyes on Hitats'uu spread wide beneath fine-spun vapor. Cedars elbowing firs and swinging their branches pushed against the village from behind. One wayward fir had fallen and lay uprooted with its foliage battered by waves and tangled in kelp. Wind whipped up a froth of sword fern sprouting in its bark. At last, she was right here, where trees had some get-up-and-go to them, where the ocean was wetter than mere water, where forest and sea crashed against each other with the Nootka pressed between them.

She had been to San Francisco and found it cramped, to London and found it stifling. She had ridden the Canadian Pacific Railway across the Rockies, breathless at their jagged power, and had galloped bareback across a ranch in the Western Cariboo, swinging her hat and whooping to the broad sky. She'd gone home to the starched and doilied parlor of the yellow, two-story bird cage of a house in Victoria, British Columbia, where she'd been born, and found only hypocrisy and criticism there.

But this, oh this, the west coast of Vancouver Island, wave-lashed and smelling of salt spray and seaweed, the teeming, looming forest alive with raven talk and other secrets, the cedar bighouses scoured by storms to a lovely silver sheen, the whole place juicy with life, was more wild, more free, more enticing than she remembered it when she'd come here eight years earlier. Or was it she that was different?

Lulu, grown into a young woman now, clamming on the beach, remembered her as soon as she'd climbed out of the hired canoe that had delivered her here from the steamer dock a mile away. Now, with Lulu carrying Emily's canvas sketch sack, a pack of barking, leprous-looking dogs came tearing toward them. "Stay down," Emily ordered, planting her feet wide apart.

Lulu ran them off, her braids flying, her long indigo skirt billowing, clams clacking in the basket on her back. She came back to Emily. "Sorry. They awful mean."

They approached the largest of the bighouses, ancestral dwelling lodges of many families, this one painted with a huge faded red sun. Lulu held open a hide hanging in the doorway, and motioned her inside.

Don't you dare go. Her sister Dede's angry command issued in their parlor two days before still grated on her mind. *Just who do you think you are . . . ?*

A thrill of defiance rippled through her as she stepped in.

Smells of fish and grease and the rich spice of wood smoke engulfed her. Women in striped cotton dresses sitting on tiers of platforms around the fire murmured and gave her curious looks. Some stopped what they'd been doing. An old woman in a red head scarf watched her with narrowed eyes, probably wondering what a white woman wearing a strange plaid English tam perched on her head was doing in their isolated village.

"Hello," Emily said.

Only a twitch of her bottom lip showed that she'd heard.

"The Nootka aren't much for friendliness," the captain of the steamer had told her a couple of hours earlier.

"But I've arranged to stay with the missionaries," she'd said.

"They packed up and left a month ago. I'd reconsider if I were you."

She'd felt the captain's words as a blow beneath her ribs. Dede would have gloated if she knew. As it was, Dede had given her a tongue-lashing about her mania for tramping through the wilderness with Indians, calling it a disgrace to the family. Still, she'd stepped off the steamer onto the dock at Ucluelet, and now, in this bighouse, she shoved back the fear that she'd made a mistake.

Lulu nodded to a man who spilled himself out of a hammock hanging from thick beams still shaped like tree trunks. His hair was cut bluntly at his shiny copper jaw, and he wore loose woolen trousers and leather shoes, but no socks.

"Chief Tlehwituua," Lulu announced, full of respect, and spoke a few words to him in Nootka, to which he responded.

Emily felt his milky-eyed scrutiny go right through her. Who are you? she was certain he was asking. It was the same question she'd often asked herself. Impulsive rebel or lonely old maid? Aimless hobbyist or committed painter?

"Chief Tlehwituua say he knew another missionary family would come. Tide that go out always come back," Lulu said. The chief spoke again. "He want to know where is your husband."

"I'm not a missionary's wife! Tell him, Lulu. I only came to visit the missionaries before. Tell him you remember me. Emily Carr." She set down her bags and took off her hat.

"Not a missionary wife!" some other voice said in English.

Murmurs. Smiles. Someone laughed. A man slapped his thigh. The chief held up his hand and the room fell silent. Apparently he didn't remember her. Maybe it was her close-cropped hair. When she'd been here before she had long hair, wound and pinned up like any proper Victorian lady. Now, to them, it probably looked like a bumpy brown knit cap.

The chief consulted with Lulu. "If not a missionary wife, why did you come? He want to know," Lulu said.

"I came to paint this time. Ask him if I may. The village, the beautiful canoes."

She dug out her half-filled watercolor book from her sketch sack to show her paintings of Beacon Hill Park in Victoria, woodland and seacoast in England. She felt apologetic. The English trees were puny compared to the mighty Douglas-firs and cedars here. Namby-pamby. A pathetic offering.

Why paint here, he might ask, and what would she answer? That she hoped that here she might discover what it was about wild places that called to her with such promise.

The chief made a circle with his hand, as if holding a brush, and nodded at her tablet.

"He want that you paint now."

"Now?"

Was this an invitation or a command? Better to assume it was a command. Could she paint under the heat of watching eyes, paint without sketching first? The years in art school in San Francisco and England hadn't taught her that. Time to prove to herself what, for the last dozen years, she'd only hoped she was.

She opened her watercolor set, a curiosity to him. He stuck his nose down over each color and sniffed while she looked for a subject. The raised platforms along the walls converged at a corner post carved into a man holding a fish, the most striking thing in the house. That would do just fine. It was a difficult perspective. She faltered. It wasn't right. She ripped off the page and people murmured. She began again, adding the fishing-man figure, baskets, stacks of blankets, carved cedar chests, coils of bull kelp hanging on the wall, and, draped over poles, strips of dried fish looking like curled brown rags. She tried to work quickly, in case they made her leave. But where would she go? The steamer wouldn't call again at Ucluelet for a week.

When Emily finished, Lulu asked, "You want to paint me?"

Ugh! Portraits were either stuffy or dead. She wondered if Lulu had ever seen her own face. "Do you really want me to?"

Lulu thrust her head forward. "We don't say things we don't mean."

"Sorry."

Lulu knelt by the fire, and Emily began. Each time she looked up, Lulu's dark expressive eyes were watching her. Older children and the woman in the red head scarf cast surreptitious glances but did not venture to come close.

"You see Nuu'chah'nulth women in Victoria?" Lulu asked.

"You mean what white people call Nootka?" Emily felt embarrassed. She couldn't tell the difference between Nootka and Songhees. "Sometimes. Songhees women too."

"Where do they live?"

"Songhees live at a reserve. Maybe Nootka camp on beaches."

"What do they in Victoria?"

"Sell berries and fish and baskets."

She didn't want to tell her how the Songhees were being pushed out of the reserve in Victoria's Inner Harbor that had been promised to them forever.

"What more?"

She thought of Wash Mary starching her pinafores on the back porch when she was a girl. "A Songhees lady used to wash our clothes, but that was twenty-five years ago."

Lulu's eyes burned with intensity. "She lived with you?"

"No. She lived in a little house beyond Chinatown."

Emily rinsed her brushes. "There. Finished."

Lulu studied the painting as if looking away would make it disappear. "That's me? You make me nice."

The red-scarfed woman came forward to have a look. Her expression revealed nothing. She walked away, opened a floor chest, wrapped herself in a dark blue blanket decorated with rows of mother-of-pearl buttons, made her way back to the fire, lowered herself onto a wooden box, pulled two hanks of gray hair bound in red cords forward over her shoulders, tapped her chest, and raised her chin in a pose.

"My grand auntie," Lulu said.

Emily grinned. What she'd really come for could wait. She wiped sweat from her forehead, and set to work again.

The auntie was of this place. Wind and sun had sculpted her face as they had her cedar house. Her laugh lines and sorrow lines were like gullies in a rugged landscape. Flames lit one high cheekbone, left the other in shadow, giving her a secretive look.

Joy rose in her. They were letting her. The wonder of it.

The auntie grinned and said something in Nootka that made Lulu giggle. "She remember you."

The auntie passed her index fingers over her own eyebrows and flapped her hands outward at her temples.

"She remember your eye hair, like wings."

Emily laughed. Her one eyebrow too widely and highly arched gave her the look of someone questioning everything.

"She remember you laughing. You're bigger now, she say."

True. She'd gone to England a shapely hourglass and had come home as what polite people would call solid, filled-in at thirty-three. Eighteen months imprisoned in that rod-rigid Suffolk sanatorium where they promised to heal homesickness and anything else that ails a body with imposed bed rest and force-feedings of honey and jam and mashed potato mountains—that's what did it.

"Bigger? Tell your auntie I can laugh bigger now."

When she finished Auntie's portrait, she set all three watercolors on a sleeping platform and stepped back, every muscle tight. "They're for you."

People crowded to see, speaking in Nootka. They opened a path for the chief and closed in behind him. After a few moments, he turned to her, nodded, and went outside.

"Does that mean he'll let me stay and paint?"

Lulu snickered. "He always was let you paint. He just want to see you do it."

Emily laughed a laugh of relief.

Auntie thrust at her a bowlful of salmonberries and said something Emily couldn't understand.

"You sleep here," a woman said. "Auntie wants."

"That's my mother, Rena," Lulu explained.

Sleep with all these people? Married people? Old men? The chief? All in the same room? She didn't belong here, but she didn't belong in a starchy missionary house with the Ten Commandments plastered on the wall either. Too much like her sisters' house embroidered with homilies everywhere she looked—enough to squeeze the spunk right out of her. But at least there she wouldn't be squeamish about what went on around her.

"Tell her thank you. I'll sleep in the mission house."

The auntie scowled when Rena translated.

Damn. She'd made a selfish mistake.

"Sure not a missionary wife?" Rena asked.

Good Lord. A missionary's wife, like Dede and Lizzie's praying ladies stirring tea with Lizzie's sacred disciple spoons, or wearing out the parlor carpet on their knees. She never knew when or where she'd trip over one. The mere thought of the missionary families' Sunday School sprawling into every room of the house, and Lizzie and Dede's double fury when she refused to teach a class, prickled her skin. That she hadn't come to Hitats'uu for a missionary purpose inflamed Dede's provincial propriety screaming against her "degrading notion to live with heathen aborigines in a siwash village. And for what purpose? Some unfathomable, unnecessary search for the authentic BC. Rubbish. It's right under our roof."

Emily heard herself laugh, throaty, deep, and loud. "No. Not a missionary's wife. That's one thing I'm sure of."

"Klee Wyck," the auntie said. Others repeated it, grinning.

"What does that mean?" Emily asked.

"Laughing One," Rena said. "You."

Emily laughed again to please them.

2 : Cedar

In the morning, with her sketch sack slung over her shoulder, she took a walk far down the beach in the mist. Breathing in sea tang, she felt like her mouth and throat were coated with brine. She looked back at the forest—more dense and tangled and full of mystery than the forested part of Beacon Hill Park at home. How could she ever paint it? No art school taught how to paint such immense, paralyzing magnificence.

She felt about to burst. She'd walked too far to make it back to the mission house. She hurried into the forest, hid behind a cedar trunk, lifted her long skirt and petticoat, and squatted. Dede would have been appalled. Well and good. Dede fancied herself above human urges.

Thunder cracked the sky and startled her. Rain worked its way through the canopy of boughs. The watercolors in her pad would be ruined. She went deeper into the forest for denser cover and saw a small wooden house painted with a curved symbol surrounded by figures of children frolicking. A hide hung at the entrance.

"Hello," she called, but heard only the rippling of chickadees. She went in. In the middle of the packed earthen floor, a fire pit caught rain from the smoke hole. Against the back wall a cedar platform was finely chiseled in a herringbone pattern, the edge fluted vertically. Someone had taken great care. She passed her hand over the subtle texture. Only love could make of such a simple need an elegant thing.

Wash Mary had mentioned that Indian women came to such places during their time. An aroma seemed familiar—coppery, fishy, a smell like hers but blended with cedar, moist ashes, and rain. Maybe sacred rituals known only to Nootka women were performed here. How could she act the same with them after she'd intruded in their private place?

As soon as the rain stopped, she went back to the beach. Three small boys sidled toward her, giggling. One had scabs under his nose. None of them had shoes. There wasn't anything that hit her so hard as a barefoot child in the cold. The smallest boy, trailing a rope of seaweed, wore only a shirt. "A-B-C-D-E," he sang in rising notes, looking to see if she heard. The others laughed and poked him. He dropped the seaweed and ran.

"F-G," she sang out, laughing at his brown fanny bouncing.

A menagerie of canoes hewn from cedar logs were beached along the tide line, each one with a tall, graceful prow painted imaginatively. A sardonic wolf face in black and white and red seemed all teeth and a human eye. A proud Thunderbird with blue and yellow wings spread across the side made the whole canoe into a bird about to take flight. A green sea serpent with red eyes and a long red tongue looked about to lick up waves.

She'd loved Indian canoes since childhood when she cheered at the tribal canoe races held every year in Victoria on the Queen's birthday. She'd always flailed her arms and hopped with excitement at the race of the *klootchmen*—native women in print dresses, their ten spear-shaped paddles dipping in unison, driving the craft forward, as fierce as men. Dede had always smacked her bottom and said, "Stand still and act like a lady."

Now, finally, she could paint them. She made a zigzag course toward the canoes, looking for the best angle, but stopped. There was Lulu on the ground leaning against a rock. Would Lulu guess that she'd been to the hut?

Lulu looked up and saw her. "You like our canoes?"

Relieved, she said, "They're beautiful. This place is beautiful."

Lulu nodded. "Right here, good place for looking and listening. Being real still here feed us back again."

"Yes. Just what I need." Emily sat next to her.

"In Victoria too—nice places?"

What would Lulu think of the new Provincial Parliament Building, all domes and arches plunked down on what was once forest? Every inch was stone. Not a scrap of wood on it. And what about carriages, rickshaws, bicycles, streetcars with clanging bells? Businessmen in top hats on horseback? Cattle herded through town to Goodacre's foul-smelling slaughterhouse? Derelict hulks stuck in mud along the waterfront? Saloons on every block? Chinese opium dens?

"Different."

"Does the Songhees lady wash your clothes now?"

"No. I do it myself. So do my sisters."

"How many people you live with?"

"No one."

"Not your family?"

"My sisters live in Victoria. I live in Vancouver. It's sixty miles away from Victoria, on the mainland."

Lulu scowled. "No one live with you?"

"A bird. He keeps me from being lonely," she said to answer Lulu's puzzlement, but how much could a bird do? The irony of it—she had four sisters, yet loneliness still gouged deep.

"I like the way you live, though. Many families together. Nobody lonely. Nobody an outsider."

"Yes," Lulu said, an exhalation more than speech. She was bending shreds of cedar bark to break their stiffness.

"That smells nice. What are you making?"

"Diapers for my sister's baby. And for *hisyuu*. I pound it. It get real soft."

"*Hisyuu?*"

"When we feel the call of the moon and go to a woman's hut."

Emily gulped. "You mean a little house where you just sit?"

"No. Not just sit. The old women teach us things."

"You stay there the whole time?"

"We can't do things some times."

"Like what?"

"Fishing season we can't step across streams or walk in the sea. Salmon get mad."

Lulu's solemn, unblinking eyes told her she believed in fish fury. A concept so curious, yet so appealing—fish and people interacting. Salmon in a quivering silver frenzy, leaping harum-scarum, tails flapping, eyes bulging, on the verge of speech.

"Our time to hear birds and breezes. Feel day and night. The blood go into *hisyuu*. We burn it there. Ashes go back into earth. *Hishuk ts'awaak*."

"What's that mean?"

"Everything is one."

She mulled over the idea, and wrote it on her drawing pad.

"Your English is so much better now."

"I learn at the cannery in Ucluelet. English, Chinese, Japanese. All words together at the cutting table." Lulu giggled, and her hands flew in circles near her ears. "But Chinook everybody understand. We talk and talk."

"What did you do on those call-of-the-moon days when you worked at the cannery?"

Maybe that was too personal. Lulu's face clouded and she stopped bending the bark.

"Sometimes, I went to work. One time I stayed in the hut. When I went back to work, a Chinese girl was in my place. So I don't work there more."

"I'm sorry."

Some dark thought pulled in Lulu's lips. "What do Nuu'chah'nulth women in Victoria those times?"

Emily shook her head and said softly, "I don't know."

Anguish threaded Lulu's voice. "I know it's not Christian, the woman's huts. I told you because you knew, no missionaries, and you came. No one here is Christian same as white people. When the missionaries go, no one does the Our Father prayer. Don't tell the mission ladies."

"No, Lulu. I won't. It doesn't matter."

But something else did. She had to find that hut again.

• • •

In the afternoon she walked behind the village in the tangle of salal bushes edging the forest to search for it. Stalwart gray-brown trunks of Douglas-fir soared two hundred and fifty feet and crowded against white pines sending out their aroma on the breeze. Her favorite, sturdy western red cedar, sheltered the droopy-topped western hemlock whose feathery tips of branches hung like graceful dancers' fingers. She inhaled deeply, hugging herself, wanting to fill her lungs with forest scents.

A crow cawed and landed on a large, square wooden box wedged between the boughs and trunk of a cedar. What was that doing there? Something man-made that high in a tree? She sidestepped through a salmonberry thicket to get a better look, and came into a soggy clearing smelling of algae and humus. Seven cedars without lower branches had boxes high against their trunks. Some had disintegrated and only a few planks remained in place.

Beneath one of them, a carved animal mask and paddle lay in the moss, neatly placed. Bones lay scattered on the ground—human bones grown green with algae. They must have fallen out of the boxes. Shock lashed through her. Slugs crawled over a green skull. She shuddered. How could they just leave it there? Seedlings had split the boxes, nourished by what remained in them. This must be a sacred place too, and here she was, her feet sinking into spongy moss right in the midst of ribs and thigh bones. How could something so repellent be sacred?

Wind whistled, or was it spirits? She thought of the handwritten paper she'd found in the mission house, *Sermon for March 17, 1906. Blessed are the poor in spirit.* The Nootka were *not* poor in spirit. Lulu running off the dogs was full of spirit. This place vibrated with spirits. She felt surrounded by them peering at her through the foliage, breathing down her neck.

Maybe she should leave and not tell anyone she'd seen this. Slowly, she backed away, but a powerful urge to paint here stopped her. Slowly, she sat on a moss-covered log. Other than dampness seeping through her skirt, nothing happened. Slowly, she opened her watercolor box. It creaked, too loud against the hush.

She reached into her sketch sack for her watercolor book. Rena's bannock bread spilled out. Instantly four huge crows cawed and swooped down to fight over it. Others dove at her, flapping their wings against her face. She didn't belong here. Crows must be protectors of this secret place.

They devoured the bread, belted out curses that she had no more, and disappeared back into the forest. Fine thanks she got.

They were only birds.

She opened her watercolor book and saw on the first page a woodland study she'd done months earlier in England. Her breath drained out in a thin stream. There was no backbone to that yew on the page. It was poor in spirit, without any earthly mystery, a ho-hum composition meaning nothing. Technique—interpretation—subject matter—all three had eluded her. She had fished five years and caught nothing.

She tore out the page. Strip by strip, she shredded the yew.

She stared at the shorn, tapering trunks before her, the grim boxes, the bones. She couldn't paint them as she had painted trees in England, meek little puffs of greenery without connection to the people who lived among them. The algae-covered skull sucked in her stare. Did she dare use a lime green that bright? An unreal color, yet those bones were real. They'd belonged to a man or woman loved by people who had let her stay and paint, by people who went about their lives today not knowing what she was about to do. Her hand squeezed the brush.

The terrible sacred privacy of the place repelled her intent. Without painting a stroke, she retreated.

• • •

After a short walk she saw the roof of the hut above some high-bush cranberry. She listened for any noise, but heard only the croaking of frogs, so she crept around the bushes to study the sym-bol painted on the wall. Not quite oval. More pear-shaped, upside down, outlined in black with concentric bands in red following its inner perimeter. She sucked in her breath, and teetered a moment in disbelief. A womb?

To put that most private thing on a building! Her sisters would be horrified. They never even whispered about women's privacies. Only Wash Mary did, happily, with congratulations, when Emily had hidden her first soiled underpants in the laundry. She'd never told anyone Wash Mary's reaction, held it as secret as a buried seed, and felt a part of her belonged to a different world.

She entered the hut, and imagined Lulu there, her full skirt pulled up and wrapped around her shoulders like a shawl, beating the cedar filaments into fluff, her bare legs, still girlish, stretched out wide, a dark, wet smear between them, and the old women teaching her some truth of womanhood.

She knelt. Slowly she ran her hands over the platform, its re-fined texture and fluted edge a pleasure to her fingertips. The same person who built a square coffin for his mother and hauled her up to the treetops might have crafted this. She stepped outside, hug-ging her sketch sack. The walls, hewn by a husband, the corners tightly slotted so no wind could chill, the paintings of children born and children to come, the man entering in his imagination a woman's private place, the womb itself, in order to paint it— everything about the hut told the woman she was loved. How could she make a drawing speak of such things?

Wanting to touch something intimately native, to have it seep into her pores to feed her art and her life, she placed her palm on the womb.

3: Lady Fern

"I think it's a menstrual hut," Emily said, spreading out drawings and watercolors on a table in the Vancouver Ladies' Art Club for Jessica to see before class. "That symbol may be a womb."

"Oh, my God. And you went in?"

"Not when anyone was there."

"This girl. She let you draw her there?"

"No. I drew her in a bighouse. Putting her here is my imagination, but these of the village and canoes I did right as I found them."

"What about this?"

"The place of the dead? From memory. It was too morbid to sit and paint right there as if I were painting petunias."

"But you liked it."

"Yes."

She'd felt pleased with her drawing of Lulu coming out of the hut, but it was such a private place, the coffin trees too, and here she was, showing them like postcards. She quickly stuffed them back into her portfolio when she saw two women bringing in the tea service. "Don't say anything," she whispered. "These were only for you to see."

Emily wanted to pose Jessica on the platform. Slender, with red hair and a graceful bearing, she'd be elegant, but she knew from their days at art school in San Francisco that Jessica wanted to get the most out of each session, yet never practiced on her own. It exasperated her. She wouldn't make Jessica give up the class time.

She posed Edwina instead, seated, ankles crossed. "This week, try not to scratch so tightly," she said as she adjusted the drape of Edwina's skirt. "On her skirt, let your stroke run loose as the wind." She doubted they could. Freedom was hard to achieve.

The studio door banged against the wall. Emily turned just as Priscilla Hamilton, madam president, sashayed in, head high, hand extended. Late, as usual. Everyone stopped working to twitter compliments on Priscilla's huge, flamingo-pink feathered hat, such a hat as would frighten a goat.

"I bought it in a wee shop on Regent Street where the Queen shops. I wore it to the Ascot races with a pretty little summer frock the same color. We were seated right near the Royal Enclosure. Shall I tell you what *they* wore?"

Emily noticed Jessica's head bent over her drawing, the only one working.

"No!" Emily bellowed. "A disrespect to ignore the model. Stop dithering and get back to what we're here for."

She let them work on their own until mistakes began to appear. "You have to define the elbow, not let it slide down the arm and melt away," she told Priscilla.

Priscilla's head popped up. The flamingo on her head jiggled, as though it were about to flap skyward.

"You may gaze at my work all you want, but I do not care to hear your criticisms."

"If I'm not mistaken, that's what you hired me for."

Emily turned to someone else. "Work the line from your forearm instead of your fingers. Working from your fingers makes your drawing too tight."

"I happen to like tight work."

Emily glimpsed Priscilla's mouth twitch upward. Sweet Jesus! Was this some conspiracy? Hold your tongue, she told herself. These butterflies with sketch pads are paying your rent.

"Can you tell me please what's wrong with this hand?"

All eyes shot across to Jessica Howard. Emily couldn't control her smug smile. Jessica, the outsider, an American. Teacups clinked in saucers.

"Look at your own hand, Jessica. How long are the fingers in relation to the palm?"

Jessica examined her hand, then her drawing, and looked up bright-eyed. "I made the fingers too short, didn't I?"

"You'll get it eventually. It's a matter of training your eye to measure one part against another."

All afternoon she itched to get home to paint for herself, but Jessica asked to go with her to pick out a sketching site for the next outdoor lesson. She was the only person in Vancouver she could call a friend. Taking a walk with someone didn't happen often. She said yes.

They followed the plank boardwalk of West Hastings Street past the packing houses and Klondike outfitters to get to the wharves. Emily rolled a cigarette from her tobacco tin and blew an agitated puff skyward.

"Dilettantes. What do they expect? Only the goo of praise?"

"Let them talk. They'll never be artists—not like you." Admiration glistened in Jessica's eyes.

"They pay more attention to the way they hold their teacups than the way they hold their brushes," Emily said.

"What? Don't tell me you think they're serious about art."

"Humph. Priscilla and her phony Knightsbridge accent posturing with that flamingo on her head. Now if she'd worn a hat with ferns or crow feathers, at least that would show she knew where she was." She was pleased when Jessica laughed.

They left muddy Cordova Street at Water Street, and walked quickly past saloons, tobacco shops, peep show wagons, bawdy houses, and Indian prostitutes, to get to Burrard Inlet. At the Union Steamship dock, they bought clam soup from an old Chinese woman tending a brazier. Under a paper parasol her grateful smile showed brown teeth. Fish smells from the packing houses mixed with the aroma of wet wood shavings from Hastings Sawmill shrilly chewing up a grove of cedars, spitting them out in planks. She grunted. Progress, Father would say. Colonialism, she'd say. While Victoria strove to be more English than London, Vancouver was busy being the Liverpool of the Pacific.

A log boom made herringbone patterns on the water, the same pattern as on the tooled platform in the hut. Was that what Lulu had meant by everything is one?

"Now that log boom is a possibility, with that three-master in the mid-ground, forest and mountains in the distance."

"Mm, too industrial for their tastes," Jessica said.

"But that's what buys their trips to the Ascot races."

At the Canadian Pacific Railway dock, an Empress liner rode high in the water. Emily stopped.

"Whooh, wouldn't you give a tooth to go north in a ship like that? My father did. I begged him to take me. He said that was inviting trouble. He left England for adventure, but denied it to his family."

"Why don't you go now?"

Emily uttered a coarse, quick laugh. "There's always that pesky living to be made."

"Then why not go west to that Indian village again?"

"Hitats'uu? Too hard to get to. It's on the *west* coast of Vancouver Island. That means either a six-hour or an overnight ferry to Victoria, an obligatory visit to my sisters there, another day and a half on a steamer up the island's west coast, and that only runs once a week, in fair weather."

"That didn't stop you before. What's the real reason?"

"The inevitable argument with my skin-and-blisters."

"Huh?"

"With my sisters. About disgracing the family by 'socializing with primitives.' " She snickered. "That made me want to go there all the more."

"That's a dumb reason. You ought to go because you love it."

"How do you know I love it?"

"Because of your drawings, silly. And your face when you looked at them."

"Love can take many forms. Even self-denial. Hitats'uu is terribly isolated. I waltzed in not even thinking about what effect I might have. The girl, Lulu, was inordinately curious about Victoria. I don't want to speed up change."

"One person? Aren't you overestimating?"

Emily shrugged, letting her gaze roam over the ship. "Look at the line of that prow. All swooped up in a luscious white arc."

"You see everything in terms of line and color, don't you? It's an obsession, looking at everything and everyone as possible paintings. Isn't life bigger than that?"

"It *is* big. Take those grain sacks and Chinese fishermen wearing those coolie hats. Strong repeated shapes. Good accents."

"But they're not people to you. They're shapes in a scene."

"What I painted at Hitats'uu was more than shapes."

She gazed across Burrard Inlet to North Vancouver and the Squamish Reserve hugging the shore—so close to Vancouver that the whole city would have an influence, not just one lone visitor. Maybe the Squamish living there had coffin trees too. Maybe it was a place that could feed her back again, as Lulu had said.

At the east end of the wharf they took a path past waterfront shacks. Down a grassy incline lay a narrow muskeg filled with skunk cabbage, moss, and lady fern. Beyond that, partly hidden by trees, a cove sheltered a tent and campsite, a beached skiff and a larger boat at anchor—funny-looking, stubby, with a tall, faded red pilot's cabin much too large in proportion to the hull, a sleepy animal's eye painted near the prow, and a crazy crooked stovepipe topped by a tin coolie hat. And on the cabin roof, a small French flag.

"Now that's a boat with spunk."

Jessica cocked her head. "What about him?"

A short, broad-shouldered, bearded man wearing a slouch hat stepped out from the shadow of trees, crossed a rivulet, and dropped a load of branches by the fire pit.

"Fits the scene, doesn't he?" Emily picked some lady fern.

They walked part way down the incline and the man looked up. Jessica nudged her. "Say something."

"Do you own that boat?" Emily called out and fanned the fern toward it.

"*Non, mademoiselle.* She owns me."

"We like it," Jessica chimed in.

He guffawed. "Suit yourself."

Emily murmured to Jessica, "Those driftwood drying racks would make interesting shadows if it were sunny." The camp looked fairly permanent. "How long will you be camping here?"

"Depends."

"On what? The weather?"

"Depends on when I sell all my furs." He moved a bundle of pelts from the skiff to the tent.

"We want to draw this." Jessica held both arms out.

The man gesticulated broadly, exaggerating her movement. "This isn't going anywhere."

"But with your boats and camp and everything."

He laid an otter pelt on his arm and moved the animal's little head as if it were speaking. "*Moi aussi, s'il vous plaît,*" he said in a squeaky voice and wagged his head.

Emily and Jessica turned to each other, dumbfounded, and laughed at his peculiarity. "They'd like this," Jessica said.

"You mean him," Emily whispered. "In two weeks," she said louder, "many ladies will come."

His hands flew up. "Ah, but none as beautiful as you, mesdemoiselles."

· · ·

She swung open the door to her rented flat on Granville Street. Joseph's gray feathers and red tail ruffled in the breeze. "I'm no English crow," he said, as well as he could.

"Right you are. I like your sense of identity." She shook out rain from her cape, put the ferns in water.

"Don't talk rot," he muttered.

She put her finger in his cage, and he let her stroke his breast. "You know how touching live things makes me crazy happy, don't you, Joseph? How lonesome I get."

He belted out a long, old-fashioned "Awk!"

Had someone knocked? She opened the door. A lean native woman, mid-twenties perhaps, stood on the stoop, her square shoulders wrapped in a shawl. She held a large lumpy something in a cloth which she carried by the four corners.

"Baskets? You want a basket?"

Half hidden behind the woman's full brown skirt stood a girl and a boy, maybe four and five years old, each carrying a smaller bulging flour sack. Rain fell like it meant it now and the girl wiped her cheek. None of them wore shoes.

"I'm sorry. I have no money for baskets."

"No money? Maybe you got dress, shirt for a basket."

The boy sneezed and buried his nose in his mother's skirt.

"Come in."

The mother hesitated, then wiped the children's feet, touched her hand to the girl's back, and waited for the boy to follow his sister in. The woman wiped her own feet, stepped in, two steps, toes placed down first, and knelt, straight-backed, to lay the bundle on the floor. The part between her braids cut an unwavering line. From another bundle cradled in the shawl on her back, a small wet face peeked out.

Emily took out a handkerchief, held her hand toward the baby, and looked at the woman. "May I?"

The woman froze, surprise written on her face, and then nodded.

Emily wrapped her index finger and dabbed at the sweet brown cheeks wrinkled as a walnut and the nose hardly a rise at all. Bow-shaped lips pulled inward at the touch. It was a moment of exquisite pleasure, passing too quickly.

The woman spread the cloth to display the baskets. Round ones, squares, rectangles, flat trays, all coiled, with intricate diagonal and geometric patterns or with animal and fern shapes.

"These are fine baskets."

The woman emptied out the children's sacks and smaller baskets tumbled out. One rolled against a table leg and the boy jumped to retrieve it.

"What are they made of?"

"Cedar root."

"What about this?" She pointed to a contrasting pattern.

"Cherry bark."

"These black ones too? That zigzag?"

"No. That one different. The bark of horsetail root. It means lightning and rainstorm. Use for holding water."

"Ah." The woman had made a connection between purpose and the source of her design. "And this?" Emily touched one with a cherry bark line undulating around the belly.

The woman laughed in a soft, abashed way. "Snake." She moved her hand to imitate a snake wriggling forward.

The design was its track in the dirt. A keen imagination. She looked at the woman's face—round nostrils, sharply edged mouth neither turned up nor turned down, dark eyes tucked under delicate eyebrows, and smooth, cedar-colored skin. A little older than Lulu.

Emily held up a basket with short vertical stripes crossing a long horizontal center line. At one end a half dozen slanted lines sat on top of the horizontal. "Salmon?"

The woman nodded, pleased. "Bones of salmon. These not the old ways. They my own."

"You're an artist."

The young woman shook her head. "I just make baskets."

The largest oval one had a lid. Emily picked it up. The inside was as smooth as the outside. The design seemed to represent open wings. "It's a handsome one. How much?"

The woman's eyes widened. "One dollar. It's Eagle."

"One dollar isn't enough for a basket this fine." A smile skipped over the woman's face and she rocked back on her heels. Emily set it down. "I can't buy it today, but it's beautiful."

"Old clothes are good enough."

"I don't have any here, but when I go home to Victoria, I'll bring some back. Maybe you will have one basket left."

She noticed another which had a rectangle outlined in black with a narrow peaked roof, a door, and two windows. "What's this?"

"The Squamish Mission in North Vancouver. That's my church. I live at the Reserve."

"How will I know whether you have one basket left?"

"Come and ask. I'm Basketmaker Sophie."

"I'm Emily Carr."

The parrot squawked, surprising the children. "His name is Joseph. Talk to him and he'll talk back."

They inched toward him as if he'd fly away, cage and all, and the boy said, "Hello, bird. Hello."

"Hello bird," Joseph said. "Don't talk rot."

They gasped and backed away, turning to their mother in wonder. In a few moments, they crept back to the bird.

Emily watched Sophie take in the paintings, the plaster casts, the paint supplies and brushes. "An artist."

"Anartist. Awk! Em'ly zanartist."

"My sisters explain me that way to their friends and he learned it from them."

"He makes strong talk. Like Eagle for Squamish people." Amusement played around the woman's mouth. "Only more loud."

Emily chuckled. "I guess I'd better listen."

Sophie was more at ease with her than Lulu had been, maybe the result of living close to a city. She seemed to have a contentedness in her own person that Lulu didn't have.

"Would you like some tea? May I give them bread and jam?"

Sophie hesitated. Her full lips parted.

"Why don't you stay awhile to wait out the rain?"

"Rain no matter," she said, glancing at her daughter whose big eyes pleaded. "All right. Only for the children." She turned to Emily. "You have children?"

"No. I'm not married. I can't be a wife and a painter."

"No? I'm a wife. I'm a basket maker."

"Lots of things here," the boy said with wonder in his voice, saving her from having to answer.

"Hard to throw things away. Clutter and putter, that's me."

Emily spread the bread with a thick layer of grape jelly. The boy ate quickly, his cheeks soon streaked purple, but the girl savored hers.

Sophie inspected each painting. "You like trees." She giggled. "But you don't know forests. Forests are dark. More dark. More . . ." She wrinkled her nose and shrugged.

Her bluntness stung. Emily looked at her Hitats'uu watercolors. More what? How dark should she get them?

Sophie's eyes ignited in front of the drawing of Lulu at the hut. "Squamish women do that long, long time ago. No more. It makes church priest mad, so no more."

"But this is at Hitats'uu."

"You went to Westcoast village?"

"That's my Westcoast friend, Lulu."

Sophie scowled. "Lulu is not a Christian."

"She's a good person."

"She is not a Christian."

Sophie knelt to wrap her baskets. The large one with the eagle she left sitting on the floor.

"What about this?" Emily said, picking it up for her.

Sophie stood up, rigid, and shook her head. "By and by, you come to Squamish Mission Reserve and paint a Christian village. We have a church. You remember me, Sophie Frank. Jimmy Frank's my husband. I call him Frank. He works longshore. We live right by the water. You ask for Basketmaker Sophie."

Emily smiled. "By and by, you come here too. Come soon."

4: Douglas-fir

"Good of you to come for Father's birthday," her sister Lizzie said.

"His birthday? Today? Imagine that," Emily said, piling on the innocence in a voice higher than her usual deep tone. "I came for the old clothes." She moved a blouse from the questionable pile onto the discard pile on the chesterfield.

"Don't tease us." Lizzie dropped her old pink Easter dress onto the pile, her long, thin fingers extended a moment in midair.

"I'm not going with you, if that's what you have in mind."

"Honor thy father and thy mother, Millie."

"There's no heavenly grace earned by visiting graves, Lizzie. Now if their bodies were folded up and put in boxes in trees like the Nootka do so they could feel a breeze or two, I might go." She chuckled, and held up a worn, flared skirt. Its forest green appealed to her.

"Every Carr daughter goes on his birthday. Mother's too," Alice said. "Why won't you?"

"Seeing his grave would only whip up my anger over some things he said to me."

Rebels like you are burned or hanged in public squares, was one thing he'd said. The house still echoed his words.

"You used to go with us. You used to like going with us," Lizzie said.

"No. You wanted to think I liked going." She hated all that sham homage she'd performed since she was seventeen, the year he died.

Dede came into the parlor, and Emily glanced at her to see if she'd heard. Uniform creases in formal balance, like parentheses around her mouth, stood guard against any random and unreasoned smile that might escape her.

"You'll go with us now or—"

"Or you'll send me to bed without any supper? Please, Dede. Is playing parent the only role you know? I'm thirty-three, if you haven't noticed, and I'm bored with it."

It was their great gap in age that made Dede capable of breathing in loudly through her nose for an interminably long time before exhaling, as she did now, her sign of exasperation.

Dede folded carefully her old blue serge skirt and matching jacket, and set them on the pile. "Are these for a church or an orphanage bazaar?"

"Neither. They're for a Squamish woman at the North Vancouver Reserve."

"A siwash?"

Emily prickled at the ugly term.

"You're wicked not to tell us that straight out." Dede looked at her suit as if she wanted to snatch it off the pile.

"She came to my flat selling baskets. I'm going to take her the clothes next weekend."

"She can get clothes from her mission," Lizzie said, tucking a loose strand into her brown bun. "You don't have to take them to her yourself. It's too personal."

"I'm not going for charity. I'm going for friendship."

"Honestly, when will you get it in your head that we can't condone this unwholesome socializing with primitives? It's a disgrace to the family." Dede's breath was loud and long. "If Father were alive, he wouldn't approve."

"No, he wouldn't—he who sold sacks of raisins crawling with maggots to Songhees lined up at his warehouse."

"Millie! How can you make such a hateful claim? He most certainly did not," Dede screeched.

"I saw it. He even told me, 'Indians don't mind maggots.'"

"That's a lie."

"Convenient for you to think so." She flung her arms to shoo her out. "You'll be late for your appointment with his bones."

• • •

The buggy wheels crunched on the gravel, an irritating sound. Even the parlor irked her. Father's raspy voice lay like a residue on his black, imitation-marble, English-style mantel, clung to his fox-and-hounds wallpaper, rested on his English primroses and cowslips peeking through the bay windows. His photograph leered at her from above his horsehair side chair. She hadn't realized until she moved across the strait to Vancouver how much these reminders of him chafed her like sandpaper.

She picked up the dark green skirt, and took the stairs two at a time to the bedroom she shared with Alice when she was home, to get the sewing basket. She cut through the hem and made a slit up the front of the skirt, made another cut straight up the back. She stitched the front raw edges to the backs to make a split-legged skirt. Now this was what she needed to ride a horse the way it ought to be ridden. She put it on, tucked a small sketch pad into her pocket, and went out to the barn to look for her old riding reins.

When her sisters returned, she unhitched Wilma from the buggy, attached the riding reins, climbed onto the fence rail, and swung her leg over Wilma's rump, bareback. Wilma skittered sideways, and Emily grabbed a hunk of mane to seat herself.

"What do you think you're doing?" Dede said.

"I'm going to make my peace with Father in my own way."

"Millie, no lady rides astride. This is *British* Columbia."

"But *we're* Canadian." She dug her heel into Wilma's side and took off at a canter. The thunder of Wilma's hooves overpowered the rest of Dede's outrage.

· · ·

Beacon Hill Park was only a few blocks away, the site of happy childhood bird-watching with Father and her first sketching trips. The memory of how she'd lugged the drawing easel she'd made of pruned cherry branches amused her. She headed toward the virgin woods, her favorite part. On the hillside she looked at the five tall Douglas-firs in graduated sizes. The Five Sisters, Father used to call them, straight and stately.

Except for one, the smallest, a bit crooked, its position buffeted more by offshore wind. That was her. Next to her and two years older than she was, the tree for Alice, who knew all about family tradition. Four years older, long-nosed, pray-to-be-perfect Lizzie knew all about God. Fourteen years older, Clara, elegant and statuesque, knew enough to escape the family into an early marriage. Fifteen years older, Dede, angular, straight-backed, *thought* she knew all about everything.

Still astride, Emily drew four straight firs, but the fifth she drew with exaggerated crookedness, leaning outward, its branches spiky. There were the good girls with clean fingernails, and there was

Emily, preferring mud pies in the cow yard to tea parties in the parlor. How odd that they all sprang from the same roots.

Father must have thought that too. She was the only one he used endearments for—wild one, witchwife, and nympholept, which sounded like something wasn't right with her, until she'd looked it up: *a frenzy of emotion for something unattainable, an ecstasy inspired by wood nymphs.* Yes! That was dandy fine.

These trees had seemed so mighty when she was growing up. Now they struck her as less dense and powerful. She directed Wilma toward the picnic area. There it was, the Garry oak. There was the notch. How could she have sat in it for hours, the bark so rough and scratchy, to look at a bird's nest? She was probably only seven, peering down at her sisters not venturing beyond the picnic blanket. She'd refused to come down when Father commanded her, so he'd left her there to teach her obedience. He loved birds as much as she did. He should have understood. She'd decided to wait him out. Certainly he'd come back for her, regret wringing his heart. He never did. Toward dark, she slunk home by herself. She was still glad she hadn't acknowledged him when he said, "My little nympholept, you can't always do what you want in this world."

· · ·

At home, she curried and fed Wilma, and sat on a crate in the floored half of the barn, the half Dede had rented to a clergyman as office space while she was in England. She shook her head at the fussy wallpaper scraps Dede had pasted up, as if to please Queen Victoria, five years dead.

Alice came in bringing her a cup of tea. She'd taken down her hair and it cascaded in chestnut waves over her shoulders.

"Convicted of impudence and waywardness, at thirty-three." Emily smirked. "We're like alley cats spitting at each other."

"You can't expect them to be different than what they are."

"I know, I know. Doers of good works. Chalking them up on God's tablet to be prepared for doomsday." But there was a difference between good works and good work. If only she knew which, in the summation of a person's life, was more important.

"Maybe I'm so cantankerous because I'm floundering. Each of you has a purpose in life. Your kindergarten. Lizzie's missionary society. Dede, the makeshift parent, now her orphanage auxiliary. Clara, marriage. But me? What am I here for?" She looked at Alice, wanting to read the answer on her face. "If only I were sure it was to paint the places I love, to paint them well enough to mean something to people, then I could take joy in every step toward that and not grumble about other things that don't really matter. Then I might not be such a thorn."

"You may be on the threshold of finding out and just don't know it."

Idly, she picked off a shred of wallpaper and took a deep breath. "Oh, those lifey smells of hay and horse and earth." She dug her fingernails into the English ivy wallpaper and ripped off strips down to the bare wood. "A barn's a barn."

"Millie! Reverend Strathmore wanted to buy this barn when you were gone. Dede didn't sell. She thought you might want to paint here again."

She stopped. "I had no idea. How can she be so kind one day and mean-spirited the next?" She crumpled the torn strips into a ball. "I can't even remember when all this squabbling started."

"Maybe the bites." Alice stifled a giggle.

"You think so? I was probably only eight or nine."

It was during one of those interminable Sunday evening scripture readings around the dining table. Father with his full beard and his eyes closed looked like Moses praying on the Mount. When her reading turn was over, after having to be told how to pronounce practically every third word, she'd stood up her Bible like a screen and went back to drawing. Lizzie elbowed her roughly in admonishment, so she'd slammed shut her Bible to hide the drawing, and bit Lizzie on the arm, just enough to shock her into silence. Dede, sitting across from her, let loose her swinging leg in a well-aimed wallop on her shin.

When Dede tucked her in bed, her duty instead of Mother's whose illness prevented it, she bit Dede too, clamping her teeth down hard. On her own bed across the room, Alice gasped and her eyes went wide. Dede hissed one of Lizzie's religious texts against wickedness. With that, the lines were drawn, and afterward Dede found a new use for the riding crop.

"You smiled a wicked smile when I bit Dede, as I recall." She showed Alice her sketch. "That's how the fifth sister should have grown."

Alice's cheek twitched. "You like to be different. You thrive on it."

"It always makes me an outsider."

"Don't fool yourself. You live to be an outsider. You can't have it both ways." Alice stood and picked up the teacup. "I miss you, Millie. They do too even though they don't show it. Will you do one thing for me?"

"What's that?"

"Paint a self-portrait, for our parlor. I want to see that one eyebrow permanently arched, permanently skeptical—the look of someone who doesn't suffer prudes easily." She winked.

"Ugh! Portraits stink of pretense. People strangled in fancy high-necked dresses, trussed up like cooked poultry." She held out the drawing of the five firs. "Take this instead."

5: Eagle

The next weekend, Emily stepped from the small ferry onto the North Vancouver dock half an hour across Burrard Inlet. A crudely painted placard advertised *Town Site Properties* with an arrow pointing right. Emily turned left onto a plank walkway toward some beached cedar canoes, which would surely be the Squamish Mission Reserve.

After walking for ten minutes, she began to breathe a soup of smells—sea salt, smoke from stovepipes, dead fish, and garbage scattered on the beach for the tide to carry out. Gulls picked over the refuse. There were no bighouses. Instead, a few rows of whitewashed clapboard cottages huddled around a church. From the walkway, paths threaded through new spring weeds to each front door. Hens strutted between the stalks. A woman digging with a stick in a potato patch stood up.

"Good morning," Emily said. "Do you know Sophie Frank?"

The woman nodded. "Two more houses. Basketmaker Sophie."

Behind mounds of bark and roots and firewood, the second house leaned slightly on its drift log foundation. Clothes strung on a line flapped above salal bushes and salmonberry. Emily glanced back at the woman who made no attempt to hide her curiosity. Sophie's front door opened. Her little girl, barefoot, wearing a skirt much too large, skipped out, saw Emily, and froze. She whirled around and ran back in, her braids swinging.

In a moment Sophie appeared in the doorway smiling a welcome. "Come."

"It wasn't hard to find, just like you said."

The odor of fish grease leapt out at her. Two homemade wooden chairs, a plank table, dishes and pots in an open trunk, an enameled wash basin, a Royal Crown soap tin with Buckingham Palace on the lid, red Hudson's Bay blankets stacked on wooden boxes, two braided rag throw rugs in native designs, and a settee—not squalor, just sparseness. Remembering the boy's awe in her own house, Emily felt a touch of discomfort.

A hump of blankets on the floor practically hid the boy wrapped up in them. He watched her every move. Although only a faint warmth issued from the wood-burning stove in the center, she wanted to gather him up and put him next to it.

The girl kept her chin glued to her chest but managed to take surreptitious peeks at her. "What's your name?" Emily asked.

Instantly the girl flattened herself against the wall.

"This one's Annie Marie. Named after our Holy Mother." Sophie gazed toward a paper image of the Virgin stuck on a nail.

"How nice. I like the Virgin Mary. She wasn't a blabberer."

Sophie pushed out her lips and nodded in satisfaction.

"You have long beautiful braids, Annie Marie. Did your mother braid them for you?"

The girl raised her chin an inch in a nod.

"That one's Tommy." Sophie tipped her head toward him and smiled with every muscle in her face. "Oldest one."

"Hello, Tommy." He only blinked. "Do you remember my bird who talks?" He opened his mouth to say something, and coughed.

Two more girls crept out of a second room.

"How many children do you have?"

"Three." The word rang like a declaration of victory. "These are Margaret Dan's. Go home now, Shaula. Go home, Rosie. Tell your mother Em'ly came to visit Sophie."

The girls raced out the door, giggling, nearly knocking over the oil lamp sitting on a chair.

Sophie lifted the cloth cover on a shallow basket cradle hanging from the ceiling. Emily peered at the small face, so wrinkled it took something right out of her.

"No worry. He grows fat by and by." Sophie stroked his cheek, inviting Emily to do the same. Emily shifted her bundle of clothes to one arm and touched the baby's brown skin, so smooth and cool it sent a tingling up her fingers. Sophie set the cradle in motion. "Three live babies. Four dead ones. I show you."

"Four! That's terrible, Sophie. How come?"

Sophie straightened and turned away.

Emily blenched. She shouldn't have asked. To lose even one! But four. And she appeared to be so young.

"I brought you some clothes." Another bad response, she realized, too late. Sophie reached for the bundle. Her scowl kept Emily talking. "The ones that don't fit you can give away."

Coolness filmed over Sophie's eyes. She let the bundle drop to the floor and spread out the clothes with her bare toe.

"I should have tried to find some children's clothes too."

Sophie fingered the fabrics, rolled them up again, stood, shoved them to the edge of the floor with her foot. She pulled her shoulders back with an air of weariness and drew in a long loud breath. "They not for wearing. They for rug making."

"Oh."

A horrible moment. Silence.

"You want to see our church house?"

"Yes, I would like to." What did she think—that all white women went around visiting churches? "I want to see everything."

Sophie went into the other room and came back wearing a full plaid skirt with black velvet bands around the bottom, unlaced the baby, wrapped him in a woolen shawl, tied him across her back, and walked out the front door and down the path. Emily, Tommy, and Annie Marie followed. As soon as Sophie stepped onto the plank walkway, she turned and went back inside. When she came out, she had on shoes. "Nice ladies wear shoes to church," she said.

Sophie turned left at the walkway, the opposite direction of the church steeple. The heels slipped off her feet at each step, and when they approached the house where the woman had been digging, Sophie let the shoes smack the planks even louder. The woman came to the doorway.

"Hellooo, Miz Johnson," Sophie said without a pause in her clomp-clomping on the planks.

Emily saw expectancy on the woman's face darken to disappointment as they passed.

After a moment, Sophie whispered, "She thinks she's better because she married a white man. But he's dead now."

"Oh, that's too bad."

"No, it's not too bad. She doesn't do anything. She doesn't make baskets. She doesn't have babies. She doesn't work at the cannery. She all the time talk about her poor Johnson dead at sea, and washes tablecloths and dries them on the salal bush so we see them and think she's a white lady. Her husband's ship sends her money. She doesn't make anything."

Emily cleared her throat. "You're right. It's better to be making things."

They continued on the walkway going away from the steeple, and then cut back to the second row of houses to head toward it. Curious. The circular detour could have been for no other reason than to walk by Mrs. Johnson's house.

"That's our schoolhouse. Frank and I learn to read and write there, and my babies too, by and by." Sophie designated, openhanded, two buildings as if introducing them. "Schoolhouse. Church house. Mission Church of the Sacred Heart."

"Handsome."

A single white octagonal spire rose behind two cherry trees flocked in blossoms. It was a simple, plank Gothic, standing foursquare facing the beach, not particularly remarkable in its own right, but mightily impressive here.

Inside the church, the cooler musty air hung heavy with incense. Soft light from an oil lamp bathed the floor and pews in a golden glow. A chipped clamshell held holy water. Emily examined its carved wooden pedestal, a long-robed saint with almond-shaped eyes. Something about them seemed furtively animal.

Sophie dipped in her fingers, crossed herself, and turned toward Emily, waiting. Emily resisted. Rituals were for those who needed props in their religion, but Sophie's steady look signaled expectancy, and she didn't want to offend Sophie again. She dipped in the tip of one finger.

She felt calmness settle over Sophie sitting at the edge of a creaking pew. She sat beside her, and Annie Marie squirmed across her knees to be between them. Emily was overcome with longing to touch the dark sheen of Annie Marie's hair, but she held back.

She looked above Tommy's head in front of her and winced. Behind the altar hung a painting of the Sacred Heart, a pulpy mass of cadmium red extra deep shaded with Indian red, misshapen and dark, looking like a human organ entwined with a vine of thorns. It was a miracle of Christianity how that muddy-colored bloated tomato could inspire worship. She glanced sideways. Sophie gazed at it in adoration. How could she, after losing four children?

In niches on either side of the heart stood small wooden statues of Joseph and the Virgin holding baby Jesus. Candle flames trembled. A devilish thought tickled her. Lizzie was a staunch Episcopalian one week, Presbyterian the next, one religion not enough for her. The next time her sister pressed for a report on her church attendance, she'd say she'd been to an Indian Catholic church. That ought to frost her eyelashes for always being so nosy.

Once they stepped outside, Sophie took a beaten path through tall grass. "Now I show you my dead babies."

Her matter-of-factness was baffling.

The cemetery sloped up from the beach to the woods behind. Sophie plucked some violet blue camas blossoms and held open the cedar strip gate. There were no coffin trees here. Instead, a tall white cross in the center of the cemetery cast a lean shadow over the graves placed helter-skelter, not in rows. Some graves only had wooden crosses nearly obscured by thickets. A few had headstones and some were surrounded by picket fences. Sophie danced her fingertips across the picket points. "Very Christian," she whispered.

She turned toward a granite headstone. "That one for my friend Margaret Dan's baby. See his cross carved in? Bigger than him. But Margaret Dan only has three babies here." They passed into the newer section. "Casamin I show first. My first boy." His grave was marked by a narrow wooden cross, unpainted, with only his name gouged in. Sophie squatted to brush away leaves.

"How did he die?"

"Every day I brought him to lie under the old Ancestor. Maybe that made God mad."

She'd expected Sophie to name a sickness, not give a theory. "I'm so sorry. How can you bear it?"

Sophie rose and her chest expanded. "A baby for a while is better than no baby." She barked out the words as though she were defending a principle.

Emily followed her to a sagging wire fence tangled with blackberry bushes in some places, broken and leaving gaps in others. "Whooh!" A wooden figure on the other side of the fence surprised her. Minimally carved, not clearly a man or a woman, but definitely human, chin lowered, shoulders square, he brooded over the graves outside the fence. Ten feet of austere sorrow. His surface had weathered to silvery gray, and a vertical crack split his torso.

"Who's *that?*"

"The old Ancestor. Chief Mathias raised it. Even after they die, ancestors keep to helping Squamish."

Sophie lifted her chin as though she'd made it herself, and nodded over the fence to two short humps of earth side by side. "My first babies," she said. "Trina and Lucy. Twins."

The number of her pregnancies sprang into reality. Sophie must have had the twins when she was only a girl herself.

"Why aren't they in here?"

Sophie chewed on the pad of her thumb. "Not baptized. Died too quick."

Emily felt herself drawn into Sophie's pooled eyes.

"Now I show you Maisie." Sophie brightened, as though . . . as though what? Maisie meant more? The babies outside the fence weren't as important? Or was she trying to ward off pity? Sophie turned slowly, lifting her skirt away from the thorny berry bush.

Emily turned too, and saw that the Ancestor figure and the large cross faced each other across the fence, one artful and expressive, the other plain and flat. She could not detect any difference in the veneration Sophie showed for both of them. Emily read some inscriptions. *Mary Chepxim 1893–1897. Matthew Chepxim 1896–1902, drowned in river. Jack Henry, loved, 1881–1889. Marcus Thom 1901 only.*

"So many are children. How could that be?"

Sophie moved only her eyes, giving Emily a scornful look. "You don't know much. No."

Emily bristled for an instant, about to retort. She felt Sophie wanting her to understand. Smallpox. Measles. Influenza. Were they always more deadly for Indian children? Apparently birth was never a guarantee of life. It was true. She didn't know much.

Sophie stopped at a gray humpbacked stone bearing the words, *In Loving Memory Maisie Frank 1903–1905.*

Those were white man's words. Had she gone to a cemetery in Vancouver to learn them?

"She came too soon after Annie Marie. Good sisters but one died. It's good to grow up with a sister. Share things. That makes good sisters."

"Do you have sisters, Sophie?"

"No. Only brothers. In Squamish. You?"

"Yes. Four. Not much sharing, though."

Sophie squinted at her curiously, as though what Emily said were impossible. "Too bad."

Maybe it wasn't bewilderment in Sophie's look, but judgment.

She watched Sophie stroke the curve of the headstone lovingly. She'd probably done it hundreds of times, and was as devoted to those graves as she was to her living children.

"That's a fine marker, Sophie."

"The grave man made it cheap for me. He said maybe I will bring him more dead babies by and by so he made it cheap."

"No!"

Sophie tipped her head to the side as if to say, Who's to know?

Emily checked to see if Annie Marie heard. What effect did Sophie's coming here have on her children? At least it would let them know how much their mother continued to love each one. Annie Marie sat in the weeds a ways off, absorbed by twisting grasses together to make a basket. Her round face tipped down like a copper moon and the sunlight shimmered some strands of auburn hair.

Her legs stuck out akimbo from under her print skirt spread like a fan. Maybe someday Sophie would let her paint Annie Marie, but for now, it was the Ancestor she wanted.

Sophie's eyes were drawn upward to the trees. She touched Tommy on the shoulder, glanced at Emily, and slowly tilted her head back. Emily looked up in time to see an eagle soar over the graveyard in a big arc, gain height, and swoop down to land with utter precision on a high jagged branch.

"Tremendous. The power of his wings," Emily said.

"It mean something when you see one."

"What?"

"Different things to different people." She turned from Emily and smiled lovingly at Tommy. "You sleepy now? Rest." She indicated a sunny patch of grass alongside Ancestor. Tommy stepped through the gap in the fence, and curled onto his side next to the figure.

"It's a perfect picture. Would it be all right if I painted that figure?"

"Ancestor would make a good picture."

"And with Tommy there?"

Sophie's eyes opened wider and her lips formed an O before they sprang into a proud smile. "Yes, I share him with you."

They approached the Ancestor, and Emily began by sketching with charcoal to get it bold enough for the stark figure. Annie Marie crept up behind her to watch. Emily liked her small, quiet presence. She did two sketches from different angles, and then two watercolors. She showed them to Sophie. When Sophie whooshed air out of pursed lips, Emily felt happiness bubble up her throat.

"Now Ancestor will not forget him," Sophie said.

· · ·

At the little two-room house Sophie made tea. "Juniper berry. Good for ..." Sophie patted her hands over her belly. She poured the tea into a chipped china teacup. Emily held it up to examine it. Queen Victoria's insignia was stamped on the side.

"She was my Queen too," Sophie said, seeing her surprise.

"Yes, I ... Yes. We share her."

Sophie nodded definitively.

The tea would take some getting used to.

Tommy played, wistful and sneezing on his blanket at her feet.

Emily reached into her pocket for her handkerchief and offered it to him. He raised his face to her. "Blow," she said softly, and it gave her pleasure when he did.

He climbed onto the settee next to her. She lifted her arm and he nestled against her, leaning his head against her bosom.

"You fit me," he said.

She smiled and sat still so the moment would last. Out the open door, she watched Annie Marie squatting near the salal bush with her knees wide apart. She patted the dirt smooth, picked out stones, and began to draw with a stick. When she was dissatisfied, she rubbed it flat and started again, concentrating, hope freshening her face each time. When Tommy moved away, Emily picked one of the watercolor studies of him with the Ancestor and offered it to Sophie.

Sophie's hands shot up to cover her mouth. Her head turned from side to side.

"Yes, Sophie. It's for you."

Slowly, Sophie lowered her hands to reveal a proud, high-cheeked smile, her eyebrows arching, even her ears lifting. She made a small, careful hole in the paper with the sharpened tip of a reed and hung it on a nail opposite the Virgin Mary.

6: Muskrat

The fur trader's wooden boats were as ticklesome as she remembered them. From where she stood on the bluff above the cove, the red pilot's cabin on the larger boat looked much too tall and narrow. The crooked stovepipe had so many angles it didn't know where it wanted to go. And to have it topped with a tilted tin coolie hat! That stern pole had no purpose other than hoisting aloft a French flag and a foxtail. The boat gazed back at her through its sleepy animal eye, a faded black circle painted on its prow surrounded by the same almond shape as the carved saint's eye in Sophie's church, painted in red and black. As for the skiff tied alongside, it was a creature, really, not a boat at all. Its bow had sprouted red whiskers and an impressive set of white pointy teeth stretching back half its length, and near its stern, red flippers.

Even the man's tent had character—taller on one side than the other, patched in places, foxtails hanging from the tent poles, and a furry little head attached to the tent peak. Two pairs of long johns hanging from driftwood drying racks flapped in the breeze like nervous specters frantic to find their bodies. It would be a dilly of a painting. "*Oui, mesdemoiselles,*" she said and wagged her head. If she were going to get any decent sketches for a painting later, it wouldn't be the next day, when she had to teach the butterflies. She walked part way down the incline to a ledge above the skunk cabbage muskeg and set up her canvas stool.

Midway into a sketch, she heard clamoring from the larger boat. "*Mon Dieu! Porquoi tu me tourmentes?*"—the words uttered with the vehemence of an oath. The man flung two skin bags into the skiff, lowered himself into it, and rowed ashore. He carried them to the creek that ran out of the woods, filled them with water, and was walking back toward the tent when he saw her. "*Attention, mademoiselle!* You're going to slide down that hill and land in the muck."

"What kind of a boat is the big one?"

"She's *une bateau sauvage.*"

"She? What does *she* do?"

"Fight. Always she wants to go one way, I want to go the other."

"Why do you paint your boats?"

"To beat back the dark wilderness with something light."

He set his water bags on the ground and came over to the opposite side of the narrow bog. His cheeks above his beard were burnished by wind and sun. His thin nose and small ears gave him a refined look in spite of his beard and tousled brown curls. He wore buckskin trousers and shirt—a man out of James Fenimore Cooper's *Leather-stocking Tales.* As a girl, she'd reread them until the pages were soft as tissue paper.

He scowled in a playful way that wrinkled the skin around his eyes. "You draw that boat, mademoiselle, and she'll put a curse on you."

Emily laughed. "What is it called?"

"*La Renarde Rouge.* She's a vixen."

"Where do you go in it?"

"As far north as she decides to take me."

"Alone?"

"Alone."

"To Alaska?"

"Sometimes. Or up rivers. Wherever they'll trade for furs."

"What is it like in the north?"

"Wild. Forests so thick they can't be logged." He threw his arms wide. "Vast territory. Weeks to get anywhere. *Tout le temps,* rain. Rain like waterfalls. Always branches dripping on you. Make you crazy." He made a funny face, upper lip going one way, lower lip the other way.

"What else?"

"What do you want? Glaciers crashing into the sea? Birds that shriek like demons or grumble like old men? *Oui,* that too." His eyes opened wide and his voice became throaty. "It's wilderness so *formidable* it can turn you inside out and leave your raw flesh quivering." He made his hands tremble.

Her mind reeled with painting subjects. "Sounds like one glorious adventure."

"What? Are you a child? It is merely mercantile." His words were clipped.

"Are there bighouses?"

"Villages of them, some painted to look like animals." He waved his arms upward. "And poles stacked with queer creatures."

"Totem poles?"

"And potlatches."

"What are they really?"

"Won't tell you. Can't."

"Why not?"

"Secret. You want me to shout it up the hill at you?"

"Yes."

"Can't. You have to come here, to my camp."

He turned and got into his skiff and rowed out of the cove. Was that it? He was going to leave her wondering?

Well, she was here to draw, so she drew, one sketch after another, different distances, different angles. Bad, happy drawings, done recklessly. Her charcoal broke. No matter. She ripped off a page to start another sketch. Wind whipped it out of her hand and blew it onto the beach. She started another, and another, filling her drawing tablet.

· · ·

At home, a letter was sticking out of the mail slot. She ripped it open.

Dear Miss Carr,
At a meeting of our board, we have decided that your teaching is inadequate for our purposes and must inform you that we shall no longer need your services.

Mrs. Priscilla Hamilton, President
Vancouver Ladies' Art Club

"What!" She stormed across the room, unable to believe the words in front of her. "Inadequate! Pish! What do they know?" she told Joseph. "They're beastly and ignorant. They have prehistoric ideas about art. I'd rather starve than teach them."

"I'd rather starve," Joseph mimicked, saying it twice.

"Good thing, because if I go, you go."

She slammed the teakettle onto the stove. Jessica was right. They weren't serious about art. They only wanted to paint flowers and themselves. Flamingo-hatted pretenders. She rolled a cigarette from her tobacco tin, lit it, then touched the match to the letter and watched the blackening edge of the paper advance toward Priscilla's graceless signature.

What would she do? She'd earned enough for only a few more months. Going home was unthinkable. She'd just begun to establish herself here. Jessica was here. Her new friend, Sophie, was here. The reserve was here. Possibility was here. The city was growing. Every month there were new houses of lumber barons to fill with paintings. But her trust fund wouldn't last forever.

She surveyed her recent work. Were they any good, or did she only like them because of the associations? Art couldn't just be personal. Her old flop fears crawled up her spine. The Ancestor was a strong composition, though Tommy under it might be too precious. She'd try it without him. She wanted to draw Annie Marie too, sometime. Annie, so curious when she watched her from behind. She probably had never seen anyone draw before. The Ladies' Art Club prima donnas never watched her draw. Annie watched, and then drew in the dirt. It was natural that children imitated what they liked in adults.

She rolled and lit another cigarette, and discovered the first one still burning in the ashtray. She pushed it aside and wrote out an advertisement: *Emily Carr, Classes in Drawing and Painting, Children Only. 570 Granville Street. First class free.* She'd never teach adults again. Ingrates. But children, that was a different kettle of fish. Jessica would enroll her daughters, and they had friends. She might even have a ripping good time of it.

· · ·

At the top of the incline above the cove, Emily dug her fingers into the shaggy black and white coat of the dog's neck. He'd behaved himself well coming here, their first walk together. His lumbering gait had made her take long strides, swing her arms, breathe deep, feel plucky.

She saw a long plank placed across the muskeg, and on the far end, the drawing that had blown away on her previous visit, weighted on four corners with stones. "Besides you, pooch, that plank's the best thing that's happened today."

She stepped carefully down the slope, the dog close to her on a leash, and crossed the muskeg on the plank, squeezing her toes to keep her balance, and urging him across.

"Good boy!" She chucked him under the chin. "You'll be good with the children, won't you? You'll keep them together on our drawing outings just like they were sheep."

With his mauve tongue on the back of her hand, he seemed to promise that he would. He was a business necessity, she'd tell Dede in case she rapped her knuckles with the bank book.

She picked up the drawing. It wasn't so bad after all.

"*Mademoiselle!*" The man smiled as he came out of his tent.

"Emily. My name is Emily."

"*Une dame courageuse* to climb down that steep hill." He waved a rag in a flourish and executed a low bow. "Claude Serreau, fur trader. One of the last, and best. From Poitiers, where all the good ones came from. You may call me Claude du Bois, considering where I live." His lips poked out of his beard in a funny grin and he gesticulated toward the woods behind his camp. "You came to draw again?"

"Yes, and to find out what a potlatch is."

"Sh." He put his finger to his lips and looked around at the trees. "The woods can hear." He raised his bushy eyebrows in mock fear.

Amusing to see a rugged outdoorsman act so queerly.

"Where are the ladies you promised?"

"They'll never come."

"Phuff? Disappeared into thin air?"

"Transformed into an old English sheep dog. His name's Billy. I just bought him. I went into a pet store for a goldfish. Came out with him."

"*Mon Dieu.* He looks like a rug. Any eyes?" Claude lifted the shaggy hair on Billy's head. "*Ah, bon. Les voilà.* What? No tail? What's he good for?"

For filling her emptiness, she thought. "For loving," she said.

His mouth dropped. "What? You choose a dog instead of a man?"

"Dogs don't go off in rowboats when you're talking to them."

"I went to the sawmill to get a plank for you to come across the bog, but when I came back you were gone!"

"I—I didn't know."

"So, now I tell you about the potlatches."

He drew her toward the opening of the tent, his fingers pressing her wrist. He hummed a tune as he built a fire. She gazed at the back of his creased neck.

He laid out a blanket of pelts, burnished brown and creamy fur. "Sea otter. Almost hunted out now. Very rare."

Billy sniffed them. She pulled him away and tied his leash to a tree out of range. He seemed content to take a snooze. Sprawled on the ground, he did look rather rug-like. She opened her campstool to sit near the pelts.

"*Non, non.*" He gestured, openhanded, toward the pelts. "For you. Not for anybody else. Even me." He arranged thick, sleek beaver pelts at the opening to his tent. "The big fur trade is over, but there's still some fine pieces if you know where to find them." He swept his hand over the fur and invited her to do the same. She bent down at the tent opening to touch them.

"Oh, my! Something in me loves to feel the liveness in things like grass and moss and feathers and fur."

He brought out more. "Feel these. Muskrat and mink."

His brown eyes fixed on her as she stroked the fur. She could dig down with her fingers like roots in the mink, or just thread them through the longer filaments. The sensation melted her. He piled them at the entrance to the tent to make a backrest. She nestled herself into them.

"*Ah, bon. C'est bien?* Now the fire crackles. No one can hear us. Now I tell you. Potlatches. *Grandes fêtes* lasting days. One chief invites other villages to witness the raising of a pole. He gives away hundreds of things. Dried salmon, Hudson's Bay blankets, basins, tools, English dishes." He waved his arms in circles outward. "Cloth, oil, sacks of grain, sugar. Even sometimes a sewing machine or a canoe."

"Why?"

"To show that he can afford to. To shame the other chiefs who did not give as much at their potlatches. Good business for me, *oui?*"

"Where do they get these tools and English dishes?"

"From me, of course." He slapped his chest.

"Is that all that happens at potlatches?"

"No. There are proud speeches, feasting and drinking and drumming. Feathered bodies dancing, stepping lightly on the earth. Ravens that talk like men. Men that dance like ravens. Moving in a trance." He squinted and leaned toward her, smelling of smoke and buckskin. "Wild things happen."

Her imagination soared. "I'd like to see one someday. Maybe to paint it."

He puffed out his cheeks. "*C'est impossible.* Not for white people. Or ladies. They're against the law."

"But you. You've seen them."

"Business, *ma beauté.*"

He leaned toward her, stroking the muskrat delicately for someone used to rough living. He seemed half native to her now, primitive, son of the seasons, a man who knows tribal secrets. She looked at him raptly, and a slow, knowing smile came over his face.

"You don't come here just to draw, *non?*"

His eyes softened, gleamed, came close, roamed over her face. The pores of his cheeks were deep bronze. He placed his hand on the back of her head and kissed her lightly. He drew back to see her reaction, smiled wryly, and kissed her again, his beard soft, his lips pressing. She resisted. The firmness of his palm on the back of her head released, but she didn't move away. They sat locked in looking, breathing together.

This was wild. It surprised her, and didn't.

"Can you hear them? The drums?" he whispered.

She listened, and felt her own heart beat.

"Once you hear them, you'll never forget."

He leaned her back and their kisses were longer. Fur caressed her arms. He trailed his finger down her neck to her collarbone. His eyes reflected points of light from the fire, a man of forest smells and animal instincts.

Father's voice rattled at her, in her. *You'd better know what being a woman means, so you won't be tempted.* She jerked away, stood up, reached for her sketching stool and held it in front of her, its legs pointed toward him.

He burst out laughing. "I see. You are merely a girl in a woman's body."

She set it aside, feeling heat in her cheeks.

He made a great show of putting his hands behind his back. "I will do nothing." He patted the pelt beside him. She sat down again.

"Now I tell you about the poles."

She hardly listened. Everything was stirring inside her. ". . . Trunks of cedars carved into animals to represent their clan. . . ." His voice seemed muted. She couldn't grasp all he said. ". . . Or to tell history." She watched his hands stroke the muskrat lightly, sensuously, yet that was so opposite to what Father had said about men. For Claude to stroke her face like that . . . She felt the drumming inside her.

But he was true to his word.

· · ·

She went home out-and-out mad. At Father. At herself too. After all these years, that awful day when she was fourteen still had a hold on her. Damn that man.

Untamed. Like a wild Indian, Father had said as she'd sat on the bench in his big gardening shed. He claimed that's why he did it, to tame her innocent wantonness. *Emily, you'd better know what being a woman means, so you won't be tempted. . . . A man pushes it, hard, and you have to take it in you.* He pointed, palm up, right between her legs, and was about to touch below her bone—or so she'd thought. She'd shoved his hand away and clamped shut her legs, couldn't bear to be there with him, and ran into the house. It had filled her with brutal images for years, spoiled what ought to be beautiful, and now, it still made her act like a silly, frightened girl.

That night she slept fitfully. Images of Claude on the pelts and feathered bodies dancing in firelight slid through her dream. She dreamt of Father, too, in the gardening shed, thrusting a narrow trowel between her legs. Of Dede, hands on her hips, laying down the law. *Ridiculous for you even to consider going north alone. Who do you think you are? I won't allow it.*

But this wouldn't be alone, she said back.

She woke up swearing that she'd get over Father's crudity once and for all. Where was her gumption? She fed Billy, gathered her drawing things, and they set out.

How would Claude act after she behaved like a fool with the camp stool? How would she?

7: Fox

When she and Billy climbed down the slope to the cove, Claude had a fire going with skewered potatoes roasting on a rack above it, and had spread the otter pelt blanket and other furs.

"How did you know I'd come back?"

"You didn't finish painting." His mouth formed a teasing grin.

She grinned back and held out her empty hands.

"Oh-ho!" He wagged his head.

She tied Billy to a tree again and sat on the pelts. "I came to ask about totem poles."

His bottom lip protruded in a pout.

"I have a Squamish friend in North Vancouver," Emily said. "She took me to the cemetery there and showed me a carved figure of a man. I want to know. Are the totem poles like that?"

"How tall is it?"

"I'd say ten or twelve feet."

He laughed. "See those cedars? Imagine them stripped of branches and carved all the way to the top. Creatures with eyes and beaks and teeth and wings stacked on top of each other staring at you out of the forest." He spread his arms like wings and bent over her. *"Comme ça."*

"Aren't they in villages?"

"Most of them. Some villages have been abandoned, but the poles are still there. You can come upon one suddenly, or you can hear wind moaning—whooh, whooh—like a ghost, and then you know there's one nearby, and so you creep around like a fox." He hiked up his shoulders and stepped his hands forward, placing one on her knee. "But even if you know it's there somewhere, it hits you when you see one. Right there." His fingers tapped her chest under her collarbone, dangerously close. A vibration shot through her.

"I want to see them."

"They might frighten you."

"I want to be frightened."

"Oh?" He leaned toward her.

"I mean I want to see the whole coast, and go up the rivers too. To paint."

"Not possible. Not for a woman alone."

Yes, but here he was, wind-burned and capable, a man of earthly resources who faced raw wind with a laugh, who lived free, answering only to the pull of the tides. And there was his funny little boat. And what tied her here? Certainly not any heaps of money she'd earn from teaching children. She imagined embarking north with him. Just for the summer. A practical arrangement.

"Not even possible for"—she worked to remember his words— *"une dame courageuse?"*

He laughed at her pronunciation. His amusement made her feel pretty.

"A fair-weather adventurer. Wait till you learn what rain really is. And mosquitoes with jaws as big as a crocodile's."

He made quick little pinching motions up her arm and neck to her earlobe. Goose bumps rose on her skin.

"I went to Hitats'uu alone."

"Alone you went?"

"For a whole week. I loved it."

"What's to love in a mean little row of bighouses?"

"The whole place. And the people. They are what they are. No pretending. I loved how they all live together. How they make what they need. Fine things. Cedar mats, baskets, hammocks." She thought of the platform in the menstrual hut, so carefully crafted it had made her ache with envy for such love. "Everything so full of feeling."

"Maybe it's you who is full of feeling." His eyes gleamed. "More than you know."

"They live by tradition and in harmony with nature too."

"Puh! You see with storybook eyes. You think they laugh at storms? Frostbite? Cougars? You think they smile at the place where they die?"

He opened a potato for her and laid it on a tin plate. "*Attention.* Hot."

"I mean, like you do. Cooking and sleeping outdoors."

His bottom lip protruded in a droll way. "I have no choice."

"Whatever the reason, they have something we don't."

"We?" He took a bite of potato.

"The we that live in cities."

"And what might that be, *ma philosophe?*" He grinned, half indulgence, half mockery.

"They know things about the workings of nature."

He pushed out his lips and scowled.

"And how places can feed us back again."

"You're sure of that now? After one week in a southern village, you know what they're like in the north?"

"I know what I saw." She stroked the pelts in nervousness—the otter so sleek, the mink making her palm tingle.

"Haida, Tlingit, Tsimshian, Kwakiutl. You think those tribes are all alike? Gitksan, Nisga'a, Mamalilikala. All the same?"

Those names, so full of mystery, vibrating in his accent. Maybe each one was different. All the more intriguing. "I want to find out. Everything."

"Everything?"

"*La Renarde Rouge.* Is she big enough for two?"

"And a four-legged rug?"

"I could paint the villages where you trade."

"You can sleep in a tent?"

"Yes."

"Cook over a fire? Live in the rain?"

"Yes. Yes!" Her splayed fingers moved through the muskrat.

He scratched behind his ear as if considering.

"Sleep in furs smelling of north woods and musk," she said.

He took a mink and stroked her cheek and throat with it. "It's warmer when you're bare against the fur." His breath came close in quick bursts.

"Yes," she whispered.

His lips grazed her skin, kissing. Murmurs of pleasure in exotic words. A brief flutter of tongue-touchings. A tightness and a trembling, a light-headedness too.

Her imagination sped ahead in confusion. She had to make him stop. Soon. In a minute. He pressed her shoulders, leaning her back, kissing, licking her neck. *He shoves it, and you have to take it. The first time rips you open.* Stop. Stop now. She pushed his chest a little, firm beneath the soft buckskin.

"Vixen, you tease me."

He opened his arms, and she scrambled to her feet.

"You go too soon."

She untied Billy's leash and began to climb the slope.

"You come tomorrow?" he called. "We talk about the north."

She had no breath to answer him.

She dragged herself home in delirious misery. She was not herself. Going up the stoop, she held on to the railing, her legs rubbery.

That night in her room she stared through the window at a moon like a shaving off a pearl, and buried her fingers in Billy's shaggy coat. What did she really know about love? Not much. Rushing back to her out of the past, the only other man in her life was Mayo Paddon, the ship's purser she'd met coming home from her first trip to Hitats'uu, acceptable to Dede and Lizzie because of his fine record of church attendance. Puh! He'd followed her to London, fawning, proposing six times, annoying her, interrupting her painting study. She hadn't felt a thimbleful of desire, not like she had with her childhood dream boy who knew how to whistle like a killdeer. He had smelled like acorns and sweet hay when she'd nestled in his arms on a white horse as they galloped in the sky to rest in the cup of a crescent moon.

Maybe Claude was right. Maybe she did see with storybook eyes. Dede told her more times than she could count how immature she was. Still, what if real love was even half as wonderful as that childhood fantasy? How could loving a place even come close? She felt wrapped tight as a bud. What if Father had exaggerated in that brutal telling? What if she'd confused his warning about sex with real love, and she would miss out for life and die a lonely old maid? She'd be a damned fool to let Father still have such power over her.

Besides love, there was the northland. She had to find out—would he or wouldn't he take her with him? In the joy of kissing, she'd felt momentarily free, but nothing was really free. She was prepared for that now, a give and take.

. . .

This time, she left Billy at home. She walked quickly and stopped at the top of the incline, stunned. The boats were gone. The tent intact, but no boats. He wasn't there. Her lungs stung with cold brine. She'd said no and no, and now that she might say yes a little, he wasn't there. She huddled against the tent to stay out of the wind and waited an hour. Two. She smoked four cigarettes, and watched the moving pattern of whitecaps. Wind lifted the feathers on the backs of black gulls and snapped the tent like a lightning crack.

At dusk his boat chugged into the cove, towing the skiff full of crates. A cry rushed out of her throat. She flung herself toward the water's edge.

"Mademoiselle Courageuse!" he called, smiling with all his might as he climbed out of the skiff, dragged it on shore, and bent her head back kissing her, all in one smooth movement. He drew her into the tent. No stories this time. And no furs in the tent. They'd all been sold. Instead, there were stacks of blankets for northern villages. How much longer would he be here?

He dropped to his knees and rubbed her hands warm, made a nest of blankets, rubbed some more, her arms, her thighs, briskly, his eyes deep and limpid.

"Why didn't you come inside the tent to stay warm?"

"I wanted to see your boat the minute it came. And to show you I'm not afraid of cold up north."

He raised one eyebrow. "Up north?"

His eyes told her he knew she was different than she'd been the day before. He yanked off his moleskin shirt. She stared at his shoulders and chest shaped by years of rowing. His hands on her face, her neck, her shoulders urged her to lie back. His face, a tawny moon, came down to her. He whispered in French. She threaded her fingers through his hair. His lips parted hers. He cupped her breast. "Round and full," he murmured. A quiver ran through her somewhere new, low, deep, and she was overcome by a moist presence. She felt his other hand under her skirt sliding between her knees.

"Like a salmon swimming up river, no?"

There will be thrust and tearing and blood. She clamped her legs shut.

He stopped, waited, kissed her. *"Comme ça. Doucement."* The words, his voice, gentle.

She trusted, relaxed her legs, and opened herself. They rolled together as if at sea until something else stopped her. Not Father. Grimmer than Father. She pushed against Claude's chest, his hair coarse under her palms.

"Don't tease me," he said huskily.

"I'm sorry. I don't mean to." Any second she would cry, right in front of him. She ducked out of the tent and scrambled up the incline. She looked back, hating herself for being wishy-washy.

He stood at the tent opening, shirtless, hands on his hips, and shouted into the wind, "If you go now, mademoiselle, don't come back!"

· · ·

Dumbly, she watched sheets of rain slide down her window the next day. Like liquid glass, she thought. Water poured out of the eaves troughs. Sitting on her bed, she fed dog biscuits to Billy, one at a time, and looked into his loving brown eyes. He'd begun to worship her, but probably only for the treats.

If you go now, mademoiselle, don't come back. Mademoiselle—the word he'd said so playfully had turned ugly. He didn't even say her name. Father might have clamped shut her body, yes, but not her heart. She couldn't deny the sting of Claude's last words.

She tried to become absorbed in painting the cove and camp from her sketches, yet something stopped her each time, just as it had with him. That panic was ridiculous at her age. But now it wasn't fear of the act of love. It was how the act might make her live, as Mother had, worshiping, a minion to a god, never having a single desire of her own that didn't fit with Father's plan. That was the grim thought that had stopped her.

The day after Father's brutal telling, when Mother had told her to meet him at James Bay Bridge to walk the last stretch home from work with him, as she always had, she'd refused. She turned silent and grumpy for weeks until Mother demanded to know why.

"He sits in church like some holy man. Why should he act as if he's God, because he's not, Mother. He's not," she'd said. She was too shocked and embarrassed to tell her why.

"You're a spoiled black crow, Emily. Pecking at him like a crow," Mother had said, the words coming in shallow, tubercular breaths.

"He's not." Whispered this time, because she knew the repetition was unnecessary.

Mother's hurt expression softened, as if she felt a double embarrassment that Emily knew that Father wasn't God, and that she, his wife, had known it all along, yet lived as though he were. Mother had seen judgment in her eyes for what she saw, and hadn't countered her. Right then, she'd said to herself that she, Emily Carr, would never live that way with any man. Never live in a house that pretended piety and concealed indecency. Would rather live in a teepee or a burned-out tree trunk than such a house. She'd screamed it to herself. They had stood like statues, face to face, two identical pairs of gray eyes looking at each other, both of them knowing that Mother was a woman in a way that she, Emily, would never be. Two women, both of them waiting for the other to speak, and neither did.

Would going with Claude mean a life like that? Going where he wanted to go, when he wanted, for his trade, regardless of what she wanted to paint? Still, it would be better than being stuck here only imagining love and all the rest.

Her pulse beat with urgency as the rain beat on the window. She waited for either one to let up. Neither one did. What would he do if she came back in this downpour? He'd have to take her into the tent. He'd see that she couldn't be deterred by mere rain, that she was an able woman to travel north.

She was stronger than Mother. She could still be herself, do what she hungered for. She would not be a shrinking violet, or a servant. *Une dame courageuse.* She heard the drums within her. She was ready, mind and body. She placed two dots of lavender toilet water on her throat, another between her breasts, and set out for the cove, in her cape, with an umbrella.

· · ·

La Renarde Rouge was gone. The skiff was gone. The tent was gone. The fire pit only wet ashes. The sea pocked and gray. The empty cove humiliated her. Wind knifed through her flesh to her womb.

She had come so far. He didn't know what she'd had to wade through to stand here, ready. He'd lost patience. She would shrivel. She was sure she would dry up and shrivel.

She slogged home dragging her umbrella, plodding through puddles, every splash reinforcing a promise to herself—no one would ever get her to reveal the sorry spectacle she was.

Billy was waiting for her inside the door. She passed him by without so much as a touch. She kicked off her shoes, stepped out of her dress, and crawled under her quilt. Billy put his chin on her pillow. His liquid eyes six inches from hers told her he was sorry. She reached out to rest her hand on his neck.

No, she wouldn't shrivel. But nothing, not his name or the sound of his words, could she allow to remind her of him. She got out of bed, tore up one of the cove sketches, lit the oil burner.

She stopped. Ridiculous to give up good work in the heat of the moment. Now that was immature. She tossed the rest onto a pile and flopped on the bed again.

"Come on, Billy. Come on up."

8 : Spruce

When Jessica came to the studio to collect her daughters after class on Saturday, a line of girls marched out the door, grabbing a cookie and singing.

Em'ly is an old maid.
All her clothes are homemade.
She's getting plump and dumpy.
All her shoes are clumpy,
But she's NEVER grumpy!

"Why, that's horrible!" Jessica said. "Who made that up?"

"I did," Emily said, deadpan, and the girls exploded into laughter.

"She taught us 'Hiawatha' too," said Megan, Jessica's oldest. Her voice became mysterious. "And, 'This is the forest primeval, the murmuring pines and the hemlocks bearded with moss.' "

"Look!" Louise, the youngest, displayed her fingernails.

Emily chuckled. She'd painted faces on them.

"Six new students today. Five new last week. I'm going to open a second session. And Megan's school wants me to start next week. For once, I don't have to worry about money."

"Where did they all come from?" Jessica asked.

"Apparently the society madams don't think I'm too critical or too cranky for their daughters, only for themselves."

"You're not too critical for me. I'm not making any progress."

"Why not?"

"I dropped out when they fired you."

"More than a month and you haven't told me that? You come with the girls and I'll murmur a critique in your direction once in a while—for what it's worth."

"It's worth the world to me."

"Then come woodsing with me Monday when they're in school. Sophie, my Squamish friend, and I are going to Stanley Park, the interior. I've never been there. She said you never know forests until you get inside. We could paint together."

"Honestly? You said you'd never teach adults again."

"Prattle. Besides, I didn't say I would teach there."

· · ·

Without a path in sight, Emily pushed through a tangle of honeysuckle behind Sophie and scrambled over fallen logs, feeling for the bottom below a blanket of needles and humus. She tugged on Billy's leash. Anything sniffable, he sniffed, blew scents out his nose, and stopped to sniff again. "Keep moving, Billy." Tommy and Annie Marie padded alongside him, and Jessica brought up the rear. Towering conifers made a canopy a hundred feet in the air, with the tops of trees a hundred feet beyond that. She felt small for a change. Only twenty minutes' walk into the interior and she'd lost all sense of a city nearby. Every branch stirring in a breeze became a threat, a cougar stalking, its hot snorting breath on her neck. This wasn't a park. It was wilderness, untouched by axe or footfall. Just like Claude had said about the north, *wilderness so formidable it can turn you inside out.* And then his eyebrows had popped up in awe.

She stepped unevenly on a cone and lost her balance. Pay attention! Forget him! She'd lost something of herself to him and she needed to become whole again. She wanted no more weepy days.

When she'd been troubled as a girl, she had taken her hurt outside, had lain with her face pressed down to earth's cool green cheek, smelled her fresh perfumes, and tried to feel earth's buried heart throb. If only that would be enough for her now.

"Don't you have the feeling we shouldn't be here?" Jessica asked.

"No, this is exactly where we should be." She thought of what a woman on the electric tram had said soon after she'd moved to Vancouver, that queer things happen in Stanley Park—suicides and attacks by cougars and bears. That had kept her out, but now, with Sophie, she felt intoxicated by the siren call of wind through branches, by the clean after-a-rain freshness. "Take a gulp of this air."

"I'd rather be taking a gulp of hot coffee."

Tommy pointed to a fungus shaped like half a mushroom growing on a spruce trunk, ridged on its shiny red-brown top, porous on its creamy underbelly, its edge ruffled delicately.

"That's a *tc'i*," Sophie whispered. "A sign of Kaklaitl."

"What's that?" Emily asked.

"Wild Woman of the Woods." Sophie regarded Tommy seriously. "Kaklaitl leaves that thing to tell children be home at sunset or she'll put them in her basket made of snakes. She want a son like Mary wanted one and got Jesus, and I wanted one and got you."

"What she look like?" Tommy asked.

"Wild black hair." Sophie made quick circular gestures around her head. "A wood leg." She took a few exaggerated, limping steps, stiff-legged and bent, sucking in air to make her cheeks hollow. "She cries, 'Huu, huu.' Be real quiet sometimes you hear her."

They all stood still and listened, Jessica bending forward, her hand cupped behind her ear. A hollow sound rang out, like someone striking a closed wooden box with a mallet.

"It's her! It's her!" Annie Marie shouted and snuggled into Sophie's skirt. The knocking came again, and changed to a sound of scraping across a ridged surface, and a kind of clucking that Emily loved.

"That's only Raven," Sophie said.

"That's not a bird," Annie Marie said.

"He makes a hundred noises," Sophie said. A bell-like chime followed by a kind of low, throaty yodel issued from the canopy of boughs. "That's him too."

They went deeper into the forest until Sophie stopped abruptly. She seemed to be absorbing the sight or smell or spell of something, as if storing it up so it would feed her back again later, like Lulu had said. She stood in utter stillness, not reaching out, but just letting it come to her if it would. Slowly Emily turned in a circle to see what it might be.

"All those greens juicy enough to drink," she murmured. "Jessica, see that spruce trunk encrusted with filigreed lichen? Lime green shot through with yellow."

"Look up," Jessica said.

The trees bowed in arches like cathedral vaulting. Shafts of sunlight filtered down through tufts of spruce foliage.

"It's the same soft light that comes through the windows in your church, Sophie," Emily said.

"What about the green?" Jessica asked.

"I'd call that Prussian green, like the sea when the sky is overcast."

Emily swept her hand across some moss thick as a looped rug turning rocks into hummocky pillows.

"Brilliant emerald," Jessica said.

"Except in shadow. There it's Hooker's middle green."

"A hundred of kinds of mosses," Sophie said proudly. "All different colors."

"Look at this." Jessica pointed to a rotting log sprouting saplings and licorice ferns. "Sap green like new spring leaves."

"For that cedar foliage, I'd use viridian. It's deeper. And for those lichens trailing from hemlock boughs, chromium oxide with gray to get that dull olive. Don't you want to just inhale those colors?"

She imagined them cleaning her lungs, and felt cradled in the bosom of the forest.

They set up their flat watercolor easels.

"Are you going to paint now?" Annie Marie asked.

"Yes. Now you have two people to watch."

Annie Marie snapped her head back and forth. Her mouth fell open when she realized it was true.

Billy sniffed until he found a half-dry bed of needles suitable for a snooze. He turned in circles, deciding how to position himself.

"For God's sake, Billy. Why don't you just sit down?"

After a few moments, Jessica asked, "How do you pick out anything as a subject? It's all so meshed together."

"That's why people say it's unpaintable. Don't be in a hurry."

The sun shifted and sent a shaft of light to illuminate a puddle, like molten brass. Perfect. That would be the point of highest light. The closest trunk on the right would be the darkest value. Everything else would be in between. Feelings came in words, and she wrote at the base of her painting: *The solemnity, the peace of this place, a lovely thing.*

· · ·

Still in her chenille housecoat and scuffs the blustery day before her student-and-teacher exhibit, Emily was printing out cards with the students' names when she heard a soft knock. Her sisters, she thought, and opened the door.

Sophie stood on the stoop with only the baby. "You need help to put up the pictures?"

"Oh, Sophie, you came across the inlet for that? But you have your own work to do."

"Any day for baskets. Today for pictures."

"You must be cold." She made her tea and warmed up some leftover vegetable soup. While Sophie ate, she seemed troubled.

"What's wrong, Sophie?"

"Mrs. Chief Joe Capilano. She saw you and me sitting on church steps. Now she wants me bring you to her house."

"That would be nice. I'd like to."

"No." Sophie's bottom lip pooched out. "I don't want share you with her. You're my friend. Not for her."

"Yes, but I have a heart bigger than for one friend."

"No. I don't want Mrs. Chief Joe get you."

"Sophie, no one will ever take your place. You'll always be my best friend. We have good shares."

Sophie's face lifted, her cheeks pushing up and making her eyes squint. She slurped the last of the broth in the bowl and they set out for the studio a few blocks away.

"You have two houses? Only one person and two houses?"

Emily unlocked the door. "This one isn't where I sleep. It's where I work."

"Why you don't live and work together? One work. One place."

It did seem extravagant. What was she hanging on to? Hope of a life other than painting?

Sophie surveyed the row of children's watercolors already tacked on the wall—driftwood with seagulls, the Billingsgate Fish Wharves, boats and fishnets, creatures they found in the tide pools. She scratched her forehead. "Too high."

Emily stepped back. "They're just right. Chest-high."

"Not for babies who made them."

Emily let the head of the tacking hammer fall into her palm. "All right. You win." She took them down and let Sophie set the height—low all around the room—while she drove in nails where Sophie told her.

"Why do you call these older children babies?"

"Because their mamas love them when they old same as when they babies."

The contentment of working together, humming, giggling when they both chose the same one to put up next, filled her, and she thought, This is the joy that sisters might feel.

"Annie Marie would like the ones of Billy," Sophie said.

"You know, she could come to my class. I'd love it."

Sophie shook her head. "Only white children."

"That's only in your head, Sophie, not mine."

They hung Emily's work, many of them from Stanley Park, on a row above the children's work. The two largest watercolors they hung opposite each other, shafts of light in a cedar grove, and the Ancestor. Sophie stood in front of the Ancestor with her hands on her hips. "Maybe Ancestor will make strong talk to white people too."

They finished as it was beginning to get dark.

"Will you be all right going home?"

Sophie made her hand cut through the air in front of her. "I just put the canoe straight and keep to paddling." She wrapped the baby in her shawl.

"That's not much warmth for going across the water. Do you want to stay here tonight? In my house, I mean?"

"No. My other babies and Frank won't know where I am."

"Then take my coat." She put it over Sophie's shoulders.

Sophie stroked the lapel and gazed at Emily in wonderment. "Only for borrowing. I bring back soon."

"Come tomorrow night for the show. Bring Jimmy."

"No. Ancestor is enough."

Her baby's eyes were closed as she went out the door. Sophie turned back and grinned. "Next time, make the forest more dark."

· · ·

"Did Lizzie and Dede even think about coming?" Emily asked Alice the morning of the exhibit.

Alice stuffed her gloves into her handbag as though the act required total concentration. "No. Yes. Lizzie's a bit under the weather and—"

"It's all right. You don't have to say."

Alice pulled in her lips and quickly turned toward the exhibit. She gushed over the children's drawings, but in front of the work from Hitats'uu, she didn't utter a syllable.

"Even a grunt is better than dead silence."

Alice stopped in front of the small drawing of Lulu at the menstrual hut. Without knowing the custom, a person wouldn't understand it, but maybe the womb and infants painted on the wall would give her a clue. If it were Dede, she'd be tempted to shock her with the truth and snicker over it in bed that night, but with Alice, she hoped for a spontaneous moment of intimacy.

"She looks dreamy."

At least that was something.

Alice passed over the Ancestor figure quickly.

"That's the largest thing in the room and you act as though it's invisible."

"I . . . He's so severe." She turned to the watercolor of the cedar grove. "I like this best. How the light falls between the branches. Why don't you call it *Cathedral Light?*"

"Does it look like that to you? Oh, Alice, I wish you'd go there with me. It's Stanley Park. The interior. It's so deep and quiet and still. It could heal a person, body and soul. I get a sense of some presence breathing there. God's too big to be squeezed into a stuffy church, but I feel Him there in the spaces between the trees."

Alice observed her a moment, dewy-eyed, as though through all the years she had doubted whether her rebel sister even believed in God, and now she was relieved.

Emily felt a sheepish smile form. "It's good to have you here. At least I can say one third of my family supports me."

"One fourth," Alice corrected. "Clara."

"Yes. Clara. Only one in five a married woman. Hasn't that ever struck you as odd? As meaning something?"

"Not particularly. It's kind of sad, though."

They were quiet awhile, and peaceful. She might not have another chance to ask for a long time. "Was there ever some injury Father did to you? Was he ever crude to you?"

Alice gave her an odd look. "No. He was never warm to me, but I never hated him like you did in your black crow period. We couldn't understand it because he loved you best."

"He did not."

"Of course he did. We all knew it. He even looked at you differently than he did at the rest of us."

"How?"

"More lingering, I would say. Protective, maybe—you being the youngest and prettiest. 'Oh, those exotic eyes and dark hair. She'll be a beauty, that one,' he used to say."

Emily snorted. "Flat eyes, you mean, the right one larger than the left. Right eyebrow too heavy. Face too wide. Cheeks like biscuit dough. Hair crinkly. Shoulders like a stevedore."

"All right, all right." Alice pushed her palms against the air to stop her. "Still, his attentions to you enraged Lizzie. That's what made her so fierce in winning his love the only way she was sure of, by being more Christian than you."

"She won that just by the way she opened the Bible."

Alice snickered in a very un-Alice-like way.

"He never spoke bluntly to you—about men or sex?"

Alice looked at her, not with the offended astonishment Lizzie or Dede would have wielded to affirm their moral superiority, the overdone shock that couldn't be trusted. Alice's look was genuine innocence—the way she negotiated life. And in that look, with Alice slowly shaking her head, she knew. It had only been her. Thank God. Father hadn't with any of the others.

• • •

Jessica and her family were the first to arrive. Parents and grandparents poured in. The Vancouver Ladies' Art Club arrived in a group, overdressed. Emily snickered to Jessica as they entered. "A parade of ruffled layer cakes." When the last one came through the door, she added, "Interesting. No madam president."

"You think I'd invite her?"

And no Sophie. She wished she had insisted that she come.

Most said the children's work was fresh and original. Parents glowed. "You're a fine teacher," one woman said. She nodded her thanks. They called her drawing of three Nootka girls in shawls "charming," and a pen and ink of the village "quaint."

"Why are you scowling?" Alice whispered. "Those words should make you float."

"I don't want to be charming and quaint. Leave that to the jabber-and-scratch ladies."

"For God's sake, Millie, what *do* you want?"

Emily caught sight of the womb on the hut. "Something deeper."

She overheard a man say, "I don't care for Indian things."

It made her skin crawl. She took the tray of cookies out of Alice's hands and walked through the room offering them just so she could pass him right by. Later that same man bought two small coastal scenes for twelve dollars each. Heat flushed her cheeks. She fetched the cookie tray. "Here, take some home with you."

At the edge of the room she whispered to Alice, "Nothing like cold hard cash to make a body feel all puckered up."

In front of a watercolor of Hitats'uu with the sea serpent canoe, she told several mothers of her plan to take the older students to the Mission Reserve in North Vancouver to draw canoes. "They're simple shapes to draw. The children will learn about line, and they'll like the animals on the bows." The women exchanged glances, stood more rigidly.

Jessica was the last to leave. "I feel I have to tell you. They don't want you to take their children to the reserve."

"Just to the beach."

"The parents don't want pictures of canoes." Jessica rolled her fist in her palm. "It's just that I think you ought to know. They may pull their children out if you do it. I wouldn't, you understand. My girls love you, Emily, and you know how I feel."

She felt Alice's anxious eyes on her, waiting for her answer. Jessica put on her coat.

"It's not the canoes, is it, Jessica?"

Jessica finally faced her, as pained as Alice. "No. It's not. It's fear."

"All those pious wives of timber merchants and shipping clerks despise anything native. They want to make Canada an imitation Europe and ignore the rest." She picked a cookie off the table and bent it until it broke apart in her palm. Alice immediately swept up the crumbs.

Living with that neatness, and Lizzie's judgment, and Dede's iron rule—she'd have to if she lost her students and couldn't make a living here. Or, living her own life, living close to the reserve, living to paint, a devotion as absorbing as Alice's kindergarten, Lizzie's missionary society, Sophie's children—that would cost her. The children's classes were too lucrative to risk. Any risks she took would have to be where it counted, for her art.

"Thanks, Jessica. You can tell them I'll keep them on the *civilized* side of Burrard Inlet."

9: Mew Gull

Wind blew Emily's skirt between her legs as she and Billy walked the wooden path at the reserve. She put her hands in her pockets and felt the smooth shell Sophie had put there when she returned the coat.

It was February. Snow runoff streaked mud on the walkway, and the freeze had caused some planks to warp. As she stepped on a spot that gave way, dirty water squirted up her skirt. Billy zigzagged in front of her sniffing for salmon heads, new grasses, any sign of life. A mew gull gave an agonized, mournful cry. She sympathized.

She hadn't seen Sophie since Christmas time when she'd brought a cherry pie, a rag doll with black yarn braids she'd made for Annie Marie, a kite for Tommy, and a tiny black-and-white-striped knit cap for the baby. Too long a time, but winter was basket-making season so Sophie hadn't come for tea or soup on her rounds of peddling as she had during warmer weather. She'd gone to the reserve to see her once since then but Sophie wasn't there, and Mrs. Johnson said, "Gone today. Don't know where."

Fog obscured the mountains behind the reserve, and a heavy charcoal sky pressed down the sea. Beached canoes covered by gray tarps lay like stranded whales. Gray-green scum floated on puddles. The village seemed to be sinking into mud, more forlorn than ever, empty, waiting for a single green shoot. Her heels on the planks jarred the leaden day.

The mewling came again, and chilled her.

She knocked at Sophie's closed door. It inched open. Women's cries burst through the crack. She saw a sliver of coppery face, iron gray hair and a large abalone earring stretching down to a purple shawl. The eyebrow lifted. The door opened. Aromas of smoke and wet wool seeped out. She made Billy sit outside.

In the center of the floor, a small pine coffin rested on a tule mat. Her watercolor of Tommy under the Ancestor lay on the wood—Tommy, the sweet boy with trusting eyes who had let her blow his nose. A lump swelled in her throat. Sophie slouched against the wall, her ashen face blank with grief. Across the room their eyes met, and Sophie broke into a cry.

A circle of women wrapped in shawls and blankets wept on the floor. Eyes and lips pinched closed, some of them coughing, they didn't notice her. All but one, a woman in a rust-colored blanket whose narrowed eyes drilled into her. Next to her, she recognized Mrs. Johnson's head hooded by a brown shawl. The older woman who had come to the door rejoined the circle. Emily felt dizzy in the pungent air of the closed room, and lowered herself to the floor.

Sophie poured water from an enameled basin into a smaller, shallow one and carried it around the circle of women. One by one, they washed their faces. When Sophie offered it to Emily, the woman in the rust-colored blanket shot her a cold stare. Maybe joining in would make it harder for Sophie with her friends. Sophie inched the basin toward her and lowered her eyes to the water. Emily dipped in her hands. "I'm so sorry," she whispered, hating such easy, incapable words.

The women crooned in Squamish to Sophie, to each other, to Annie Marie huddled in the corner in a daze. Something seemed missing in that corner. The basket cradle! She scanned the room. The house was in disarray. Cherry bark, cedar roots, beargrass, and finished baskets lay scattered instead of in their usual neat piles.

The gray-haired woman in the purple shawl motioned for Emily to follow her into the other room. "I'm Sarah, Sophie's auntie," she said softly. "You are Em'ly?"

She patted the bed, inviting her to sit. The handmade featherbed was thin and lumpy. The window near it was broken, and stuffed into the open space was some blue print fabric in a familiar pattern—one of her cast-off dresses, too tight.

"Sophie likes you. You're honest, she say."

"So is she."

Folds of skin lined Sarah's eyelids, and one eye opened wider than the other. In the grooves that ran bow-shaped from her wide nostrils around her mouth to her chin, there was something motherly and aristocratic.

"How did it happen?"

"A hard winter. Many die. Margaret Dan . . ." She looked through the open doorway to the woman sitting stiffly beside Sophie in the rust-colored blanket. "She lose a baby too."

Margaret Dan must have heard. She gave Emily a cold look. You don't belong here, her eyes seemed to say. You don't know what suffering is.

"Some older ones die too."

Influenza? Whooping cough? Measles scuttling through the reserve?

"What about Sophie's baby?"

"Gone. Not baptized. Sophie thinks she made Ancestor mad when she baptize babies."

That child was on Sophie's back when she paddled home across the inlet at dusk. She should never have let her go home that night.

"The little one, Sophie held him four days. Touch is medicine. Then Tommy got sick and coughed blood. Sophie had no more touch for Tommy too."

If she'd only known, she would have been here, feeding him, keeping him warm, giving him medicine, helping Sophie. "What can I do? Is there anything I can do?"

"No."

Annie Marie waddled into the room dragging a blanket, and snuggled into Sarah's lap. Sarah stroked her hair, and Annie Marie slumped against her breast and played with her purple fringe. Sarah rested her cheek against the child's head. Emily held Annie Marie's bare feet, as cold as if they'd been fished from the sea. She rubbed them until they were warm, and then wrapped them in her skirt.

"A bad spirit come to the reserve," Sarah whispered. "Don't say anything. The *nipniit* fine me in church for say that. Church priests can do that, you know. But I am an old woman. I know spirits. Sophie and Margaret fight. The bad spirit doesn't like. Margaret's baby dead. Now Tommy dead too."

Wind whistled through the floorboards stirring the odors of damp and sickness and bodies. The keening started again. "Three days going like this here," Sarah said, "until *nipniit* come."

Sarah gestured toward the door to the main room and they re-joined the circle. The women rocked. Emily rocked too, forward and back, folding herself over her crossed arms. At some cue she couldn't detect, the women stopped, and Margaret Dan brought the water basket around again but passed her by without pausing. She wished she were invisible. The women clucked their comfort to Sophie as another woman went around the circle and put some small thing into each of their hands. When the woman's wool skirt brushed Emily's arm, she felt, pressed into her palm, the cool disc of a quarter. She turned to Sarah, puzzled.

"Sophie pay you for witness," Sarah whispered. "To thank you for cry."

Emily puffed out air. "Thank me!"

Those quarters were harder for Sophie to come by than baskets. Her hand curled around it and held it to her ribs.

"What happens next?"

"The *nipniit* comes here. Father John. We go to the graveyard. He talks. Tommy's soul goes to the sunset."

Everyone stood up. Emily moved close to Sophie and opened her arms to enfold her when Margaret Dan scowled at her. She hadn't seen anyone else embrace Sophie. She let her arms drop.

"Tommy never cried," Sophie said.

Emily nodded.

"It feel like I lost my Casamin twice. Six babies gone."

"I'm so, so sorry. Is there anything I can do?"

"Margaret Dan has four now. You see this coffin?" The rough wood, split and warped, was pulling away at one joint and nails showed in the opening. "The coffin maker in North Vancouver, he thinks good enough for Indian baby." She turned and smiled. Incredibly, she smiled, as genuinely as if she had no sorrow. "Look, Em'ly! Lots of baskets. Tommy's going to have a big white gravestone with a cross carved, like Margaret Dan's boy."

The door opened and two men entered. Billy nosed his way in behind them as though he had already met them.

"Frank," Sophie said. "This is Em'ly."

Jimmy Frank and Sophie spoke softly in Squamish, his face without animation. The oily skin under his eyes drooped. He was stocky, with thick hair and muscular arms. He wore heavy work boots and a rumpled coat. She couldn't tell what color it had once been.

He turned to Emily. "Sophie talks about you all the days. The white lady that paints. In my house, you're the same as family."

"Thank you. I always like to be here." She felt a seed of happiness drop in her lap which would nourish her at some more appropriate time. "I'm so sorry about Tommy."

Jimmy Frank nodded, and stroked Billy behind the ears. "This your dog?" His fingers lingered at Billy's neck.

"Yes. His name's Billy."

Jimmy crouched down, his big hands over Billy's body steady and firm, calming him until they were friends. "You're a good dog, Billy. My boy told me about you," he said softly.

He went into the bedroom and pried loose two bottom planks

of the back exterior wall. "Old Indian way," Sophie said, her eyes darting from Sarah to Emily, her lips pinched.

"So death will not come through the front door," Sarah explained.

Sophie turned away from Jimmy as he pushed the coffin through the opening to the other man standing outside. Was she turning away because it was the custom that the mother shouldn't watch, or was Sophie embarrassed by the native custom in front of her white friend?

Except for Annie Marie and Sarah, everyone went outside into the drizzle. The women lifted shawls and blankets over their heads and the men wore felt hats. Emily had nothing. When Sarah noticed her bare head from the doorway, she stepped outside and draped her purple shawl over Emily's head. It smelled of smoke and wet wool.

"Thank you," Emily said.

Billy moved excitedly from person to person, sniffing. "No, Billy, stay down," she said several times until finally she had to tie him to a bare bush. He whined a little. "I'm sorry, Billy, but you have to be good and stay here."

The priest arrived to start the procession. Jimmy Frank and the other man carried the coffin. Jimmy sang his hurt in hollow, hypnotic tones. *"Aadidaa, aadidaa, aadidaa."*

Sophie followed the coffin. Margaret Dan sidled in front of Emily to walk with Sophie. Emily fell into step with Mrs. Johnson, who stiffened at her approach. "Poor Sophie," Emily whispered.

"You can't be her friend in the way you think," Mrs. Johnson said.

"Why not?"

"We're different. You're different. You shouldn't expect so much. It will only hurt. I know."

They walked the rest of the way to the cemetery in silence.

The procession passed the cross, streaked pearl gray in the dim light, to the newer area behind it. Emily's shoes sank into mud, and rain drilled on her shoulders. The priest droned his *"domini spiritu sanctu,"* then spoke in Squamish or Chinook, she couldn't tell which, then in English. From the back of the group, and under wheeling, crying gulls, she heard only bits of phrases riding on the wind: "The face of the Lord shining upon the little ones." She couldn't hear him explain why "His mercy cannot be measured," but she had a clear line of vision to the little coffin resting near the small hole. Rain darkened the yellow wood to ochre and ran in rivulets around its base. She stared at the crack in its seam, and hoped this *nipniit* wouldn't take much longer.

Sophie had no tears at the grave. Weathered resignation lined the women's faces, as though this were just life. She looked past the cross to the Ancestor, but couldn't see beyond the fence where Tommy's baby brother had been laid among the heathen.

After the reciting and responding, after the sprinkling, the lowering, the covering, people murmured in flat voices, nodded goodbye, and went off to their houses. Sophie dropped back to walk with Emily, and Margaret Dan whirled around, leveling at Emily a look vibrating with resentment. What was she to do? Shrivel up and disappear?

Their footsteps thudded dully on the wood. "I want lots more babies," Sophie said. "Frank knows. He wants them too. Indian men drink medicine to stay strong until they old."

Ahead, under slumped shoulders, Jimmy Frank walked with a tired stride, his hands cracked and grimy.

Sophie slowed, and Emily watched an idea take shape in her mind. Her eyes glistened and her voice took on a bright earnestness. "When I get more babies, I share one with you."

"Sophie! What are you talking about? People don't share babies."

Sophie's face fell into a pout, and she marched ahead.

Could she have been serious? Emily felt her breath knocked out of her. She had offended Sophie in the deepest way.

"No worry. It's only for borrowing," she said over her shoulder, her words clipped.

In a few minutes Sophie waited to walk with her. "When I get a girl, her name will be Em'ly Maria."

Emily breathed more easily. "That would be very nice."

A short way off, Emily saw Sarah bareheaded in the rain, whisking Sophie's house with a small cedar bough.

Sophie lunged ahead, shrieking, "No! No, Auntie! This is a Christian house. We don't need the old ways."

Sarah continued to brush. "Wash away death," she murmured.

Sophie snatched the branch from Sarah and threw it onto the mud. "No. I am a Christian woman. I have a Christian friend."

Emily flinched. Was this tirade for her benefit? She glanced at Mrs. Johnson, who raised her shoulders and tipped her head, as if to say, See?

Emily handed Sarah the shawl and stepped back.

The thin skin around Sarah's wet eyes puckered as she glared at Sophie. "You don't know what you are."

10 : Killer Whale

Emily stood with Alice in their Skagway hotel room and watched ghostly figures passing through sheets of rain, the wettest summer she could remember. Fog obscuring the coastline on the way north and three days of downpour here had made any sketching impossible. The town was shut tight. The Klondike gold strike over a mountain pass in the Yukon seemed more than ten years ago. Assay offices and saloons were boarded up with weathered planks. All the hurlyburly was gone. Foghorns moaned a dirge.

"Sounds like cows with the collywobbles," Emily said.

"Our whole time here, wasted," Alice said, her forehead against the window.

It had seemed such a good idea—a trip to coastal Alaska to help Alice get over her gloom from losing half a finger slicing bread, the horrible result of her poor eyesight. Even Dede had agreed and loosened her hold on their trust fund. Best of all, it got her north, without needing Claude du Bois. But it would take dogged effort to jolly Alice out of the grumps.

"You know I'm not very good at concocting cheer, but at least I'm making an effort. Watch."

She drew a caricature of the two of them dripping wet, bedraggled, rain pouring off their umbrella, an enormous hump of a bandage on Alice's left hand, a pick in the other, shovel propped over Emily's shoulder, paintbrushes stuck above her ears, both of them in enormous overshoes leaping across a puddle. Underneath, she wrote: *Gold Rush Gals on Liquid Holiday.*

Alice smiled in spite of herself.

"I think I'll send it to Dede," Emily said.

"She should have come instead of me."

"Ooh, poor-dear-little-me. Let's cherish our misery a little longer."

"You'd be miserable too if you'd lost a finger and couldn't hold a brush."

The thought brought her up sharp. "You're right. I'm sorry."

Emily scrutinized her stubby fingers and knobby knuckles, not feminine like Alice's, but capable of steady strokes. For that alone, she liked them.

"I took my kindergartners to the park once to fly a kite," Alice said. "When it dove into a bush, a baby bird on a branch got tangled in the kite string. I wanted so much to free it, the children were crying, but when I came close, it flapped and yanked so that the string cut into its leg."

"So what'd you do?"

"It flew away, but the foot fell into my hand." A muscle in Alice's chin quivered.

"At least it wasn't a child."

Alice's right hand slid over her damaged left one. "That's not the point. That bird was damaged. Any other bird could see that. Imperfect creatures are shunned." Her voice rose, shrill but soft. "She'll probably never get a mate." Her eyes, moist now, asked for understanding.

Emily put her hand over Alice's. She'd never guessed. Even nearing forty, Alice was hoping for love. The mutilation of her finger made that hope less likely. To Alice, one small spot of ugliness was enough to kill her chance of marriage.

She felt choked with love and sadness. Of all the sisters, Alice was the pretty one—her eyes golden brown as a hazelnut, her face colored like a damask rose and crowned by luxuriant auburn hair. She knew that lemon yellow was Alice's favorite color, that Lily of the Valley was her preferred talcum powder, even that Alice slept on her right side, but this, Alice's hope and disappointment still so raw, she had not known.

What could she say? She had her own lost hope, had tried to bury it, and all that was left was a shadowy loneliness that made her wonder things at night. Did Claude ever think of her? Camping alone night after night, did he ever feel the bite of solitude? Did he ever roast a potato on the fire and remember how naturally he'd said, "*Attention*. Hot," as though they'd known each other for years?

Did he wish he'd stayed in camp just one more night to give her another chance?

She stood behind Alice and rubbed her neck and shoulders. "We start this life and we've got, most of us, all that we need. Then circumstance or accident robs us—a finger or a toe or a friend or a dream—and we go on, and maybe we even learn something. Loss or no loss, we go on."

Alice waved off Emily's hands and shook out her shoulders. "Lizzie's the preacher in the family. The role doesn't suit you."

"We go on. I think I learned that from Sophie."

"Who's she?"

"A Squamish woman I took those clothes to. You talk about loss? Sophie's lost six children. Six, and she still breathes."

Alice winced. "She mustn't have taken care of them."

"It's not that, because it happens to many native women. They die of white diseases, Alice. They die because they live exposed to the elements."

"Don't be taken in."

"She's solid, like a cedar."

"You don't see them realistically."

"I see them as people, imperfect as we all are, but real."

"You see them as figures out of Longfellow. You see everything that way."

"That's not true!"

"Your ideal Indian. There's a lot you miss, Millie. Your romanticism blinds you. None of your paintings show them dirty or drunk or lying on the street."

"What good would that do, for them? Don't they already have enough people seeing them that way? I refuse to join that horde. I may not understand things about them, but what I see, I love."

Alice rolled her eyes. "I know. You drummed it into me in bed at night when we were girls. 'By the shores of Gitche Gumee, by the shining Big-Sea-Water ...'" Alice put on a mock-serious face, extended her arm, palm down, and moved it left to right.

Grinning, Emily made a tent of her hands. '... Stood the wigwam of Nokomis.'"

"'Daughter of the Moon, Nokomis...'" Alice gazed up to her fingers encircling an imaginary moon above her head.

They burst into laughter. "See, Alice? Seeing with storybook eyes is good for something."

. . .

They left Skagway hoping to escape the rain, and arrived in Sitka harbor nestled in the V of mountains.

"A spanking fine day, eh?" Emily said. "That sky! Pure cerulean blue."

Along the dock, fishing boats and canoes rocked against pilings reeking of creosote. Emily breathed in and exhaled in a big, satisfying puff. "Take a gulp of adventure."

Kerchiefed Tlingit women squatted along the road and leaned against warehouses to sell their goods—bowls of berries, carved spoons, beaded skin bags and mittens, animal-teeth necklaces, rattles made of deer hooves.

"Did you see these, Millie?" Alice stopped at a display of miniature wooden canoes painted in red and turquoise and black. "How darling. How much?"

"Two dollar." The woman looked at Alice's feet.

"Too much. I like, but too much. Maybe I come back." Alice lingered. "Maybe I not find anything else and I come back."

Emily cringed and stole a glance at the seller, whose wide bronze face showed no reaction even while she leaned toward the seller next to her and said in perfect English, "It's the ones with shiny shoes that bargain most."

Mortified, Emily pulled Alice away.

A young man sat on a blanket behind a single flat, open-backed drum, about twenty inches across. Deerskin, his sign said. He held it toward her as she crouched to get a closer view. It was painted with an eagle shown from two perspectives, the bird's body and head in profile with one fierce eye, and the wings spread equally to the sides, as if seen from the front. He handed her a drum mallet. When she struck it on the bird's chest, a deep boom resonated, the vibration traveling up her arm.

"Did you make this?" Emily asked.

"My father."

"Tell him it's very fine." She reached for her money. "Tell him I will feel honored to own it."

His pleased look stayed with her as she and Alice walked across town to the Russian Orthodox Cathedral of St. Michael, a blue-gray clapboard with an onion dome and cupola. The dim interior smelled of incense and melting wax. She examined a row of ornate icons depicting The Last Supper—sad faces and downcast eyes painted flatly on yellowed ivory above torsos draped in tarnished silver. Positively medieval.

"It's like we stepped into Poland or Russia," Alice said.

"Sophie would love it. 'Very Christian,' she'd say, and kiss her fingertip and dare to touch a disciple's foot."

Alice gave her a wry look. "Do I detect a note of judgment?"

"No. Just sympathy."

A mass was in progress. The parishioners were mostly Tlingits, but they sang in some ancient Slavic tongue.

"What could those sounds possibly mean to them?" Emily whispered. "Their songs should imitate wind or ravens."

"Sh."

She held the drum by its back crosspieces, raised the mallet, and struck the stretched hide at the eagle's chest. A deep resonant tone went out in waves. Heads turned toward her. Alice grabbed the mallet and hurried her outside.

"You're incorrigible, Millie. It's embarrassing being with you."

Emily laughed. "Just imagine what those people are going to remember right before they fall asleep tonight."

· · ·

They checked into a hotel, sent for their bags from the steamer office, and Emily asked if there was a native community nearby. The proprietor directed them out Katlian Street along Sitka Channel to the Tlingit village.

Rockweed and alkaline tidal deposits gave off a potent smell. Clouds scudded swiftly, letting bright sunlight through one minute, leaving cold shade the next. They stopped at the edge of the village and peered through tall rice grass that caught the sunlight like polished swords. There weren't any traditional bighouses like Hitats'uu's. The place was more like Sophie's reserve, with separate houses. One had a cormorant painted under the gable. Only one.

"It's so dreary and poor," Alice said.

"There aren't any totem poles." She couldn't understand it. Claude said there would be poles everywhere in the north.

"What do you think those red flannel rags hanging on that rack are for?"

"They're salmon filets. Very thin. I've seen them at Hitats'uu and at Sophie's reserve."

The sun came out and shone right through them, illuminating them like red-orange flames and showing striations in the flesh.

Beyond fishnets strung on willows, she saw beached canoes and dories. "Maybe those canoes have creatures painted on them," Emily said. "Come on, a little closer."

"No. It stinks here," Alice said.

A woman stepped out of a doorway, sauntering in their direction with a slow, hip-rolling gait.

"Let's leave," Alice said and retreated.

Emily followed. Had Claude only told her stories she wanted to hear? She shook her head slowly. "I can't understand why there aren't any totem poles."

· · ·

Morning fog was lifting as they walked beyond the town in the direction opposite the Tlingit village. While Emily stopped to sketch a wooden ore sluice, Alice strolled ahead. In a few minutes she hurried back and tugged Emily's arm.

"Stop what you're doing. There's something here you'll think is worth the whole trip."

Around a bend and hidden by spruce trees, a totem pole stood right there, not twenty feet from them.

"Whooh! God Almighty!"

A bear, a man holding a fish, a bird, and other creatures she couldn't identify sat atop one another, all painted in shiny red, bright turquoise, white, gray, and black.

"I knew there had to be," Emily said, looking up its length.

"Gaudy, eh?" Alice said.

"Granted, but the inventiveness."

"Lizzie would call them graven images."

Alice pointed to a sign announcing *Totem Pole Walk*, explaining that Haida and Tlingit poles had been removed from their villages on islands and the mainland, repaired, repainted, and moved to this government park.

They entered an alley of spruce with poles at regular intervals. The next was more strange than the first. The bottom creature, whatever it was, had black eyes, but not like the eyes on Claude's boat. These eyes had lids, like human eyes.

"It's grotesque," Alice said.

"Maybe the notions of ugliness and beauty we're used to don't apply here. Maybe we have to grow a little."

Alice cleared her throat and tipped her head. "Over there."

A middle-aged white man was sitting before an easel. Emily and Alice exchanged glances and walked toward him.

He touched the brim of his felt hat. "Afternoon."

Alice returned a greeting. His canvas was nearly finished, a composition of three poles, but only one stood in front of him.

"That's fine draftsmanship," Emily said.

"My sister is an artist too," Alice said.

He nodded an acknowledgment. "Ted Richardson, from Minneapolis."

"Do you always paint Indian things?" Alice asked.

It sounded like criticism. Alice's crisp way could be taken wrong. She probably only meant to keep him talking for her sake.

"Poles mostly. There's a big market for native motifs. I've been coming here every summer for twenty years."

"Here? This same park?" Emily asked.

"Not here always. Sometimes to the interior, or to islands."

"How do you know where to go?" Emily asked.

"Indians will guide anybody for a price. Money talks. The old ways are fading. They know what gold is. One chief sold his father's pole for gold. They won't last, these old poles."

"Where are there more?" Emily asked.

"Up the Nass and Skeena Rivers, you'll find Tsimshian bands. Haida are mainly on the Queen Charlotte Islands. And Tlingit in Alaska."

"What's that on top?" Alice asked, pointing to the actual pole he was painting. "Is that a derby?"

"Yes. To signify a white man. It's a shame pole. A chief found a Boston man starving, brought him home, and his daughter nursed him. The man repaid him by teaching him how to gamble. He won all the Indian's furs, then took off with the daughter."

Good Lord! Emily hoped Claude didn't do things like that.

"That's awful," Alice said. "They don't worship these carvings, then?"

"No. They just represent powerful ancestors that they identify with."

"Where do you sell your work?" Emily asked.

"A gallery in New York takes as much as I can turn out."

Outside of England and San Francisco, she didn't know anyone who made a living by painting. What's more, he was painting totem poles!

"Are you working here tomorrow? Could I join you?"

"Yes. My pleasure."

Safely out of hearing, Alice asked, "Was his painting good?"

"Good composition."

"He wasn't painting what was in front of him, though. He moved them all together."

"But he arranged those three poles nicely—the dominant one up close showing only the two lowest figures on it, the two other poles farther away to show their height."

Alice shook her hands. "But on the real pole the man wearing a derby wasn't standing on the bear. He was way at the top. That might mean something."

It pleased her that Alice cared. "Hm. Maybe changing it is going too far."

· · ·

She brought lunch for Ted the next morning in case he might be tempted to go back into town in the middle of the day.

"Which one do you want to paint?" he asked.

"All of them." She grinned. "I want to stay here the rest of the summer."

A slight scowl wormed its way across his forehead.

"But I can't, so tell me everything you know in one fell swoop, and then we'll paint."

He turned to the first pole. "You can tell the difference between Tlingit and Haida. This one is a Tlingit house post, which means it was in or on a house, so it's not as tall. Each figure is separated from the ones above and below it by a groove, and the forms are rounded." They walked past another and stopped. "Here the forms are intertwined without a horizontal groove."

A beaver's stretched tongue lay on the forehead of a bird beneath it, and some creature's legs were coming out a bear's ear.

"Ingenious. Haida?"

"Yes. You've got it. Haida poles are more massive, taller. More sharply edged, and unpainted."

She saw that the animals were stretched or compressed. The carvers had divided space in proportion to the tapering width, not according to the relative size of the real animal. A beaver could be as large as a whale, a bear smaller than a raven. A beak could be larger than the bird's body, or the angle of a wolf's eyes could be slanted to look wicked. Carvers must have chuckled at the liberties they took. But they were taking liberties with the animals' forms, in the first act of creation. That was different from the liberties Ted had taken in re-ordering them on the pole.

"Do you know what all the animals are?" she asked.

"Yes. You'll catch on to traditional characteristics the more you see. Two teeth for a beaver. Hooked beak for an eagle. Straight beak for a raven. Short snout and round ears for a bear."

She was swept away by their depictive power and ingenuity. The more she learned about them, the less bizarre they seemed.

"Each one seems greater than the last one."

"Chiefs competed to build their reputations by the impressiveness of their poles." He cast a sideways glance at her. "Competition thrives here."

If only Sophie could see them. They'd make her feel proud and strong.

"Of course, you can't get a true picture from these poles in the park," he said.

"Why not?"

"The colors are inaccurate. That's white man's bright manufactured paint. Tlingit colors were more subtle to begin with, and they were allowed to weather naturally."

"How did they make their paint?"

"They ground minerals into powder and mixed it with chewed

salmon eggs as a binding medium. Black is made by burning red ochre from an iron-rich spring near Ketchikan. The rust red is from a cinnabar deposit at Yakutat Cave. The turquoise from the clay of Kruzof Island. The greenish copper from Copper River."

She imagined Tlingit families loving the pole-to-come enough to travel great distances in canoes to get the minerals, transporting the powders in painted skin pouches cradled in hands that knew their worth. The thought made her inexpressibly happy.

Ted scratched his bushy sideburn. "Which one do you want to paint?"

"Why not that diving killer whale? I like the way it's balanced on its nose."

They moved their equipment in front of it and Ted identified the forms—the bottom, most important figure first, a stocky eagle. Above it a whale dove. The dorsal fin, shaped like a tongue, was an added extension of wood sticking out of its back. Above its tail a wolf crouched, then a frog, then a man with a cormorant on his head. She liked that mix of human and animal.

The pole had a subtle interior upward line connecting and defining the main shapes. Ted hadn't told her that. He hadn't seen it. On his painting of the day before, he'd broken the line to place the figures in a different order. She felt the violation for a different reason than Alice had. For the carver's sake, she would paint this pole exactly as she saw it.

She watched Ted dab his brushes in Chinese red, turquoise green, Payne's gray, straight from the tube. Maybe that was why his figures seemed flat. But what did she know? She'd never painted with oils. In England, lady painters had to paint in watercolor. Instruction in oils was reserved for men.

After a while, she felt him studying her work. "I wish I'd painted that," he said.

"Really? Thank you!"

He gave her a long, analytical look that showed he knew he had by accident touched and opened her in a powerful way. Abruptly he packed up his paints.

"You're not going, are you? There are six hours of daylight left!"

He folded up his easel.

"Where can I find more authentic poles?"

He didn't answer. He knew, but didn't want to tell her. She felt cheated. He snapped closed his campstool and walked briskly down the alley of trees and totem poles.

She was stunned a moment, and then ran after him. "What's wrong?"

He kept on walking, faster now, facing straight ahead. "Nothing. You should be proud."

She dropped back, letting him go. Had her painting made him leave? She returned to study it. Yes. It had promise. She had promise. She could do this. She wanted to leap and shout.

A raven uttered a commanding *kraaak*, swooped over her head with an eerie *kloo klak*, and wheeled back into the forest. Strong talk. Approval, she hoped.

· · ·

Other than wisps of vapor floating up the valleys, no rain or fog hid the forest and coastal villages on the trip home. Emily gripped the ship's railing and couldn't look away from the parade of poles slipping past, even to eat the apple and sandwich Alice was feeding her.

"Too bad we can't stop close to shore long enough to have a decent look."

"Whales a'starboard!" a crewman shouted.

A fin broke the water, then a huge black body with white markings. Then two others, blowing out mist in breathy gushes.

"There's more over there," Emily shouted.

"Where?" Alice cried.

Emily stood behind her to get the right angle and pointed. Alice gasped. They arced again in a slow, rhythmic gallop. First their rounded backs and fins broke the water, then their flanks, showing only part of their bulk at any one time. A moment later they flashed their flukes and dove, deep and long, all of them, and were gone.

"And God created great whales," Alice said in awe.

"Mysterious things humble a person, don't they?"

She thought of the weird beauty of the whale totem. There were hundreds of poles just as mysterious that few people had ever seen, would probably never see. But paintings of them—that was something different. It was something she could do.

She'd have to plunge into dark waters. Only part of the idea would be visible at any one time—a fluke, a flank, a fin—but the whole of it unfathomable. She felt the whales below pulling her, the forest nudging her, the totems tightening their grip on her.

"I'm going to teach the children about Alaska next year," Alice said.

"You know, your life is fuller than you think. You have a mission, to teach all the 'difficult' children the public school can't." She linked her arm around Alice's. "Now I have one too."

"I know. I knew when you didn't come back until midnight."

"But it was still light. I was still painting."

"That didn't mean I didn't worry."

"I'm sorry." She waited until Alice nodded her forgiveness. "Other than Hitats'uu, I haven't found anything mysterious enough and true enough to help me say what I feel, but yesterday changed that."

"So, tell me. Your mission."

"To preserve the totem poles in paintings. That art is vanishing, Ted said. In another generation, it might all be gone. There needs to be a record of them, in their own village settings, before they rot back into the forest, or before the missionaries burn them down in some righteous Christian frenzy."

"Millie!"

"The poles are reminders of past glories, of healthy communities before Indian mothers wept or turned hard when baby after baby died. It's something I can do. To counter that sadness."

"You think Dede's going to let you? Not in a hundred years is she going to release a dime from our trust fund for you to traipse through heathen villages painting their idols."

"Then I'll have to earn those dimes myself."

"Won't it be awfully hard to get to those places?"

Impossible for a woman alone, Claude had said. She gazed out to sea. "Easy things don't interest me."

11: Horsetail

Emily set the chicken she'd roasted on Sophie's table. "Where's Annie Marie?" she asked.

Sophie gestured toward the other room. "Sleeping."

Emily poked her head in the doorway and saw Annie Marie curled onto her side, thumb in her mouth, the shoes and socks she'd bought for her on her feet. "She wears them to bed?"

"'Em'ly's shoes,' she say. She won't take them off inside, won't wear them outside. 'Get dirty,' she say."

Emily chuckled as she sat cross-legged on the floor next to Sophie and held up a purplish black strand from a pile. "What's this?"

"Horsetail root bark."

Sophie wound a cedar root coil with cherry root and stitched it to the coil below it with an awl. Her fingers flew, tugged, twisted the strands. The basket was a flared rectangle decorated with a long horizontal shape worked in horsetail root stretching upward at each end with bumps along the top.

"What's the design?"

"Canoe."

"Ah." The bumps were heads. No bodies. Just heads. Seven of them peeping out of the canoe like peas in an open pod. Under it was a band of peaked waves. "Why is the middle head bigger?"

"That's Annie Marie."

Sophie's children, all seven of them living and dead, embarking over the waves to the unknown.

Sophie looked at the place where the basket cradle had hung and her eyes filled with tears. Emily lay her hand on Sophie's wrist. Sophie dropped the awl in Emily's lap, went into the other room, and came back with the drawing of Tommy under the Ancestor.

"Little baby I didn't even get to know, but Tommy's still in my heart so he stay on the wall." She hung it again opposite the Virgin Mary.

"That's good, Sophie."

Sophie sat beside her again and held the unfinished basket in her lap but couldn't seem to begin work on it again.

"I remember when he taught me the three-pebble game on the beach," Emily said. "He was so happy when I finally threw the stones quick enough so they all landed, plop, at the same time. He squealed and jumped in the shallow water so much he got us both wet."

Sophie smiled in a far-off, misty way. Maybe she'd said too much. Emily gave her back the awl. "Is that made of stone?" she asked, trying to bring her back.

"Bone. Bone of an ancestor."

"A human bone?"

"No. An animal ancestor."

How could Sophie believe that and the Bible?

"This was my grandmother's awl. It has wise stories."

"Does everything you use have a story?"

"Most everything. You don't have a story for every color?"

"There's a feeling for every color. Red for passion. Yellow for happiness. And green, oh, green—the glory and spirit of growing things."

"Stories come from feelings. In the old time, all the grandmothers told stories."

"Why don't they anymore?"

"Nobody listens. No bighouses, so not a lot of people around one fire. Now the church priest tells stories."

"That's not the same, is it?

"No. Singing not the same either. My grandmother said at the first mass the *nipniit* told everyone not to sing anymore the old songs. They go to hell."

"Did she stop?"

"No." A sad smile streaked across her face. "She sang when she felt a hurt inside or a heat."

"Sometimes it's important to do what you feel, no matter what."

"When I was little, she sang to my baby brother because he was sick. He couldn't sleep because crows kept to cawing in the salal bushes so I threw a stick at them. They cawed more loud and flew into a tree. She took me there and said to the crows she was sorry her granddaughter did that. Now that she knows better she won't throw things at crows again."

"Did you?"

"I hope not, but I loved my brother. In the story time before humans, Crow was the basket maker. Now he helps basket makers."

"Does Crow help you?"

Sophie tipped her head. "Hm. Yes. Like this. My grandmother told me her grandmother saw a crow. He cawed at her all day. She asked him why he kept to cawing that way. Crow said once he could make lots of sounds, like Raven, but he lazy. He only made one. Then he want to make different sounds. He tried. Nothing. Only that ugly one. So now I make each basket different. That's how Crow helps me."

Her fingers started to move again, as if by their own will, holding the coils together, poking in the binding strand. She pulled it taut with her teeth.

"Do other basket makers make each basket different?"

"No." She rolled down her bottom lip, and screwed up her nose. "Same ones over and over. Puts a person to sleep. Me, this is only one with a canoe. Now you tell me a story. Tell me about Alaska."

"I thought you'd never ask." Emily shifted to stretch her legs. Out spilled everything about Sitka and the totem poles. "Each pole is different, you'll be glad to know. I wish you could see them, you and Jimmy."

Sophie straightened her back. Had she blundered?

"I want to paint the poles, all of them, before they disappear. They make strong talk. There should be a record."

Sophie's expression darkened, and Emily felt an invisible wall rise between them.

"What? Is it wrong to do it?"

Sophie shrugged and pursed her lips into a tight wound.

"Sophie, it's something I can do. Do you understand? Like when your brother was sick and you threw a stick at the crows. To help him."

Sophie's hands stopped working.

"Would it make any difference between us if I painted in other villages?"

"We used to have totem posts," she said sharply. "In the old days before I was born. Inside houses. Long time ago a logjam made the river flood. All the houses and posts washed away. The church wasn't washed away, so people here don't make them more."

"Because of that?"

"What do you think? Of course because of that."

"Will it be hard to find them all?"

"Yes." The word shot out.

"Impossible?"

"Maybe."

"A fur trader told me that it's impossible for a woman to travel alone to native villages in the north."

Sophie yanked a binding strand roughly.

"My sister Lizzie, the missionary one, says some villages don't want white visitors. Is that true?"

"Yes. Frank's brother, he knows. He went north to work for white man logging job. He knows." She scowled and pulled in her lips into a wrinkled wound.

"What's wrong? Do you think I shouldn't do it?"

Sophie gave her an irritated look. "You just said it's important to do what you feel. So do it."

"But do *you* think I should do it?"

Sophie held the cherry root strand between her teeth, making her wait. Mrs. Johnson's words, *Don't expect so much,* rattled in Emily's mind.

"How much you want to give up?"

She felt reckless with words. "Whatever it takes."

"Then I think *you* can do anything."

That wasn't as specific as she wanted, but at least it was something.

She noticed a picture next to the Virgin Mary, Moses and the tablets of stone with the words *Thou shalt have no other gods before me* printed below it. "Is that picture new?"

"Father John gave me it when I told him about you."

"About me?"

Sophie smiled in that abashed way of hers, turned the basket to do the corner, and held it with her feet. "You aren't Catholic. At mass he said anybody had other gods go to hell. He said that mean anybody not Catholic, so I don't sleep for nights. I told him you love my babies and you're a good white woman. He said that don't matter. I said you paint the Holy Spirit. Then he said maybe it's all right." Sophie's face glowed with triumph.

"Paint the Holy Spirit? I've just been talking about painting animal ancestors. Is that why you wouldn't answer when I asked if I should do it? Because totems aren't the Holy Spirit?"

Sophie hugged her basket to her chest. "I was afraid for you."

"How can you say I paint the Holy Spirit? You've never seen any painting of mine with God or any saint or angel."

"You know. Green." An impish grin flickered, her eyes shot through with sparks, so pleased she was with herself. "Like you said. Glory and spirit of growing things."

12 : Bear

"Come on, Billy. Up!" Emily said from the rickety dock. "We're here! Alert Bay, so snap to it."

Billy whined in the bobbing shore boat.

"What is it? You've got the wiffle-woffles?" The shore boatman tossed her the leash. "Up!" she ordered.

On the peak of a swell he gave Billy's rump a firm push. Billy got the idea and scrambled up onto the dock. He shook himself, looking smug, as if it had been his own idea all along.

At every swell raising the boat, the crewman handed up another thing—her small carpetbag, sketch sack, food box, and the strapped bundle of her folding watercolor easel and stool. The large canvas knapsack was the last. He grunted and heaved. "What do you have in this? Lead weights?"

"Yes. Bibles."

She strapped her easel and stool onto Billy's back, the knapsack onto hers, and hoisted her bags, out of breath already. This village on tiny Cormorant Island, two hundred and twenty miles up the east coast of Vancouver Island, and the people she'd meet, would either launch her project or kill it. Jimmy had said as much.

"One week," the boatman called, and revved up the motor to head back to the steamer.

"I'll be waiting." She walked with wide footsteps trying to keep her balance, always a problem. Billy pulled at the leash, only too glad to get off the dock. "Slow down and act respectable. We're guests," Emily said.

On firm ground, she took a look around. What a weird, won-drous sight. A congregation of birds, wolves, bears, saw-toothed sea creatures, all carved and painted, some stacked on poles, some on roof peaks. A ferocious zoo! Sophie would love this. If they had voices, they'd be howling, croaking, screeching, growling. Was that the kind of reception she'd get?

She headed away from the row of bighouses toward the mission where she'd arranged to stay. Three clapboard houses and a two-story school hugged the Anglican church. Emily screwed up her face. A crenelated roof and a frieze of wrought iron? What in the world was it trying to be? A white picket fence bravely separated the mission from what it was supposed to save.

Billy stuck his nose into a soggy hole. "Billy, no!" She yanked his leash. "At least for a first impression it would be nice if you'd be clean."

In the parlor decked with doilies and embroidered Bible verses, Reverend Alfred Hall welcomed her and introduced his gaunt wife, and bird-like Miss Winifred Crane, missionary-in-training with a pointed nose and an unfortunate name. She was making a chart of the occupations of Jesus' disciples, the fishermen printed boldly in red with a drawing of a salmon by each appropriate name. Emily unloaded the slates and chalk from Alice and twelve pounds of used Bibles from Lizzie.

"Oof! One pound for each disciple."

Mrs. Hall gave her a censuring glance, but didn't turn them down as payment for room and board. "Would you like tea while we tell you about our missionary work at Saint Michael's School?"

"No. Thank you. I'd rather get right to my work."

Mrs. Hall squared her shoulders. "Indeed."

"While there's still good light. You can tell me at supper."

"Five o'clock. Do you have a watch?" She smoothed a crocheted antimacassar on the back of a chair.

"Yes."

· · ·

The pebbled shore made walking difficult. "Don't you wish you could wear men's clodhoppers like mine, eh, Billy?"

She itched to get close to the poles. Take things slowly, she told herself. She unfolded her camp stool and flat easel. From here she could get a village panorama, and then work her way closer to the totems. In the left foreground, two handsome canoes had birds in flight painted on their hulls. *Wings in dark red and green, beaks in yellow-orange and scarlet,* she wrote on the edge of her drawing paper. The ropes of kelp at the same diagonal would lead the viewer's eye across the beach to two women trussing salmon on frames in the middle distance and to the mounds of clamshells and the cannery on the far right. In the background, the houses and poles and forest would give context.

Three boys dragged the kelp out of the angle she wanted it and cut it into lengths using the edges of clamshells. So much for leading the viewer's eye, she said to herself. She caught them peeking at her, and they giggled.

"Hello," she called. She should have asked Mrs. Hall for the Kwakwala word.

The children looked down the beach at an older girl, maybe ten or eleven, as if checking for permission to come closer.

"Long seaweed, eh? What are you going to do with it?"

"Play cannery. I cut it and sell it," the older boy said, "and he buy it." The smallest boy uncurled his sandy palm to reveal a few pebbles.

"Can you tell me what bird that is?" She pointed to a large wooden bird sitting on a roof. "He's ready to fly down here and get me." She flapped her arms and pretended it landed on her head. The children laughed. "Is he an eagle?"

"No."

"Is he a raven?"

They shook their heads and said no even louder.

"Then what is he?"

"He's Cormorant," they shouted.

"A coal goose! I should have known." She noticed them watching Billy absorbed in sniffing a dead bird. "You want to touch him? He likes children." Instantly six hands were all over him, and he was doing a jig of happiness, trying to get in more than his share of licks. He woofed and posed in a play bow, head low and hind end high.

"Why he don't have a tail?" the middle boy asked.

"See that big wooden sea creature over there? Who's that?"

"He's Killerwhale."

"Well, one day Billy was sleeping on the beach and Killerwhale sprang out of the sea and bit off his tail, snap, like a crab." She snapped her hand closed right in front of the middle boy's nose. He backed away and laughed.

"What are you doing here?" the younger boy asked.

"I'm going to make pictures. Of you, if you'll let me."

"Me first," the older boy said.

"Only if you tell me your name."

"Freddy."

"Freddy Eagle?"

The others laughed. "No."

"Freddy Raven?"

Vigorous head shakes.

"Oh, I know. Freddy Coal Goose."

"No! Freddy Hannah!"

"All right, Freddy Hannah. You'll be first."

As she worked she learned the others' names. Baby Toby's older sister, Tillie, edged closer. Emily learned that Freddy was the chief's nephew and that Toby's uncle, Hayward James, was a carver of poles and masks.

"And I'm going to be one, too," Toby said.

Aha! Native arts were still alive. "Wonderful!" Such simple confidence. She could use an ounce of that. "How do you know?"

"Because my mama, she wants it, so my uncle pulled out a eyelash of me and he put it in a paintbrush and it had porc'pine hairs and he painted Thunderbird on a box to keep it and when I'm ready, he'll give that brush to me."

And in the meantime, she thought, Toby's eyelash, if not his eyes, would be close to his uncle's work. "Good," she said.

She finished her drawing of the village. The time had come. She was here for the totems. She set up in front of the wolf on the nearest pole. She drew its oval nose holes, even the crack through its right eye. She wanted to be absolutely precise about detail and proportion. She tipped her head back to sketch Bear above Wolf. His toothy mouth was pulled back into a fierce, taunting look. How dare you think you can paint me, he seemed to be saying. White curls came out of each nostril as though he were snorting smoke. How could she get that detail without being so close as to require foreshortening? From below, how would she make that bear look like anything other than an overhanging snout and nostrils? She felt trapped. She didn't know a pinprick of what she needed to.

She checked her watch. "Holy moly, Billy boy. We're late for supper."

13: Raven

"Chief Wakias summoned you to his bighouse," Mrs. Hall said, placing a basket of bread on the dining table.

"Did I do something wrong?" Emily glanced around to pick up cues. Miss Winifred Crane kept her nose in her napkin folding.

"They want to welcome you, I suppose." A coolness in Mrs. Hall's voice accompanied her glance at a portly man standing at the dining table. "Sit, everyone," Mrs. Hall said.

"This is the Indian agent, William Halliday," Reverend Hall said from the head of the table. "He's a good sort, for a Scotsman, if you forgive him his cups on Saturday night."

"Just a wee touch, Reverend. Purely medicinal," the Scotsman said, leaning back and stroking his pointed reddish beard.

"Indian agent?" Emily said, sitting down opposite him.

"Department of Indian Affairs."

What luck! She opened her mouth to speak to him just as Mrs. Hall set down a tureen of chicken and dumplings as if it were a holy reliquary. Emily waited until the Reverend intoned grace, appreciative murmurs registered, and Mrs. Hall seemed pleased.

"Do you know where there are totem poles besides here?"

"Of course." He aimed a forkful of dumpling into his mouth.

"And how to get there?"

"Yes again." Chewing.

"Then perhaps you can help me. I want to paint them, as many as I can before they're all gone."

"So I understand. You're not afraid of 'em?"

"Afraid of what? Totem poles?"

"The Kwakiutl. You can hire one with a canoe and go when the villages empty out in summer and fall for work at canneries and fish camps, but I wouldn't recommend it, especially you alone."

"More potatoes, William?" Mrs. Hall passed him the bowl.

Halliday wiped grease off his mouth. "While it may be fitting an antiquarian's interest to paint their villages and idols as vestiges of a passing way of life, to socialize with them, if that is your intent, leads me to question your character, Miss Carr."

Emily set down her fork. "My character is intact, I assure you. It's the idolatry I question. I understood that they don't worship the figures on totem poles."

"Mm. Not directly." Uttered with a mouthful of potatoes. "But totem poles and potlatches go together, and potlatches are the root of the problem."

"What problem?"

"Their heathenish ways. Wherever the potlatch exists there has been no progress, and the government—"

"And the missions," Reverend Hall interjected.

"We both want to see our native people progress so they'll be useful to the province, on an equal footing with whites. That canna happen so long as potlatches continue, so I'm committed to stop them under orders of William Ditchburn, regional superintendent for the Department of Indian Affairs." An unctuous smile slid across his face.

Equal footing? He deserved to be praised if the sentiment was genuine, smacked to kingdom come if it wasn't.

"I'm afraid I still don't understand."

"Potlatching requires outlandish expenditures of money for gift giving, encourages vanity and fanatical competition among bands, conflicts with Indian employment in logging and agriculture and canneries, and spreads disease, sloth, rowdiness, irresponsibility, and prostitution, if ye must know." He reeled this off like it was a memorized liturgy, striking the air in her direction a few times with his fork to emphasize his words.

"Couldn't have said it more eloquently myself," Reverend Hall remarked.

"You mentioned that my paintings might portray a passing way of life. What exactly did you mean by 'passing'?"

"Why, assimilation, of course. They'll bring their own ruin upon themselves surely if they resist change," Halliday said.

"I see."

"There will come a time in this province, one way or another, when they won't exist, such as we know 'em now. Mind you, the Kwakiutl are the most stubborn of the lot. Better not to get mixed up with them."

"One more question, if you don't mind. Do you happen to know a fur trader named Claude Serreau or Claude du Bois? He has a funny-looking boat."

Mr. Halliday chuckled. "Ah, Claude of the Woods, he calls himself. A queer fellow, but a good sort. The Indians like him."

"Has he ever been to Alert Bay?"

"Many times, I reckon. Any trader going north stops here."

Emily folded her napkin. "This was a Kwakiutl village first. We are all guests here. I've been invited and I'm going to go."

Mr. Halliday rested his elbows on the table, his chin on his fist, and regarded her quizzically.

"Thank you, Mr. Halliday, for your concern. And you, Mrs. Hall, for a delicious meal." She saw the vein in Mrs. Hall's temple swell violet. "Painting can make a body mighty hungry."

Outside, a few minutes later, she closed the gate against Billy's nose. "I'd better not take you, Billy boy. I'll give you a good scratching when I come back."

Billy gave her his pitiful, injured pout. She reached over the gate to touch him, and he whined in resignation.

The front door of the Halls' house opened and Mr. Halliday came out. "It's the last house in the row, the only one painted." He held a battery torch over the fence. "Ye'll need this later."

His concern surprised her. "Why, thank you."

A raven swooped onto the bell tower, its black form silhouetted against the lavender sky. *Haw, haw, haw,* it croaked. A taunt. What did it know that she'd soon find out?

Picking her way on the muddy path between the white and Kwakiutl sections of the village, she heard the dock creak, and the slap-gurgle-slap of small waves on the gravel beach. Maybe she'd been seen drawing something sacred. They might forbid her to do more. She should have asked Halliday more questions. Her apprehension grated against her excitement.

Teeth, talons, flared nostrils, open wings sprang out at her from the poles in front of the bighouses. There were beaks everywhere. Straight for Raven, hooked for Eagle, she remembered.

When she saw faded red and black wings stretched across the width of the last house, she realized Halliday must have meant painted with a design, not with house paint. A massive carved pole attached flush to the front of the house as part of its construction towered above the roof. She stopped. The lowest figure, Raven, had an enormous beak projecting out nearly ten feet over the plank walkway. No real raven's beak could be so large in relation to the head and not make the bird topple forward, but here, its attachment to the house prevented that.

Above Raven stood Bear with faces on his forepaws, a longnecked bird, a man, and Wolf crawling down the pole. At the top, Thunderbird with outstretched wings held Killerwhale in his talons. The pole made this the most impressive house in the village. The only thing was, she couldn't find the door. Was this Halliday's idea of a joke? She passed under the beak, and walked around the far corner of the house. There it was. Closed. She knocked. Nothing happened. She walked back to the front.

A loud creak issued from the raven's beak. It was opening! An orange glow issued from inside as the lower beak came to rest on the walkway, let down by ropes. Inside the lower beak was a ramp with crossbars like those on a ship's gangplank to prevent people from slipping. Her feet didn't move. The utter strangeness and the inventive design were more than she'd imagined in her wildest dreams. If Halliday was right, Claude had been here. Now, if she ever had the chance, she could tell him so had she.

She took hold of the rope and stepped onto the beak. One step, two. She placed her heels securely beyond each crossbar, and peered through the throat. Firelight softened everything. Men sat on an inner platform that ran around the central fire. Women wearing dresses and shawls of orange, sienna, and indigo sat with children one tier back. Taking one more step through the bird totem would mean crossing a cultural divide. She hesitated, not out of fear, but out of a desire to feel it fully.

Tillie, the girl she'd drawn on the beach, was sitting right inside the door. "Come," Tillie said and led her past bull kelp hanging in coils on the walls. Strips of dried salmon draped over poles had fine striations, like the cedar grain on chests, walls, rafters, like the meticulous parallel tool marks on the platform of the menstrual hut.

Tillie brought her to a man wearing suspenders whose deeply grooved cheeks had the texture of rutted paths. He didn't smile, but his expression was not unkind. A younger man with a smooth, shiny face spoke in English.

"This is Chief Wakias, high chief of Nimpkish Band. His crest is Raven. He also owns Killerwhale crest, powerful creature of the sea, and Bear and Wolf, strong and swift creatures from the forest. Chief Wakias gave five potlatches. He owns much wealth—thirty dancing blankets of mountain goat wool and four canoes. He owns five salmon streams, seven clam beaches, and the story of Huux-huuk, Man-eating Bird."

Owning a story—what did that mean? She'd ask Sophie.

The speaker gestured behind her. She turned. An awesome carved bird with open wings in red and black stood against the wall, maybe fifteen feet across. The body was shown from the front, but the head and the enormous beak were in profile, as on her drum. One fearsome black and white eye glared at her.

She gulped. "Is that the man-eating bird?" Did they have to use that term? Did its beak open too, to swallow white painters?

The speaker nodded. "Who are you?" he asked.

"I am Emily Carr, a Canadian."

But what else?

The three boys she'd met on the beach watched her intently from the hard-packed dirt floor, knees up to their chins. They probably knew what she should say next. Give me a hint, she said with a look. They only wiggled, hardly able to contain themselves. Tillie, sitting one tier behind them, didn't give her a sign either.

"I have come to paint your village and totems, if I may. They are noble forms of great strength and mystery."

The chief's mouth turned down. She should have asked Sophie to teach her a few more words of Chinook. That universal trading language all tribes spoke would be as valuable as trade beads. He nodded for her to continue.

"I own not so many goods. One Eagle basket made by my good friend Sophie Frank of the Squamish Band at North Vancouver, and thirty paintbrushes, some of weasel and mink and sable, quick and clever creatures from the woods. I own one bird who makes strong talk, and the story of Billy, the Dog Who Has No Tail."

The children exploded in laughter. She tried not to smile, but to return Chief Wakias's steady look.

"Are you a friend of Agent Halliday?" the spokesman asked.

Ah, here was the crux of the matter. Stillness descended. The fire popped. What did he want to hear?

The truth, take it or leave it.

"I have met Mr. Halliday. I am not his friend." They expected more, but what? "I am Freddy Hannah's friend." Freddy let out a squeak. A murmur went around the room. She flipped through her sketch pad and produced the drawing of him. "I give you, uncle of Freddy Hannah, this picture."

The younger man took it and showed it to Chief Wakias, whose face broke into a smile. "My house is open to you," Chief Wakias said, his voice like gravel pulled by waves.

Women brought her barbecued salmon lying on skunk cabbage leaves, and bannock bread with jam. It would have to settle on top of Mrs. Hall's dumplings. She lifted some flakes of salmon, ate, made appreciative murmurs, and licked her fingers.

"The best part is the cheek," Chief Wakias said. He held out to her a disk of dark, sweet-smelling meat.

She noticed its grain. With her finger she drew the close lines across her palm. "It's like cedar wood." He smiled. She wished she remembered Lulu's saying that everything is one, but that would be Nootka, not Kwakwala. She picked up the fish, ate it, and made her face show that it tasted rich and flavorful.

A young woman brought her a flat basket piled with silver fish about the size of cigars that people had been eating when she came in. The three boys grinned at her. One wiggled a little silver fish, and the others scowled and nudged him sharply from both sides. Tillie tapped him on the shoulder and said some word of admonishment. One boy bit off a fish head.

"I've never eaten a whole fish before. I mean the head." She picked out the smallest one, only a half inch shorter than the rest, closed her eyes, aimed her teeth well behind the gills, bit down, and chewed. "Hm, good." If she didn't think about the snapping and crunching in her mouth, it tasted all right. Full of wood smoke. "What's it called?"

"Oolichan," the young woman said.

Emily patted her belly to convince them she was full. A woman whose face was as wrinkled as a dried mushroom shuffled toward her. Her painful progress across the packed dirt floor hushed even the children. She held out an oblong bowl carved into an animal shape. Curving up at one end of the bowl was a carved face etched with whiskers, the eyes made of inlaid shell.

"That's an elegant bowl. Is that Seal or Sea Otter?" She was glad she'd picked up from the children to drop the "a."

The old woman raised the bowl under her chin. "Eat."

A vile smell, like stale fish oil mixed with rotten pork, assailed her. Her throat squeezed shut. A pile of translucent whitish meat lay in shiny shredded globs. She glanced up. Chief Wakias stood with his chest out, his shoulders back, watching. Should she ask now or later? She touched the moist gelatinous substance. "This must be very special. What is it?" she asked in the most casual tone she could manage. Without breathing she put a morsel in her mouth before the woman could answer.

"Seal blubber," the woman said with a penetrating stare.

"A seal came to our beach a day ago. Died there," the chief's speaker explained.

It didn't taste bad, meaty rather than fishy. "It's so tender. Falls apart in my mouth. How do you get it that way?"

The chief's speaker translated for the woman: "I chewed it myself this morning."

Emily gagged. Everyone else hooted with laughter.

Some joke.

The woman touched the bowl to Emily's collarbone, her expression deadpan. The test wasn't over. Obviously the second bite had more significance than the first. Emily's obligatory laugh came out a mere croak. She put the second morsel into her mouth. The dumpling in her stomach rebelled, but she forced a smile, chewed, and swallowed. The woman nodded, and passed the bowl and everyone took a small amount, laughing.

They resumed what she supposed they'd been doing before she arrived. Children played games with pebbles. Old men puffed on pipes under lazy curls of smoke. Women twined spruce root hats and wove cedar bark mats. A grandmother with glazed eyes made a warm nest of her lap and a young woman placed a baby there. This was the way of life Halliday said was doomed?

The chief and his spokesman invited her to sit at their fire. Little by little, the chief spoke to her himself instead of through his speaker.

"Have you been to Karlukwees?" he asked.

"No."

"Guyasdoms?"

"No. Are there poles there?"

"Yes. Fine painted houses too."

"How can I get there?"

"There will be a way. Mimkwamlis?"

"No. How many Kwakiutl villages are there?"

"Kwakwaka'wakw villages, we say. Many. Some for fishing. Some for potlatch." He patted his stomach and smiled. "Hidden ones. Police get lost in the islands." Under folds of skin his eyes gleamed. "Kwakwaka'wakw potlatches make good story."

"They must be grand."

He said nothing, apparently lost in memory.

Embers were glowing in the fire pit. The children had curled themselves onto piles of blankets, and hands rested unmoving on unfinished baskets. She had to ask now.

"May I paint your great Raven tomorrow?"

He tipped his head forward in a single nod.

· · ·

First thing in the morning, with Billy leaning against her leg, she sat before Raven on the plank walkway in front of the houses. Raven's disdainful eye with its lid curved down at the corner bored into her, firing her desire. On his lower beak, a human face looked back, frightened in a humorous way. She'd missed that the night before. She made tight reference drawings of the face and each of the stacked figures above. But if she were to give any of the raven's detail in a painting of the whole house, she'd cut off the upper pole.

How to accommodate a form so tall? Give its lower portion dominant placement in profile in the mid-ground with the row of houses at an angle? That way she could show a retreating line of poles suggesting what she'd cut off. Maybe a canoe prow in the lower foreground for size reference? She wasn't sure if it was the best solution.

Effective composition might come with exposure to the right examples, but where could she find any?

She set to work using Indian red, Prussian blue, and black for
the raven, burnt sienna blending with sepia umber for the pole's
raw cedar parts, bleached by the sun. It was adequate, but it lacked
the drama of the real thing.

"Billy, move." She wanted the angle right from where he was
lying. She nudged him out of the way. "To be a painter's dog, you
have to be flexible."

But I was comfortable, he said with a sigh and a whine.

"Oh, don't pout like a wilted petunia."

To depict a thing beyond objectivity—that's what that beak
challenged her to do. In it were all the croaks and squawks and
clucks and rattles a raven could make. And through it, in the bighouse itself, all the stories and laughter and keening and baby
gurgles and death rattles of generations. But how could a painting
convey that?

Sketching in watercolor, she laid in the main shapes. She
squeezed her brush dry to lick up excess paint above the beak to
lighten it where it reflected the sky. The eye had to be fierce. She
darkened the heavy bone above it. It was still too tame compared
to the strangeness and wildness of that glowering totem. She tried
to be bolder and still be accurate, but how could she with watercolor? Those British academicians passing for artists, squeezing
their brushes at the ferrules, had crippled her, made her work
timid. If only she could talk with someone who knew how to
make paintings express feelings.

The beak creaked open and Chief Wakias came out. She'd have
to show him her paintings. They weren't perfect but they were all
she had.

"Good morning, Emily Carr."

"Good morning. It's a fine morning. The best morning I've had
for months."

"Why?"

"I'm painting your magnificent Raven. He makes strong talk."

He pressed his lips together as he inspected her work. He turned
to her. "You come for potlatch by and by."

Claude had said they were illegal. Lizzie called them wild drunken revels. Halliday considered them heathen. She knew they'd be exotic and fascinating. Being invited was what walking through Raven's beak meant.

"I would like that very much."

14: Cedar

"Come in. The door's unlocked," Emily said when she heard Jessica's customary Beethoven's Fifth Symphony knock.

Jessica waved a newspaper clipping at her. "Did you see this in the *Province?*"

"I don't get a paper. Times were better when everyone went 'round shouting things to each other."

"Then I suppose I'll have to shout unless you read this for yourself." Jessica smacked it down in front of her.

Emily kept working on her drawing of Bear above Wolf from Alert Bay. What to do with the nostrils? She'd loved those curls of painted smoke coming out of them on the real totem. She put them in. "Kind of frilly, eh?" She held up the drawing at arm's length. "What do you think? Nostril smoke or plain?"

"Plain."

"Plain," Joseph echoed from his cage.

"Rats. What kind of cronies are you?"

"The best." Jessica shook her finger at the article. "You always complain that you aren't getting to the gist of your subject. Well, in Paris . . . I'll read it to you.

"The current art movement in Paris aims not to reproduce subjects but to represent them through color. It seeks to penetrate the nature of things by bolder brushwork, to interpret by exaggeration, and to convey form with light and color rather than using them as mere decoration on a form. 'The artist's goal,' says André Derain, 'should be to make the strongest possible presentation of his emotional reaction to a subject by using bold color and strong linear patterns.'"

Jessica passed her the clipping. "Isn't that what you've been talking about—emotional reaction?"

Emily practically choked. "Yes."

The nostril smoke—she did have an emotional reaction to it, but didn't know how to express it other than to draw thin curls. She read the article again, and surveyed her Alert Bay watercolors on the walls, the work of a whole winter.

"I'm not modern at all. I'm fussy and old-fashioned and I hate it. My colors don't convey form. They only decorate the poles. My work doesn't 'penetrate the nature of things' either. I don't know how." She tossed her pencil onto the table. "Oh-hh, Jessica. In England they were always talking about what they learned in Paris. I should have packed my bags that instant."

"Oh-hh, Jessica," Joseph muttered.

"But doesn't this tell you what you're always complaining about, that there's more to art than what people know here?"

"Yes, it's a damned vacuum here." She smacked the tabletop and pointed her index finger in the air. "I must be on the verge of a discovery if I can see what I'm *not* doing. Now I just need to figure out what *to* do." She glanced at the article. "But what can you tell from words? There isn't even a picture."

"So? Don't you have to go see it face to face?"

"Oh-hh. You don't know what you're asking." She felt herself sinking. "I made a horrible mistake by studying in London instead of Paris."

Jessica sat down. "I'm sure you had plenty of good reasons."

"Bad reasons. Narrow reasons. Fear of foreignness. An impossible language. Unbearable loneliness. A big city."

"London's no village, Emily."

"It didn't seem so—" She flapped her hand, trying to think of a word. *"Formidable."* She snickered at her French pronunciation. "A lot of good it did. I got just as qualmy in London as I would have in Paris—city soot and crowds rush-rushing all the time, everything all rackety-clackety."

"I didn't mean to make you feel bad, Em." Jessica patted her hand. "I know you're hungry to grow in a way I'll never be."

"What a heap I'd give to go there now."

"What's stopping you?"

"Everything. I've just put down roots. I feel a momentum building. The chief at Alert Bay welcomed me. He said he'd tell me how I can go to other islands. He smiled at my painting of his Raven house. Do you know what that means to me? If I go off to Paris now, for who knows how long until I get hold of this new art, he may not even remember me when I come back."

"And if you don't go?"

She looked at the wisp of steam coming out Bear's nostrils. "If I don't go, I'll keep *reproducing* subjects superficially, like this says." She tapped the newsprint with her fingernail.

"I don't get it. Hasn't that been what you've wanted to do? Make a record of totems?"

"Until I went to Alert Bay. Now I want something more personal, but I don't know how to get it." She sighed. "In order to escape the hold of the Old World to paint the New, I'm being yanked back to the Old."

"Then you're going!"

"No. You go and tell me about it. You can afford it."

Jessica's mouth dropped. "But my family."

"Aha! See what an undertaking it is? What a risk, all on the basis of one puny paragraph?"

"But think of all those artists in Paris discussing—"

"And trying new things together, struggling together. Maybe being bonked on the head by what someone else was doing with paint." She played with the edge of the paper. "May I keep this? It'll come in handy when I go begging before the Keeper of the Treasury."

"Who's that?"

"Queen Dede. She owns everything, and us three young 'uns too. Once I circumvented her rule and went right to the family solicitor for money. She whipped me till I fainted, screaming that I was getting too high and mighty."

"You never told me that."

"It's not an aspect of family life a person can be proud of. The next day I dropped out of high school, packed up for art school in San Francisco, and ran smack into you." She waved the clipping. "So, may I have this?"

"Yes, if you let my girls take care of Joseph while you're gone."

Emily smiled. "Not so fast, Jessica. I haven't tortured myself with indecision nearly enough."

· · ·

"You like better water or sky?" Annie Marie asked as she offered Emily the cat's cradle in Sophie's house.

Emily picked the taut strings. "The sky, I think. It can be so many colors."

"Water too," Annie Marie said. "The ocean too."

Each time it was Annie Marie's turn to hold out the string, she asked a question. "You like better . . ."—she tilted her head back—"painting or trees?"

Emily smiled. "They are the same."

Here. But not in Paris. How could she leave the place she loved?

Annie Marie wrinkled her nose. "Like dancing and singing?"

"Like dancing and singing."

Margaret Dan called from the walk, "You coming, Sophie?" She came to the open doorway and leaned in. When she saw Emily, she straightened up. "Oh." Her lips tightened. She turned and left.

Emily felt as if smelly white scum had eked out her pores.

"Her heart too small," Sophie muttered.

"Is that the problem with Mrs. Johnson too? She says we're too different, you and I, to be friends."

"She wants to be the only one here ever loved by a white person."

"Jealous? Of you?"

Sophie's frown changed into a proud grin. "Yes."

While Sophie packed a basket of provisions, Annie Marie took off her shoes. "No. Keep to wearing them," Sophie said.

Annie Marie tugged off a sock, and Emily crouched in front of her. "I'd like you to wear them outside too. Then your feet won't get hurt. Please."

Annie Marie scowled a moment at this new thought, tugged the sock back on, and let Emily tie the laces.

They set out, Billy in tow. "With all these meadow grass smells, he's in doggie heaven," Emily said.

"What's this place name, Mama?" Annie asked, patting Billy's head. She looked up at Emily. "Places have names."

"Ayulshun. Soft Under Feet," Sophie said.

Beyond some tall elderberry bushes lay another marshy meadow. "How about this?" Emily asked.

"Ay-ayulshun. 'Nother Soft Under Feet."

Annie Marie giggled and hopped along like a chickadee. "You like better Ayulshun or Ay-ayulshun?" Without giving Emily a chance, she squealed, "They are the same."

Emily twirled Annie's braid around her head like she'd seen Jimmy do, making her dance in a circle. If she went to Paris, she'd miss this precious age.

They entered the forest through a grove of maples at Kak-makulth, and went to Huphapai, where a stream gurgled through the forest. Sophie examined the cedars, choosing. Billy did too, and lifted his leg.

"Mama's going to peel cedar bark."

"I didn't think you used the bark for baskets," Emily said.

"I don't. Cedar bark can be for diapers, soft things."

She realized that Sophie must be hoping for a baby.

"Here, Mama. Here a big one." Annie Marie ran around a tree in a circle to show how big it was.

Sophie wrinkled her nose. "Oh, that's too big." She held her long skirt out wide. "When the trunk goes out like this, the bark's too thick. Too tough. Small tree is more easy."

Annie Marie's little chin quivered in a pout.

"But it's a good tree for basket roots." Sophie's cheeks rounded. "So big it has lots of long roots. It won't be hurt if we take one."

"Dig a root, Mama. I love this tree." She patted the trunk.

Sophie poked the ground with a carved yew digging stick on the side of the tree by the stream where the ground was soft and muddy. She found a root and looked up to the tree's upper reaches. "You Who Dwells Above, thank you for making this cedar to grow near this stream so the roots are straight. I need to take one from this good tree. I promise not to waste. I will use for a good basket."

Sophie waited, then knelt and loosened the dirt along both sides of the root, following it toward the stream where Billy lapped water. The water's glints and gurgles were so inviting that Emily set one hand in the mud, leaned over, and cupped her other hand to drink.

A breeze shifted the ends of foliage, like the tips of fingers moving. She sensed a presence under the tree's canopy. God didn't camp only in places where there was a steeple. But did God breathe only in BC forests and not in the woods in France? Fear and stubbornness made her want to say yes. Sophie and the tree seemed to inhale together, sharing the same breath. She breathed in too, wanting to inhale enough of its forest scent to last a year, at least.

She and Annie Marie watched Sophie pull up a long unbranched taper. Was a root able to look up through itself and see its own grand tree? Maybe it just had to keep blindly sucking its nourishment from Mother Earth and sending its spirit up and up, never knowing if what it produced was beautiful. She hoped that wasn't so.

She leaned against a log and cuddled Billy. "I feel a spirit here."

She saw Sophie's eyes widen minutely in surprise, as if she'd seen something startling in her white friend and couldn't take it in at a single glance.

"A spirit can come to a person alone in the forest," Sophie said.

"How?"

"In the cry of Raven. Howl of Wolf. Wolf makes him a good hunter. Cormorant makes him a good fisherman or canoe maker. Gives him power. Ideas. Everybody has a power spirit. You just have to find it."

"Do you really believe a spirit can come to you from a bird?"

Sophie squared her shoulders, pushed out her chest. "Yes."

"But Sophie, you're a good Catholic."

"It's not religion. It's just Indian."

"You can have both?"

"Have what you want."

Was it as easy as that?

Sophie moved to a younger, smaller tree, and studied its slender trunk. She said a second prayer, waited, and made a horizontal cut about waist high. She gouged and pried right above the cut until she loosened a handhold of fibrous bark. She leaned backward, pulled and twisted until the bark hissed and peeled off in a long pointed strip.

Annie Marie hopped. "Ooh, a good one, Mama."

Sophie looked at the two exposed surfaces—trunk and inner bark. "Like baby skin right after borning. First time in air."

The ivory surface dripped streams of clear sweet-smelling sap and darkened right before their eyes.

"It's magical," Emily said.

Sophie smiled and used a knife to separate the silvery gray outer bark from the inner bark. Once she started the split, she pulled them apart, and the inner and outer bark separated cleanly. Sophie's lips formed an O of delight, and her eyes opened wider. "See? Easy."

"It's like the tree gave of its spirit to you," Emily said.

Sophie folded the bark strip into a bundle and bound it with a cedar strip. "Sap side in, Annie. It goes red by and by."

Annie Marie was preoccupied dusting off her shoes.

"How does a person find his power spirit?" Emily asked, half to herself, musing over mysteries.

Sophie thrust her chin forward, scrutinizing Emily. Downward furrows at the corners of her mouth plowed deep, as though she were struggling to make a complicated decision.

"It's all right, Sophie. You don't have to tell. I was only thinking out loud."

Sophie untied and tied again the bundle of bark twice, her fore-head more lined than usual. "I only tell you this. No one else."

"Oh, no, Sophie. I'd never talk about it."

"To find power, people go out alone. They fast. Pray. Be real quiet. Listen. Be still. Be ready."

"Go where?"

"To lonely, wild places, hard places, sacred places."

"Why into the wilderness?"

"You make risk so the spirits know you're true. Then they speak. You need to prove yourself. Wanting hard helps too."

There was no denying her desire. Standing in front of Chief Wakias's house, she had wanted with all her might to pour the spirit and drama of that Raven beak into her painting. As for risk and lonely, hard places, she could see Paris in no other way.

"Forest spirits help you to make things, to create?"

"The spirit goes in the tools. Everything has power. Loon, Owl, Raven, Wolf, Killerwhale."

The loping whales she'd seen with Alice were full of power. But how could Killerwhale teach her in Paris?

"Only animals have spirit power?"

"Thunder, Wind, Moon, everything. Everything!" Her cheeks and eyebrows lifted, her eyes brightened, alive with possibility.

"Tree? Can a tree be a power spirit?"

Sophie raised her shoulders. "It's not good to talk about it. It might leave you or make you sick."

Yes. That she understood. If her own spirit of yearning left her, she *would* be sick. She picked up a fibrous piece of cedar bark that Sophie had discarded and held it to her nose. The tree had breathed through this. She could have this, the spirit of British Columbia, when, breathing city soot, she would crave the piquant smell of woods, or when, amid the clang of trains, she would long for its deep silent places. Hoping that cedar might be her power spirit, she put the bark in her pocket.

Annie Marie cocked her head to the side. "Why do you take that?"

Emily tapped her once on the nose. "It's not good to talk about it."

Annie drew back. Sophie smiled, a slight, fleeting movement before her serious expression returned. In that graver look, Emily saw that Sophie had stepped beyond native custom in telling her of the spirit realm, something so private they needed the whole forest to swallow its echoes.

"Thanks for telling me about spirits. That was a good share."

She waited until Sophie nodded and then took out her tin box, rolled a cigarette, and lit it.

Sophie took out a wooden pipe from her pouch, packed in it whatever she used for smoking, and lit it. "*Kinikinik,*" she said, offering her pipe to Emily. "Just leaves." A teasing grin skimmed across her face. "Leaves to make you see things."

Emily took it and inhaled a pungent, woodsy aroma. She felt light-headed as she handed Sophie her cigarette in exchange.

Sophie inhaled, exhaled, and smiled. "Not so strong, huh?"

"No, not so strong."

Emily inhaled from the pipe again. "I have something to share too. I may be going to France, to learn how to paint better."

"More dark?" Sophie blurted sharply, and then grinned.

"Maybe. I don't know yet."

A raven croaked, half human, half otherworldly—a foot in each realm. A bit like her when she'd stood in Raven's beak.

"I walked through Raven's beak into a Nimpkish bighouse. Something started for me there, bigger than I had planned on, and now I have to walk back out."

"By and by you go again," Sophie said.

"I'm afraid, though. Many things can go wrong in France."

"Go wrong anywhere. You go and find out."

"What I started was for you. To show you totem poles so you'd feel strong and happy again. Now it's just as much for me."

Sophie smiled. "The best kind of share."

Watching Annie Marie thread ferns through Billy's coat, they finished the first pipe and a second. Sophie drew out a small leather bag from her pouch. She opened it and dug her middle finger into a dark substance. With an odd smile, Sophie drew her finger across her broad cheek at a slant. It left a reddish brown streak.

"*Tamalth.* Indian paint."

"What's it for?"

"Medicine. It comes from fungus on a very old spruce. Spruce is strong medicine." She spread it on her other cheek. "Use for being close to earth in my blood season. To make me strong. To have babies. More babies."

Emily eyed the shiny substance in the bag. Billy put his muzzle close to it and Emily pushed him away. He sneezed. She inhaled its musky scent.

She needed to be strong too. To go to Paris. To birth paintings. More paintings. Sunlight cast a sheen on the mud, under which the roots of that cedar grew and took their nourishment. Vague shapes danced on the shiny mud. She blinked to clear her vision, but still paintings waiting to be born glistened on the brown surface. Her eyes locked with Sophie's. She drew two fingers slowly over the cool mud, and painted her face.

Billy watched her, nose flaring, asking what in the world she was doing, his whole body on the alert, Annie Marie's ferns quivering.

Sophie tilted her head back. Her rhythmic breathing became a quiet song. "*Ay-e, ay-e, ay, ay.*" Sophie's voice was high on the first two syllables, lower on the others. The last sound came loudly with a puff of air. She sat still awhile, then rose slowly, looking up at the tree from which she had taken the root.

"You Who Dwells Above, Creator, you make the trees and the

roots. You make the animals and the people. You see I am poor. I have six dead babies. Give power to my hands to make good baskets for selling to white people so I can buy Christian gravestones for my babies."

Sophie's yearning entered her, an inner jolt. How deep it was, and primitive, and pure. How selfless too. Could painting ever help to feed her own hunger as Sophie's gravestones were helping to feed hers? If she went down into the deep of herself, would the yearning to paint well be as pure and selfless? If it were, maybe then skill and wisdom might come. She stood in the clearing listening for a breathing through the trees, watching for a shift of branches.

"You Who Dwell in the Forest," Emily murmured into the hush. "You have given me the longing to paint. You see I am lonely, and have nowhere to pour my love. Give wisdom to my eyes to see into the soul of this land. Though I will walk through the valley of the shadow of a far and lonely wilderness, help me to hear a spirit song. Give power to my brushes so I can create something true and beautiful and important."

Part II

15: Sparrow

Madame Bagot stood in the narrow street in violet bedroom slippers with two leeks in her hand and shouted to the upstairs window, *"Maurice, réponds au téléphone."* Her fleshy jowls shook.

Emily came through the passageway and sniffed—garlic, cigarettes, and musty carpet. She tried to flatten herself against the pension doorway in case this battle-axe of a landlady would sweep back inside, hips and bosom stretching her wine-colored sweater. She knew Madame would spit the directions too fast to understand, and she'd stand there like a ninny. Madame's puff of black hair loomed like a thundercloud. Emily showed her an address. Madame's fingers pudgy as German sausages snatched it.

"À gauche au boulevard Montparnasse, deux rues, et puis à gauche encore."

Emily thrust out her hand, palm up, first to the left, then to the right. She snapped her head in both directions, then back at Madame Bagot with a look that any reasonable person could see meant, Can't you do better than that? Madame smacked the paper onto Emily's palm, turned her roughly by the shoulders, and waved her leeks to the left. *"Allez, allez."*

Emily went left onto boulevard du Montparnasse and waited while a horse-drawn hearse and cortege passed. Bookshops, cafés, and ateliers lined the street, and above them, apartment windows opened onto balconies with fanciful iron grilles, some with laundry hanging from cords between them.

Noticing the fascinating fan pattern of paving stones, Emily stepped off the curb. An old man on a bicycle with a loaf of bread and sweet peas in his wicker basket jingled his bell and shouted at her. She jumped backward to let him pass, and nearly dropped her portfolio of Alert Bay watercolors in a puddle. A newspaper skipping in the wind fastened itself onto her leg. She kicked it loose. Children laughed. She scowled and they ran off, their wooden *sabots* clattering.

She ought to be exhausted, ought to be napping, like Alice, the sensible one, but it was their second day. She couldn't wait. "Only a year," Dede had said at the bank, slapping the trust fund money into her hand and glaring. She had to make every day count.

At rue St-Beuve, she turned. Number 32 was a *boulangerie* puffing out the cozy aroma of fresh bread. She took a reassuring whiff. At number 30–28 she peered through a smeared window at a display of traps and stuffed rats hanging by their tails, plump as eggplants. And the French were supposed to love beauty! The sign on number 26 read *La Remise de l'Artiste*. Brushes, drawing paper, tubes of oil paint lay scattered in the window. The possibilities excited her, but not knowing what was cheap or dear made her feel vulnerable. *Baguettes de peintre*, a sign said. Baguette. She thought that was a loaf of bread. She walked back to the bakery shop. *Baguettes et miches*, that sign said. She shook her head. What kind of bread were painters supposed to eat?

At number 24, she pressed the buzzer and picked at the peeling brown paint on the door. A thin man with a florid complexion opened it.

"Hello. Are you Harry Phelan Gibb?"

"*Oui, mademoiselle.*" The second man ever to call her that.

"I must have been mistaken. I was told Mr. Gibb was English."

"*Oui, mademoiselle.* I am English." Not a hint of a smile.

She handed him a letter of introduction given her in an art supply store in Vancouver. He glanced at it as she said, "I want to understand the new Paris art." Damn. That sounded like the language of a simpleton. And here he could be the key to her whole Paris experience. "And this new way of seeing," she added.

He twisted his thin lips into a smile of sorts, more on one side than the other. "You're ahead of most Parisians. Van Gogh's been in his grave for twenty years, Cézanne for four, yet art collectors still don't buy them, and despise what's new now."

"What is new now?"

"Their offspring. Léger, Picasso, Braque, Matisse, Modigliani, Derain, Rouault. Many directions."

He spewed out the names so fast she couldn't fix them in her mind. Her ignorance was probably plastered across her face. His hand was already reaching for the door.

"I read that in French art academies artists convey their emotions with bold hues and exaggeration," she blurted. "That's what I'd like to learn. Can you tell me, does it have a name?"

His crooked smile twitched again. "*Les fauves.* Wild beasts, the critics call them, for their wild colors, but they're not accepted, and the Cubists less."

"Where do I see it?"

He scoffed. "Not in *l'académie.* Most galleries don't show it. You'll have to see it in the Salon d'Automne in October. It shows work *l'académie* ignores. And in private studios. In the meantime, for fifteen minutes, start here."

He ushered her upstairs into a large, light-drenched studio where a red-haired woman sat reading.

"My wife, Bridget. This is"—he checked the letter—"Miss Emily Carr, a painter from British Columbia."

Bridget, dainty as a porcelain figurine, turned her head, chin slightly raised, as if she were posing. "Ah, so far away."

"A month to get here."

"Most of these can be called Fauve," Gibb said.

The paintings shone in astounding colors. Angular and broad-buttocked nudes with pale violet and cerulean skin reclined on vermilion bedspreads and hot ochre sand. Their anatomies were distorted in an attempt to shock.

"Mademoiselle's reaction?" he asked, tight-lipped, like a bank teller demanding the next in line to step up, or step aside.

Her response would be crucial.

"Intriguing in a primitive way. Distortion I've seen in Native Canadian art, but that's done to accentuate a characteristic of the subject, not just for design."

"No. It's for more than design. It's for expression."

She turned around to see landscapes sparkling with vivid complementary colors, playing warm against cool, applied thickly with ridges of paint showing. "I'm thunderstruck at the colors. They're—" She trailed her fingers in the air.

"Fauve," he declared.

"Raw," she said. "Your color handling, this streak of red alongside that green, unmixed."

"The eye does the mixing. Impressionism. Not particularly new.

The outlines, Post-Impressionism. You have never seen this before?" His voice rose.

"No."

"But you will adapt it to your own work. However, there's more than a single new way of painting. There's a whole tribe of experimenters. Art in 1910 is broadly accommodating."

"Now that's a shred of comfort."

"*Alors*, Mademoiselle Carr." He pointed to her portfolio. "You have some work to show?"

She felt her fingernails dig into her palm. Her work was flavorless and simpering by comparison. She shook her head. "These are only supplies." She waved her hand vaguely to indicate the shop next door. "Can you tell me where I should study?"

"*D'accord.* You are a woman, so your work no doubt will need strengthening. That can be had by exposure to male examples."

So that's what Paris would be like. She crumpled the paper with his address on it and tried to control her face to be expressionless.

"L'Académie Colarossi on rue de la Grande Chaumière across boulevard Montparnasse. They have mixed classes, women with men. Not many do. Van Gogh was there for a while, and Gauguin."

"Will they teach me oil?"

"There, yes." At the door he smiled and added, "Come back and let me know how you're doing."

"Thank you!" If he said that, he couldn't be all bad.

. . .

Sweat and turpentine fumes smacked her in the face in Colarossi's cramped, humid oil studio. She jockeyed for a good position among the easels jammed so close together she couldn't squeeze through. Between that and the sewer crew clattering through the room to pump out the drains, the place was bedlam.

But she was here. She was painting. She would learn.

André Laffont, her instructor in oil, stormed through the studio, his black eyebrows joining as he stopped at the easel of the tall man painting beside her. If she painted Laffont, with his black hair hacked bluntly, instead of the table, chair, fruit, and figure on the platform, she'd name it *Medieval Despot*. He turned to her with astonishment, as if he hadn't noticed her, the only woman, for the last three weeks.

He glanced at her painting and made a face. Her stomach tightened. She had been trying to use the pure brilliant hues she saw on canvases around her, but hers seemed muddy in some places, out of control in others. The longer oil brushes were stiff and hard to get used to. She didn't move a muscle while he rattled off a stream of French, flapped his hands at her canvas, and passed on to the next. Had she been praised or ridiculed?

Her arches ached. She wasn't used to standing to paint, and with three three-hour classes every weekday, her feet screamed back at her. She gave them a sympathetic look and noticed a fresh smear of rose madder on her dress, the required attire for women painters. She tried to rub it out with turpentine to dissolve it, but knew she was only forcing the pigment through to her petticoat, already a palette of blotches.

She was working on her dress instead of her painting when Laffont came around the second time and gave her painting a scornful two seconds before he said, *"Vous avez de bonnes couleurs, mais il faut les employer à communiquer la structure, pas simplement comme de la couleur mise sur un dessin."*

She pointed to her ear, her mouth, and shook her head.

"Faut communiquer la structure," he shouted.

"But the colors?" she shouted back. *"Couleurs,"* she mimicked. She held her hand palm up, said, *"Oui?"* then palm down and said, *"Non?"*

"Oui," he said and walked on.

Bewildered, she turned to the lanky young man with tousled hair in loose, paint-smeared dungarees and striped jersey working next to her.

"He says to use *chiaroscuro* to define the shapes," he offered in a heavy accent through thin, feminine lips.

"You speak English!" Relief and anger clashed in her voice. "Why didn't you say so before this?"

"Until today, you haven't said a word. For all I knew, you could have been mute."

He put away his paints, dipped his brushes to clean them, and looked around his feet in annoyance for a wiping rag. "Never have one when I need it."

Emily thrust hers into his hand. "Take it." She gesticulated to her pile of them. "Take them all, only tell me what he said."

"Come with me for a *café*, and I will."

His name was Paul, she learned, hurrying downstairs after him onto rue de la Grande Chaumière, a street so narrow that the six-story buildings seemed to lean in. They walked toward boulevard Montparnasse. Where it met boulevard Raspail, several large restaurants and brasseries spread their tables onto the sidewalks—Le Dôme, Le Sélect, La Coupole, and La Rotonde.

"Everything important happens at one of these places," he said and gave a nod toward Café de la Rotonde jutting out into the traffic under a broad red awning. She hesitated at the curb. He clasped her wrist and they dodged an autobus, a pushcart heaped with gooseberries, another displaying silver mackerel, and a pair of screaming motorcycles.

Paul was particular about where they sat among the red outdoor tables and wicker chairs facing the street. "All the painters come here, or to Le Dôme," he said in a low voice. "See the one with the yellow scarf? Amedeo Modigliani. Italian. He practically lives here, when he's not chasing women or passed out in the street."

The Italian slurped down some raw oysters, stood on a chair, flung his scarf over his shoulder, waved both arms, and began to rail against something.

"What's he so angry about?"

"He's just reciting poetry."

Paul ordered two *cafés*.

A slump-shouldered woman sat at a nearby table behind an amber drink, a metal ashtray of crumpled butts, and a pair of red gloves. Shadows under her eyes gave her a desperate appearance. Alice would never come here, no matter how close it was to their pension. One good thing about Paris—nobody cared, or noticed, if she smoked. She lit a cigarette. The Gauloise smokes stank but they reminded her of Sophie's pipe.

The woman pantomimed smoking, said something, and reached out her hand. Emily offered her a cigarette from her pack. Then the woman wanted a match. Emily slid her last matchbook from the ocean liner across the woman's table.

"You're *américaine*, no?" Paul asked. "From New York?"

"No. From British Columbia."

"*Colombie?* You mean jungle? Parrots? Where *café* comes from?"

"No. I'm from the far west of Canada."

"Ah. No parrots."

She thought of Joseph. "No. Ravens, though. Big ravens in big forests, not jungles. Cedar trees sixty meters high. Native people carve them into stacks of animals. They're called totem poles. That's one reason why I'm here—to learn how to paint boldly and expressively enough to do them justice."

He drifted away, listening to the conversation at the Italian man's table. Her explanation was wasted. It might as well have been about parrots in jungles.

"Tell me what Monsieur Laffont said at my easel."

"He said you have to use color to communicate structure."

She puffed out a breath. "I thought I was!"

"We all think we are. He says we're not."

"Then what does he want? He could at least show us some examples."

" 'Chiaroscuro,' he says. 'Blend the colors to show curvature. Learn to see.' "

"See how?"

"The Fauves don't blend. Their colors are flat." He took a gulp of coffee. "I don't know. I've been at Colarossi a year and I'm more confused now than when I started."

He was young, but his gray eyes seemed opaque and worn. His admission shaved a chip off her hope.

More people gathered at the table of the Italian, who tipped his chair back behind stacks of saucers.

"The one on the left is Henri Matisse. L'Académie de la Grande Chaumière. I've met him. He doesn't blend. He outlines."

Paul kept glancing hungrily in their direction. Now that his acquaintance had arrived, he was itching to join them, would have if it weren't for her, an encumbrance to him.

She laid her centimes for the *café* on the table. "I have to go." She stood up. "Thanks. I'll bring you a new rag tomorrow."

• • •

Over the next weeks, she struggled with embarrassment and the French impatience with her attempts to understand. Few books had color reproductions to study, and color handling was vital. Oil paint tugged against her brush in a way that watercolor never did.

Paul stopped coming to class. Laffont gave her little attention. She tried to glean from others' work and their reaction to hers whether she was improving, but that was guesswork. Claude's Mademoiselle Courageuse did not exist here. Where was her spirit song?

Alice loved everything. She took French and history classes at the American Student Hostel, did all the communicating with wait-ers and shopkeepers, went on long walks, and noted everything in a journal. Paris seemed to wake her up. She laughed more. She for-got and fluttered her left hand with the shortened finger when try-ing to think of a word in French.

One hot September Saturday, Alice packed a cheese, a baguette, and two peaches, and insisted they have a picnic in the shade of the cemetery near their pension. They followed the spiked iron railing past raised tombs frilled with Gothic tracery. Cats slept on the granite slabs, and lovers lounged on the grass. Emily and Alice sat on a bench opposite a limestone angel.

"Stone. Paris is stone. We left the world of wood when we left home," Emily said.

"Just think how old some of these stones are, and the stone buildings. They laid the foundation of Notre Dame in the twelfth century. Doesn't that make you shiver?"

"As old as some cedars." Emily pulled the piece of cedar bark out of her bag.

"You brought that thing halfway around the world?" Alice tossed crumbs from the baguette to some sparrows.

Emily held it to her nose. "It reminds me why I'm here." She tipped her head back to see patches of tin-colored sky among the leaves. "At least they left some trees in Paris. I like this spot."

"I knew you would. That's why we came."

"You're good to me, Alice. Thanks."

They watched sparrows snatch up crumbs in jerky movements. Timid ones picked up the leavings the more aggressive ones left.

"Crumbs. I'm only getting crumbs of instruction."

"Maybe you expect too much. Of yourself, I mean." Alice clapped her hands together once. "Why don't you take the afternoon off and we could go to some galleries? They're free."

"Gibb said galleries don't show what's really new."

"Then we could go to Luxembourg Gardens. It's not far."

"Pictures don't get painted wandering through parks."

"It's a weekend, Millie. This is Paris. We'll probably never be here again."

"We definitely won't if I don't improve faster. I need to work on weekends too."

Alice tossed her last crumbs to a sparrow too skittish to join the fray. He bounced toward the stone angel to snatch them.

"Alice, look! That stone angel." She grabbed Alice's arm and spoke fast. "Amazing! Does it look bluish white on top and pale charcoal brown on its undersides to you?"

"No."

"Well, it does to me. You see its shape, don't you?"

"Generally."

"Those hue changes are what gives it shape. I see it now. It's what Laffont meant!"

Alice tipped her head and squinted.

Emily studied the angel more intensely, afraid to let it go. Yes. Definitely. The difference wasn't in the lightness or darkness of the stone but in its actual hue.

"If this is an optical principle, I'll see it everywhere, see how it's shown in paintings. All right, Alice. Tomorrow we'll go to Salon d'Automne. You'll have to find it. Just tow me on a leash."

• • •

They took the *métro* to the Champs-Élysées and walked past a puppet show under chestnut trees and roundabouts for children. Emily watched for hue changes in geometrically hedged courtyards and Neoclassical stone façades. Under a striped café umbrella advertising an apéritif, a woman dressed in fluid emerald crepe posed while sipping an opaline green drink. Emily slowed.

"Absinthe," Alice whispered, as if it were dangerous even to say it out loud. "They say it's made from wormwood."

"The dress, Alice. I'm looking at her dress."

Above the woman's bosom, the hue of her dress was yellower, and where it fell in folds from her lap, the shadows were bluer. New eyes, she thought. She was seeing with new eyes!

Fluted columns announced the Grand Palais, roofed in curved glass, the entrance topped by marble muses.

"Now that's a building built to tell you something," Emily said, feeling spirited as they started up the broad stairway to its monumental porch and arched door.

The main gallery was a madhouse of noise. Passions rendered in pigment exploded in hundreds of paintings. Sulphur yellow, crimson lake, cerulean blue sprang out of their frames hung edge-to-edge up to the ceiling.

"It's garish and unnatural," Alice said, "the colors they use. A red sky? A green and orange bridge? Blue horses?"

"They're expressive all the same. It's what that article meant. Sensations of color."

She began to glimpse things as they walked from room to room. The brushwork left visible. Ridges of paint following the direction of the stroke which followed the object's shape. Figures and objects outlined in black. The viewpoint never quite fixed. The essential exaggerated and the unimportant vague.

As if from a dream, Alice's thin voice reached her. "Do you really want to paint like this?"

"Like what? Which? They're all different."

Alice touched her temples. "The colors don't go together. I'm sorry, Millie. It gives me a headache."

Alice slumped on a bench while Emily went through the exhibit again. At closing time, she found Alice hunched over her French grammar book, her nose inches from the page, her posture just like Emily felt—overwhelmed. What technique should she try first? Images battered at her on the way home. As they crossed the pont Alexandre with its ornate lampposts, square stone towers, and gilded angels, everything, all of Paris, seemed too heavy.

"Of all the names, I don't know who are the rising stars."

"Do you have to?"

"I don't know that either."

She fell into bed exhausted.

A violin student one floor below squeaked the same four notes until they drove her mad. She closed her eyes to shut out the noise and to envision what she had seen. Vibrant, saturated color streaked across the window shade. The violin sounds became visible in orange, red, violet, and with the deep opacity of oil. She saw herself floating out the window. Above the pont Alexandre, she saw the Seine in yellow and purple. Unmixed daubs of pigment swam before her—Prussian blue trees, screaming orange faces, smeared vermilion skies. Was she asleep or awake?

Monstrous Madame Bagot shook oil brushes at her in one hand, blue leeks in the other, and Laffont shouted at her as if volume would make her understand. She felt herself sink under the bridge, plunge down like a whale to inky depths. She couldn't breathe, and woke up coughing and crying, flailing at the colored water until she noticed Alice stroking her face.

"It's all right, Millie. It was only a dream."

She shivered in sweat and clutched the blanket. She was in bed. She was safe.

"Talk to me," Alice said.

"A grown woman, nearly forty years old, crying because I'm so ignorant. I've progressed so little." She slid down and pulled the covers up to her chin. "We come from such a backwater."

Alice put her cheek against Emily's. "You've got to forgive our origins."

"Forgive the province I love for making me provincial?" She turned onto her side. "I don't know if I'm improving at all."

"Why don't you come with me to French class?"

"I need every tick of the clock for art."

"Then go back to Gibb and ask where you can get critiques in English. Only do *something*."

"All right. All right."

· · ·

She went to his studio and spilled it all out.

"Don't you ever teach?" she asked in exasperation, plunking herself down where he directed her, on the model's chaise longue.

A softness came into his eyes. "Spring and summer only."

"Then where can I go? I only have enough money for a year, so you better tell me where I can learn fast."

He tapped his lips with his fingers all bunched together, thinking, and left a magenta paint smear on his mustache. "Go to John Duncan Fergusson at L'Atelier Blanche. A Scotsman known for Post-

Impressionist styles. He'll get you to ignore what isn't right for you, and teach you in English what is. Tell him I sent you. Then in the spring, come see me again."

· · ·

Fergusson put on his red wool neck scarf and tucked it under his tweed jacket. It was late afternoon, time for him to leave. A big man with big hands and a big voice, he filled the spacious studio when he was there, and it seemed empty when he wasn't, even if other students were there. He drew up a stool next to her.

"You're working too hard on small things, lass."

She snickered, the term so inappropriate for her.

"Simplify your forms and you'll see repetitions within that composition," he said.

She studied her canvas of a figure. "What if there isn't any repetition?"

"Oh but there is, sure. See the roundness of her shoulder and the edge of the circular table? Stretch both of them until they follow the same curve. That will give you rhythm," he said. "Rhythm, that's the thing."

"To see it on my own seems beyond my reach."

Dede's words taunted her. *Who do you think you are that you deserve to study art in Paris?*

Fergusson smiled at her in a fatherly way even though he was younger than she. "It's coming. You don't see it yet. Art isn't just something a person does. It's something he is. And you are. Let go your worries a mite."

His encouragement drove her, and she exhausted herself with overwork. A headache that lasted for a week made her so nauseous she couldn't hold a brush, couldn't eat, couldn't get out of bed. Alice telegraphed home her alarm, and called for a motor taxi to take her to the infirmary of the American Student Hostel.

"What seems to be the problem?" the admitting nurse asked.

"I feel beaten and skinned alive."

The doctor prescribed bed rest. She stared at the tan blanket, cream-colored walls, white curtains hanging between beds, white uniforms. There was nothing to urge her to keep her eyes open. She slept fitfully, lost track of time, drifted.

"The nurses took my petticoat," she grumbled to Alice. "Color would at least remind me of why I'm here. I demanded it back. They threw it out. 'Unsanitary, Mademoiselle.' What cheek!"

Alice gave her a stern look. "What was that you told me in Alaska about your Indian friend going right on after she lost a child? And you only lost a dirty slip."

"Unfair." She rolled onto her side away from Alice.

"You've been here seventeen days. If you don't rouse yourself soon, we'll have to go home."

"No."

Alice put a telegram on her blanket and left.

Just like in London. Just as I predicted. This second illness in a big city ought to teach you. Give up on art. Come home. Stay home. Dede.

Emily flung it across the room.

The following day Alice brought her a crocus in a pot. Emily touched a violet petal as if it were a jewel. The bright yellow center quivered at the razor edge of sound.

"There are more in Luxembourg Gardens," Alice said in a tantalizing way. "New sap green leaves everywhere." She fluttered her hands in the air.

"How'd you know that hue name?"

"I read your paint tube and translated." Alice gazed at the ceiling and sucked in her cheeks. "All the cherry trees are budding. Too bad you won't be able to see them bloom."

Emily sat up in bed. The passing of time shocked her. Spring already. She couldn't bear to miss it, colors that produced the new art. To drench herself in apricot, tangerine, pomegranate, apple green, as fruit refreshes the tongue, that would cure her. Alice knew her better than she realized. A sister who wanted her to get out and paint.

"Thanks, Alice. It's a beaut. Better than a pill. I'm sorry I've been so spunkless."

16: Sisters

She slumped onto a bench alongside the canal. Taking the short train ride from Paris yesterday and walking four blocks on cobblestones from her rented room today was all she could manage.

Harry Gibb's promise of special attention in his oil class here had roused her to come to this village, Crécy-en-Brie.

For now, it was enough to breathe fresh country air and feast her eyes on the light washing the houses along the canal with honey tones. Women with suds up to their elbows slapped their clothes in stone wash booths along its edge. Kneeling like that, they reminded her of Sophie pulling roots. Drooping willows brushed the water. A breeze made ripples, which splintered light, breaking up the green liquid. How could she paint that action? Her brush strokes would have to be broken touches—green wisps, blue patches, red and violet daubs, yellow highlights—all to depict light bouncing off water.

Gibb came across a bridge and along the canal path whistling. Dour old Gibb, whistling! He was carrying a cheese and a bouquet of pink lilies.

"Pretty spot, eh?" she said. "In this light the water assumes so many colors."

"Same with shadows. They take on the hue opposite them."

He turned to the bridge. "Early tomorrow morning, take that bridge and follow the path to the base of a hill. Get there while the shadows are still long, and you'll see what I mean. I'll be there by eleven for a lesson. Mind you, have something to show me."

Something to show! She barely had enough energy to keep herself upright. After he left, she dragged herself back to her room and stretched out on the rose chenille bedspread. Dust motes swirled over her in a shaft of sunlight. She let her eyes close in delicious stillness. Just for half an hour.

Her own snoring woke her in darkness. She turned onto her side. *What did you come here for if you weren't going to paint?* Gibb's voice rolled like distant thunder above her bed.

She jerked awake. It was light again. Still in yesterday's dress, she gathered her supplies, folding stool, and new adjustable easel, upright for oil, flat for watercolor, and hurried outside.

It was still early enough that trees and houses laid their shadows across cobblestones and vegetable gardens. She bought a baguette and a salami and trudged across the bridge to the first rise, out of breath. Poplars with new leaves cast diagonal shadows over the path. Shadows of what color? They seemed just a darker shade of the ochre of the dirt. That wasn't what Gibb wanted her to see, was it? If he didn't think she was capable of seeing what he saw, what then? Would he dismiss her?

She laid in the cottages, hedgerows, poplars, and a copse tangled with honeysuckle and wild roses. What an astonishing miracle. Here she was, wrung-out Millie Carr, painting again, smack-dab in the middle of France, about to take a lesson from someone who cared enough not to let her waste the day.

Gibb ambled up the path wearing a farmer's straw hat and carrying two apples.

"It's a perfect whiz-bang day," she said.

He held up both apples, turning them, and gave her the more dazzling one, pale yellow generously streaked with red-orange. Taking a look at her canvas and the scene before them, he asked, "Are those shadows of the trees warmer or cooler than the earth?"

"Cooler."

"What hues?" He waited for an answer. "Wrestle with it."

"Greens and blues."

"Right. Just as if the poplars and the sky were spread against the earth."

"Why in all my years of seeing haven't I noticed?"

"We're trained by living to use our eyes to recognize objects, but not color unless we make a conscious effort." He took her brush and dipped one edge in vermilion, the other in turquoise. She gasped.

"Don't be afraid to exaggerate," he said as he blocked in shadows of the cottages.

"I'd never have nerve enough to do that."

"Now you have to. You've got to key up your palette so the rest of your painting will be in accord with what I just did. Make a few commas in red-violet next to that alizarin crimson, add a dot of red-orange and see what happens to that patch of flowers."

When she did, the colors practically vibrated off the canvas. "This is the get-up-and-go I want all my work to have."

He smiled in that lopsided, tortured way of his. "Do you have another canvas board with you?"

She pulled a small one out of her sketch sack and he set to work on the same composition but using hues she hadn't seen, even ones she didn't see now in the landscape. New admiration and gratitude flooded her. "You paint more than the scene. You paint into it what's in your mind."

"Art isn't reproducing visual facts. It's the difference between perception"—he pointed with the brush to her painting—"and conception." He tipped his head toward his own. "Once you learn that, you'll never paint the same again."

· · ·

Each week she felt more comfortable painting patches of contrasting color, and hues not in the natural scene. Each weekend when Alice came from Paris, Emily showed her something she was pleased with.

Late one morning in her room, Gibb held the bowl of his pipe and pointed to her canvas with the mouthpiece. "See how you've given contour to the hill by color, that yellow ochre next to that lime green? This is good work. When it dries, let me have it for a while. And yesterday's too."

"Why?"

"I have someone I want to show them to. Don't worry. You'll get them back. I think you'll be a fine woman painter someday."

· · ·

When he left, she set to work stretching canvases, the only thing she felt like doing. Hammering. That good solid whap when she hit one dead center. *Woman* painter! She scowled at a tack she was holding in place, hammered at it and smashed her thumb.

Alice burst into her room with her small carpetbag.

"It just gets my goat," Emily muttered. "Gibb said I'll be a fine *woman* painter someday. Might as well say, 'Fine work for a child. Or a monkey.' " She sucked on her thumb. "Haven't you noticed that he always has to smash a little spunk out of me?"

"Haven't you noticed that there's more to life than art?" Alice's voice trembled. Her face was blotched.

"What's wrong?"

"Haven't you noticed it's not the weekend and I'm here?"

Emily put down the hammer. "What happened?"

"A telegram came."

"Not another of Dede's 'come home immediately' demands." Emily drove in a tack in one wallop.

"No!" Alice shrieked. "It's from Lizzie. Dede passed on."

"Died?" It wasn't possible. Her throat swelled shut. She enfolded Alice with both arms, small against her chest, and tried to absorb her spasms. Alice's tears wet both of their cheeks.

"How?"

Alice collapsed onto the bed and handed her the telegram. Meningitis. Eight days and she was gone. Slipped away when Lizzie went out to make her tea. Lizzie would blame herself for not being there at the very last. The print swam. Dede loved her tea. She called it her cup of you-and-me, the Cockney slang. Emily rocked with Alice in her arms, crooning to her.

Dede dead. She'd hardly had a chance to live. Hosted a few Ladies' Aid meetings, helped the orphanage society, and kept the house, cooking for them all those years. Was that all there was to it? That easy to let it slip by? Fast as a blink. Fifty-five years. Older than Mother was when she died.

"I can't believe it." Some thought shook Alice with new sobs and Emily held her tighter, her thumb throbbing against Alice's shoulder.

"Remember how Dede took old ladies on buggy rides in the country wrapping them up in blankets?" Alice said. "For their health, she used to say, when it was really that she loved the ride."

"Those buggy rides were the times I liked being with her."

"It's like part of myself gone, like she's been stolen out of the house," Alice said.

"No. The mark she left on us will always be there."

She saw Dede in her seated tin soldier position the day she announced she was going to France, the thin bones of Dede's hands rising and falling as she drummed her fingers on the arm of the chesterfield, muttering that Paris was infected with Bohemians. The energy it took to control her disapproval of most of the real world had sapped her of vitality, kept her brittle. Emily had understood then, watching Dede's fingers, the truth hidden under Dede's lethal dose of protection—fear that her unruly sister would get something rich and foreign and dangerous out of life that Dede would shrink from, wouldn't have time for among her good works.

She let go of Alice's shoulder and saw that her gaze was unfocused. "Even though Dede was such a stick, she meant well," Alice said, sniffling.

"Working out her frustrations by scrubbing me raw in the bathtub."

Alice snickered. "Because you needed it when you were smeared with cow-yard muck."

"But she didn't have to whack me with the dipper handle when I squirmed."

"You didn't just squirm. You scratched her. Be a little compassionate. She was only trying to raise us properly after Mother died."

"And now that she's dead too, you make her into a saint? She didn't have to raise me with the riding crop. Compassionate! When I think of all those times she whipped me with it, how can I be?"

Alice winced at the memory.

"What hurt even more was when she had the police shoot Molly when I was away. Until Billy, I'd never had a dog so sweet-natured. What kind of a sister would do that?"

"Molly bit someone."

"Barely. A puppy's mistake. Dede was vindictive, Alice. You can't deny it."

Alice's eyes flooded.

Emily held her again and rocked. "I'm sorry. I didn't mean to make you cry. It's just that life went crooked when Mother died and Dede took over with no one to stop her."

Eventually Alice calmed and finished her tea. "Lizzie there all by herself. She's had to do it all." Alice tapped the empty envelope against her palm. "I've booked passage for us out of London on Saturday. It's the soonest I thought we could manage."

"We?"

She caught sight of the blank canvas she was going to use for a canal bridge showing the water's many colors. To give up splintered light off water just when she was beginning to grasp how to make it vibrate, to leave before she learned some elusive painting truth—that would be Dede's triumph from the grave.

She rested her hand on Alice's sleeve, and noticed that her thumb had developed a blood blister. Alizarin crimson. So sudden. Fast as a blink.

"Will you be all right if you go home by yourself?"

Alice fingered a pile of stretcher tacks.

"It's more important for me to stay," Emily said.

Alice reached for the telegram and put it in the envelope and the envelope in her pocketbook, snapping it quietly.

"Then stay."

17: Gibb

"Harry's been detained in Paris," Gibb's wife Bridget said.

"Detained," Emily said with an edge to the word. Spring in Crécy had flown by. Now she didn't want to waste time waiting for him here in St. Efflam on the coast of Brittany. She counted out the francs for the summer session. Expensive but worth it.

With a playful smile, Bridget added, "He wants you to do five local subjects so he can critique new work as soon as he arrives." Her smile became conspiratorial. "He assigned the other students only two. Of all of them, he talks about you the most."

"Humph. When's he coming?"

"Saturday."

"Five in one week! I'd have to slapdash them to get five."

Bridget patted Emily's cheek. "Maybe that's the point."

• • •

In the morning, Emily followed a hedge between wheat and corn fields to a cliff. The rumble of waves and the *kleeuw, kleeuw* of gulls sounded like the beach at Sophie's house. She'd paint right here so she could listen to them. She turned to face the high, open countryside and made a composition of two farmers in yellow straw hats mending a plow in front of a stone farmhouse. The next day, the patchwork fields drenched in golds and greens liberated her to use the brilliant Fauve palette. If she could have painted the smell of heather, she'd have splashed that on too. Later, a milkmaid with scratched legs switching her black and white cow held still for her. An old church, pared down to its peaked roof, arched doorway, and stubby dome, was the first painting she showed Gibb.

"Good. You're more assertive with form on that church, like

Cézanne," Gibb said when he saw it. "You're taking risks with unnatural color. Clumsy, but it has energy. That is to say, it has soul."

"How do I get rid of the clumsiness?"

He looked at her blankly. "Work."

• • •

"Bonjour, madame," Emily sang out every day to a stout peasant who
greeted her from her garden. One Sunday when Emily passed by,
the woman patted her chest and said, "Héloïse." She was wearing a
wide white headdress with starched wings. Emily pointed to it and
held up a paintbrush. Héloïse's face turned rosy, her hands flitted
like butterflies, and she brought out her knitting and a chair. She
struck a stiff pose and her expression turned serious, as if that were
a requirement for High Art. Emily smiled.

Eventually, Héloïse waved her inside for biscuits and milk. She
looked so absolutely right in her maroon skirt and long apron stirring soup in an iron kettle hanging in the stone fireplace. Only
a few simple objects surrounded her—crocks and ladle, oil lamp,
basket, two rush-bottomed chairs. It was as sparse as Sophie's
house. In the dim room, Emily contemplated shapes—from butter
churn to broom to bellows. Simple geometric forms—ovals, half
rounds, columns, trapezoids—that's all they were. Héloïse herself
was an egg shape suspended over a bulging rectangle. She took out
her sketch pad. Héloïse smiled and chatted gaily as though Emily
could understand.

When she finished, she hugged Héloïse and walked through the
rectangle of light past two leafy spheres and a green cone. Before
her a pale sienna strip narrowed in the distance, lined by white
rectangles. The sensation was eerie. Where there had been hay-
ricks when she walked into Héloïse's cottage, now there were giant
ochre blocks. Near them stood three connected trapezoids with defined planes, on four angled cylinders in Vandyke brown. It might
be a horse. It didn't matter what it was. It was more interesting as
shapes and planes. On the way home, shapes and planes overwhelmed her as the only reality. She breathed hard. *This* she could
use to paint totems.

A summer thunderstorm kept her indoors the next day, so she reworked her Alert Bay watercolors, simplifying to geometric shapes and exaggerating. For three rainy days she didn't stop painting in her room, transforming her native subjects. On the fourth, Gibb came to her door under a torn umbrella. She pulled him inside and laid out a display of new work and old.

"You're getting it," he said.

"Getting what?" She always had to pull it out of him.

"The difference between objects as you see them in the world and their shapes transferred to flat surface."

"And the handling of unblended pigment?"

"That too." He looked at the one of Héloïse and almost smiled. "Gauguin painted those same Breton headdresses."

"What about the native subject matter?"

"Entirely appropriate for you, with not a little aesthetic interest."

"Not a little? How much is that?"

"Some Paris dealers show African sculpture. Picasso painted in African motif and Gauguin owes much to primitive art."

"Do you think I can sell paintings of native motifs?"

"Maybe someday, but not until you paint them out of a deeper experience, with ideas out of your soul."

"I thought I was. You even told me. Soul is energy."

He wrinkled his lips. "That's not all it is. It's personal expression." With one hand he gestured to Chief Wakias's Raven's beak. With the other, Héloïse's cottage. "Which one has it?"

"Both!"

He shook his head and left.

She fumed the rest of the afternoon, paced in her room, compared both paintings for soul, couldn't decide which one had it, and felt like kicking herself for not making Gibb explain. She couldn't paint in such confusion, so she wrote to Jessica.

July 12, 1911

I may be a simpering provincial here, but oh what I'm learning! These new, joyous ways of painting blow the top of my head off some days. Other days, my flop fears paralyze me. My teacher says I've got to paint ideas out of my soul. He says he doesn't see it in my work. But it isn't a see. It's a feel—the way the forest seeps into my innards, or wind

who-whoo's through pines, or totem eyes stare back. Oh, how I miss it. I
have heaps to tell you when I get home. Thanks for prodding me to come.
                                    Your old fusspot, Emily

In the morning, she got out of bed and lifted the curtain. The
ground was puddled, but dry enough for her to work. What was
she to do but to start again and show him? She trudged out of the
village in galoshes.

The world crackled with after-a-rain brilliance. She set up her
easel and stool, loaded her brush, one side with Naples yellow, the
other with raw sienna, and quickly dashed off the rolling wheat
field without even charcoaling it in first.

Breezes rippled the wheat like thousands of fluid paintbrushes
upright and swaying, painting the air. That was an idea out of her
soul. Brushes. When she'd gotten her first ones she'd marveled at
their magic compared to colored pencils. A thin line trailed out if
she held her brush so it barely touched the paper, thicker with
more pressure. Dampened in green pigment, the brush could, with
a flick of her wrist, suggest a leaf.

Now, in the distance, she let a flick of her wrist suggest a
hayrick and peasants.

She remembered placing in her father's big hand a drawing of
the family dog. He gave it a glance, said, "Hm," and went back to
reading his paper. But on her seventh birthday, under a card in Father's broad handwriting, *To Millie, who sees glory in dogs and birds and*
cow yards, there they were, eight rectangular cakes of pigment and
three slim yellow brushes.

In a gush of gratitude, she painted out the farmers and painted
in a man dressed in pale raw sienna in the mid-ground. She put a
shape in his hand. It could be a box. A paintbox even.

When Father planted the seed, he hadn't foreseen that he'd later feel
compelled to kill it. She could hear the scorn in his voice years later
when he said, *It's one thing for a child to paint pretty pictures. It's quite another*
for a grown woman to take such amusements seriously. He was afraid it would
make her unmarriageable. He didn't care about what she wanted. She
changed his clothing to violet and Payne's gray, his face to lime green
and yellow ochre. She layered color after color, building up a thick
impasto, her hand flying, the colors coming from some inward place.

It was an experiment in painting without a preconceived plan, in moving elements around, in letting colors show her emotions. It was an experiment, and she ruined it. It wasn't soul. It was anger. She hadn't defined her feelings about the figure so it was unconvincing in shape and muddy in color. She dreaded some sharp comment about her foolishness from Gibb.

"It's going into the dustbin," she told him the next day.

"You're willing to risk your best to learn something better. That's why you'll be a fine painter someday—woman painter."

"Why can't you just say painter?"

A sound, not a word, came out of his mouth. His eyes looked like those of a small cornered animal. She didn't really want to hear what he'd say.

"Why don't you show me your work? Or other students' work?"

"They don't know what they're after. You do."

"I think I'm getting stale. I've learned tremendous lessons from you, and I'm grateful, but maybe I've painted with you long enough."

His eyebrow twisted into the same curve as his lips. He tapped a brush against his wrist and gazed at her work. "*D'accord.* A New Zealand woman, Frances Hodgkins, is teaching at Concarneau, a port south of here. I'll write to her today. Give me your home address for me to ship those paintings."

The clarity that they were parting dawned on both of them at the same instant. She felt a cord unraveling between them. For once he looked directly at her, his eyes watery wounds.

"Remember when you get home, critics' insults are medals of honor. Stay away from art jargon, Emily, and learn from your silent Indian."

She repeated it to herself, word for word.

"One more thing. Very important. See the Salon d'Automne at the Grand Palais. All your progress will become clear." He thrust his head forward, his eyes intense. "Promise me."

He reached out his hand as if to grasp her arm, to touch her to make her know the importance of what he was saying.

She held her breath and thought, Yes, touch me.

His hand, blue paint under his thumbnail, stayed suspended in midair.

"I promise."

18: Frances

Emily ran her fingers through her hair to tame it before she knocked. A woman answered. She was about her age, maybe older, nearly as stout. She wore an orange blouse, dark blue skirt, and black beret with a bold brass buckle at the front. Emily introduced herself.

The woman flung wide the door. "I expected you yesterday. Come in. I'm Frances."

Emily entered a small cluttered room and found clothes hanging on easels, dishes piled on sketchbooks, jars of brushes on windowsills, every inch of wall space filled with vivid color. Instantly she felt at home.

"It took a day for me to find a room to rent. This town's packed with visitors."

"Always is in August." Frances tossed her hat onto the bed, flumped into a sagging wicker armchair, and unlaced her shoes. "Whew! I just came in. Squeezed every drop of the day at both ends behind an easel. My feet are throbbing, but what glorious light."

"Harry Gibb said you might have space for another student."

Frances crossed her ankle over her knee to rub her arch. "He ought to have known. My summer classes are finished. I'm not taking students now. If you teach all the time, you can't paint."

Emily groaned.

"So, in that portfolio you have something to show for yourself?"

Emily pulled out everything, the recent St. Efflam scenes on top.

"I like the vigor and your loose suggestion of detail around the cottage." She switched to rub the other foot. "You use color well to give shape to that church."

Then she *was* getting it. And this woman with the ponderous cheeks was capable of saying something that wasn't brusque.

Frances uncovered Chief Wakias's Raven beak. "Gracious!" She stopped massaging her foot and pulled the string to light the bare bulb hanging from the ceiling. She spread out more redone paintings of poles, and scrutinized each one. "Bizarre."

"That may be, but they're carved with great sincerity."

"Don't apologize. Apologies are for milksops. I love these. Wait a minute." She moved some dishes and sketchbooks aside, dug through a stack of her own watercolors, and pulled out several of natives sitting on the ground wrapped in plaid blankets and wearing heavy beaded necklaces. "They're Maoris."

Green eyelids. Blue-white lips. "Surprising color handling, and interesting faces," Emily said. But no native context. Nothing to suggest their culture. Done from the outside.

"I did them on my last trip home. My father hates them. He runs an art school in Dunedin." The confession sparked a scampish smile.

"Hates the subject or the style?"

"Everything about them. It isn't just him. The more different I become, the more my country rejects me."

That sent a pall through her. What about her own country?

Frances studied the totems again. "You know, it's probably condescending of us, this attraction to the primitive. Do you think it's substituting for something in us?"

"It's not a substitute for me. And I don't feel it to be condescending," Emily said.

Frances gave her a sidelong look. "Never mind. What is it that you want in these paintings?"

"I thought I wanted to make an accurate record of the totem poles in their village or forest settings, before they're destroyed. They deserve a record."

"And now?"

"Now it's bigger than that. It's that, but also to express their spirit, or my response to them. To make them send the drumbeats I hear when I'm standing in front of them."

"Ah. And you can't do both. Express yourself and record them accurately. You need to decide which is more important—you or them." Frances's face softened in a smile. "We could paint together tomorrow if you'd like."

"I'd like that very much." Her fingers gripped the table.

"I saw them mending red fishing nets across the drawbridge on the Ville Close, that island in the harbor. You can meet me there at nine."

"I'll be there!"

. . .

Crossing the bridge, Emily felt the low-angled morning sun warm the base of her skull clear down her spine. Light brightened the yellow ochre houses edging the water and the scarlet geraniums in window boxes. Terns gave their vibrating chirpy calls, brown sails flapped, and the sea rippled in patches of aquamarine, sap green, even manganese violet. The brine of pickled herring wafted from market stalls. Stooping fishermen, their boats and the wharf piled with shipping bales and draped nets, begged to be painted. It was going to be a cracker of a day.

She spotted Frances on the quay, red jacket with magenta neck scarf blowing under a black fedora. She loved that slapdash way of dressing. Standing, Frances leaned forward and lashed out at her easel in long, decisive sweeps, working from her shoulder with her whole arm. She leaned back to take a quick look, her hip thrust out, then forward again to lay on more paint, all in one continuous, confident action, her gored skirt swaying. Every pore of her body painted. She worked with reckless grace. It was astonishing to watch. That's what she wanted—to paint just that freely, that exuberantly.

Frances noticed her but took a couple more strokes. "I'm beginning to see the point of Matisse instead of Monet. The joy he must have felt from his long, flowing brush strokes instead of broken marks."

"And here I've worked all spring to learn broken strokes!"

On top of that, Frances was painting in watercolor, exactly what she'd come here not to do.

"You work so fast. Like you're painting in a storm."

"It frees the passion. Try it. Think hard before you begin, then enter the work."

Emily set up her easel and opened her folding stool.

"Don't sit down. Move within it and don't stop. Like a dance. Don't intellectualize. Let your instincts direct you."

"I did that once when I had a mad going against a teacher."

"Harry?" She snickered. "Do it now when you're not. Load up your brush and get a lot out of each stroke."

Emily looked and thought and composed a subject. Deliberately and easily, she slipped into a consciousness which reduced the scene before her to geometric shapes and planes. Standing, she slashed a diagonal green curve for the left gunwale of a fishing boat. It was strong and true. She slashed again for the right edge. She made a mess on her oil palette mixing red and deep violet, and swept it on in one long luscious stroke for the shadow beneath the gunwale. She outlined the prow in black and it popped off the page. She leaned back to look for an instant, then leaned into the canvas for another stroke, getting into a rhythm, speeding up.

"It's like I'm careening into the painting," Emily said.

They painted for she didn't know how long, murmuring to each other when either of them noticed the light shift or the colors change. The sense of another woman swaying with her, here on this quay, painting together—it *was* like a dance. Not a waltz, a mad joy dance.

She caught Frances scrutinizing her work. "You don't need a teacher. You just need to paint."

"I need to catch my breath is what I need."

"I'm famished. And my feet can't stand it for another minute," Frances said. They moved to a stone bench. Frances wiped her hands and opened a lunch hamper and offered Emily bread and a bunch of grapes. "Where did you study in Paris?"

"Colarossi and l'Atelier Blanche."

"Colarossi! I taught there until May of last year."

"I came in July."

They looked at each other, momentarily dumbstruck.

"If only . . . No critiques in English. No books or prints to give me a clue. The instructors ignoring me."

Frances held up her hand to stop her. "I know. Impossible. I was the first woman they ever hired. Concession or experiment, I don't know. There really aren't any women in the inner circle of the avant garde painters today. Not a one. I'm only peripheral."

Information she didn't want to hear.

"Right where boulevards Montparnasse and Raspail come together the big forces of the new art meet at Café de la Rotonde and Le Dôme," Frances said.

"I know, but I didn't have the gumption to go there on my own."

"Harry Gibb sold Matisse's first painting. He could have introduced you."

"I think I saw Matisse there, but I don't speak French."

"That's not the whole problem. We're colonials, and women, and that makes us timid."

"I'm not sure which is worse. For our art, I mean."

"It's not being a colonial. Here everyone's a foreigner. Besides, they think we're English."

"A couple times Gibb said I'd be a fine woman painter, but he never dropped the word *woman*. What was he afraid of?"

Frances laid her hand over Emily's arm. "It's an uphill tug all the way. I know. But here, women have a better chance of being considered serious artists, not just—"

"Hobbyists."

. . .

They painted together every day, trading off choosing subjects—boats beached on stilts, sail makers in open lofts, vendors in wooden shoes selling pears or mackerel from pushcarts. Standing to paint all day, staggering back to a quay-side restaurant where they had their slow supper, and then to their pensions, they lived in a world of just the two of them. Emily tried Frances's heavy sweeping line. She adapted Post-Impressionist styles to watercolor, and strove for the luminosity of Frances's colors. She felt them both letting down their guards.

One afternoon a surprise thunderstorm brought them into town from the countryside drenched to the skin.

"It's been a perfectly plummy day, but I've had enough wheat fields and cows and hollyhocks. I'm getting too European."

"Never. You belong here. France is emancipating. Come in and dry off," Frances said at her doorway on the lane. "You'll catch a cold."

Inside, Frances took off her wet clothes, down to her slip, and hung them over the steam heater to dry. "Don't be a prude. You're as soaked as I am." Frances kicked off her shoes and massaged her foot.

"Too hot to work? The Indians rest. Too wet? The painters rest." Emily took off her jacket and skirt and sat on the bed to spread out her day's work.

"Just think of what we're doing, painting all day, spending our last centimes on a tube of paint or a single print, moving from place to place, living in rented rooms," Frances said.

"Not giving a bean about anything else but painting."

Frances snickered. "Thumbing our noses at stifled married women longing to be us. Creating ourselves to suit *us*, Fanny and Millie, *artistes*."

"Don't you think— Do you think creating yourself is a spiritual act?"

"Definitely not. It's a practical enterprise. It has to do with food and rent versus passion and self. Everything, *everything* must be secondary to self-fulfillment. I broke an engagement once. My parents were horrified, afraid I'd starve, but I'd never felt freer."

"Broke it for art?"

"Of course. I didn't see how I could divide myself." She changed feet. "So I came here to embrace bohemian itinerancy."

"I never came that close, but I said no to a proposal ages ago. He followed me to London promising that I could still paint. Then he said, 'We could have children and you could teach *them* to paint.' "

Frances guffawed.

"That one sentence of his toughened me enough to squash the guilt for hurting him. Oh, but he would have bored the zing right out of me. My sisters couldn't understand it—how I could reject the very thing that all of them had been praying for on their knees since girlhood."

"Being lonely toughens us too," Frances said. "Toughens us to decide what we can do without. But men? No one would expect men to give up what we have to. They have families, wives, lovers, *and* art."

Frances flopped her foot down onto the floor. "Ah, that's better. Here, let me do yours." She pulled the wicker chair up to the bed.

Emily drew her foot back.

"Yours must be aching too."

"No. It's all right."

"Then why've you been limping? You always have this hitch."

"Only when I'm tired. I usually paint sitting."

"Here." Frances reached down for Emily's ankle, and wiggled her fingers impatiently.

Emily felt the flush and urge of a rosy nakedness she'd never known before.

"You can be as stubborn as a stone."

"I'm missing a big toe." She heard Fanny's quick intake of breath. "How?"

"Amputated when I was London. My own fault. I ignored a fracture and dislocation from a carriage accident until too late and I was insane with pain."

"And here I've been complaining for weeks about fallen arches." Frances leaned forward, resting her forearms on her knees. "Let me," she whispered.

"It's ugly."

"Better an ugly foot than an ugly face like mine." Frances wiggled her fingers again.

"Don't be shocked when you see it."

Frances shook her head and closed her eyes. Emily raised her leg and rested her ankle in Fanny's palm. Fanny untied Emily's laces and slipped off her shoes and stockings. She started right in on the foot without the toe. Her hands were firm, massaging her crusty heel first, then working up her arch in long strokes with her thumb, relieving the tension of it having to do the work of a big toe to keep her balance.

"No one, ever, did this for me."

"You were too closed up to ask. Like a walnut."

"And that from a woman who preaches independence."

"Sh. Lie back. Close your eyes."

She moved her watercolors out of the way and lay back. Rain settled into a lulling drone. Her eyes closed of their own accord. Fanny's hands, gentle on the ball of her foot, pressing out the ache, gentler still, squeezing the base of her four toes. She surrendered to the tenderness of Fanny's fingers stroking the puckered stub. She felt warm and whole, unlike any other time in her life, needing nothing but more of the same.

• • •

Summer cooled to fall, their time growing short. It had been six glorious weeks. One evening over fish soup and green beans, Fanny's face caught the glimmer from the oil lamp. Her eyes shone. Emily felt as though something unacknowledged in both of them was unfurling, laying itself out on the table between them, waiting for the other person to touch with the pad of an index finger. A new aliveness made everything lovely.

The rigging of boats clanked against masts as if the boats were settling in for the night. A couple on the quay, both wearing the yellow wooden shoes of Brittany, leaned into each other, broke apart, and laughed softly. "Sweet," Emily said.

"Illicit lovers?" Frances asked.

"No. There's nothing furtive about them."

"Have you ever experienced passion, Millie? Not for art. For a person."

"Life's been a little skimpy to me in the doling out of that kind of passion. For a long time, my father paralyzed my romantic longings."

"Paralyzed? How?"

Fanny's eyes were the blue one sees when looking across an ocean for a safe harbor. The slight lifting of her cheeks offered encouragement.

"He was vulgar with me, talking about thrust. I thought he was going to touch me where he shouldn't have. His words made sex seem disgusting. I was fourteen, innocent, and horror-stricken."

Frances patted Emily's hand, and murmured sympathetically.

"He spoiled all the anticipated loveliness and joy of union. I loved him, intensely, before that, but never after."

"I'm so sorry for you."

It surprised her, how easy it was to say this, finally, like tossing a weight onto foreign soil where she'd never encounter it again, and feeling lighter afterward.

"I suppose it was an attempt to make me fearful so I would be wary. It was after an argument when he wouldn't let me go to the park alone as I'd done regularly when I was younger." She ran her thumb across a rough cuticle. "Chastity guaranteed by panic. It made me cynical. Or maybe it's just handy to blame it on him and I was born cynical."

"It's not cynicism, Millie. It's priorities."

"If I had the chance to live the last thirty-odd years over again without my father's influence, if he had died on my seventh birthday after he'd given me my first watercolor set, what then? I probably would have made the same choices."

"Maybe he saved you from the longing."

"No. Not entirely."

"Oh?"

"There was a Frenchman."

"Here?"

"No. A fur trader at home. I was naïve and afraid and lost my chance. It was all tied up in a foolish hope to go north with him." She lit a cigarette and inhaled. "But it was enough to show me what loving feels like."

Frances met her steady gaze. "Are you religious?"

"Yes. Not that I go to church. I'm the rebel in a family inflamed with piety. Those scowls glowering down from the pulpit used to wilt me like boiled spinach, and then some clergyman in a London pew slithered his hand onto my thigh. Disgusting, liver-spotted old sexpot. This country's crammed with cathedrals and I've hardly gone into a single one."

"But you say you're religious."

"God breathes in the forests. Oh, Fanny, I wish you could see them. The boughs so far above, like the vaulting of Notre Dame, and that same sacred stillness except for the sighing of wind through pines, like a sustained organ chord. If there's any kind of prayer in my life, it's that if I seek Him enough, He'll breathe His Spirit into my work."

"*You'll* breathe His Spirit into your work."

• • •

On the last night before Emily's return to Paris to collect her canvases and winter clothes, she and Frances lingered at the restaurant on the quay, sharing a tureen of mussels and a carafe of red wine. Emily gazed at the harbor. Lights winked on anchored boats and the moon cast a column of dancing silver on the water.

"You saved me from a lonely summer," Frances said.

"You saved me from a wasted one."

"It's the loneliness of what we've chosen that . . ."

"Cuts into the joy?"

"Like a claw in my chest." Frances leaned on her elbows on both sides of her cheese plate with sudden urgency. "Why don't you stay here, Millie? Paint with me in Paris this winter. We can share a stu-

dio. Live there together. I'll introduce you to the painters at La Rotonde. And dealers."

"And never paint another cedar or totem face to face? Give up
the one relationship that has fed me for years—with a place? How
many poles have been sold or destroyed since I've been gone?"

"In New Zealand women painters band together for support."
Frances's words rushed out. "They go on painting trips together.
We could do that."

Together in BC? No. She didn't want that responsibility.

"An army of two," Frances went on. "We're free as field mice to
live the way we want to here."

"I need to get home, Fanny, to use what I've learned here on
what I love. Paris isn't where I belong. I'm not myself here."

"You don't know that for sure. I tried to go home once, but I
was too radical after Paris. So they said." She laughed. "Me radical!
They haven't seen the Cubists."

"So you're never going back?"

"No."

Frances's fork scraped the inside of a shell, a shrill sound.

"When did you decide that?"

"Last week. Hearing you talk about British Columbia. I realized there's nothing at home I can't find to paint here. There's
nothing there I love enough to put up with the narrowness. As of
now, I'm a woman without a country."

"That's the difference between us. If I'm to paint out of my soul,
I have to do it in BC. You seem to find things anywhere that stir
you to paint."

"Your art will die there, Millie."

"But my soul won't." She took a long drag on her cigarette.

"Your own expression will pale before those poles you worship,
and you'll fall back to documenting them."

"I don't worship them. I love them. That's all."

"Why? What makes them so God-blessed important? Your ro-
manticized love for Indians? It's not love. It's—"

"Fanny! Stop!" She gripped the edge of the table in shock.

"Patronizing. Great White Woman saving totem poles of ruined
Indians."

"Is Gauguin patronizing? Is Picasso?"

"It's in the way you talk about them. Do-no-wrong children of nature living nobly in the dirt. You need distance to see how you idealize them."

"You're wrong." Her temples pounded.

"The center of the art world is Paris, Millie. Not some far-flung edge of the wilderness."

"You think I don't know what I'm giving up? The one place where things happen in art? The closest friend I've ever had? I never knew such joys of friendship. Yes, closed up like a walnut. Words weren't enough to say how I felt when you massaged my foot. You think I haven't considered that you might be the last intelligent person I'll ever talk to about art? Loneliness gnaws like a rat there. I'd give my other big toe to have a soul pal like you back home, someone I could lay bare my heart to, tramp the woods with, talk about anything, like we do, you and I." She took a long, uneven breath. "British Columbia may be the edge of nowhere, but it's my center."

"You want it both ways, don't you? Just like your totem paintings. Accuracy and expression. You want everything both ways. Friendship and independence too."

"Yes, Fanny, independence. Your credo."

Frances sat back in her chair as if struck.

Emily looked out across the dark water, across the Atlantic, across the plains, the bosom of her country, to the wild, wet, fecund West. She snuffed out her cigarette, bending it.

"I won't apologize because I know that irritates you, but I'm going home."

Frances tipped her face toward the pool of dark wine left in her glass, and swallowed it in one gulp. She placed her hand on Emily's. "I think I knew that all along."

19: Chestnut

Emily stepped out of the *métro* at Montparnasse station and looked up. Ironwork in sinuous tendrils arched over the stairway, and slim metal stalks unfolded gracefully into leaves and lilies. Why hadn't she noticed before?

A woman singing and a man wearing an eye patch were leading a baby jaguar on a leash. Paris. Unbelievable! *"Bonsoir,"* Emily said, but they didn't answer. Two whores in low-cut dresses came toward her, their faces painted in red and blue. They had none of the sidling carriage of the Indian women of Cordova Street in Vancouver. These women sauntered, owning the boulevard. Emily didn't sidestep to let them by, and they brushed shoulders.

The red awning of Café de la Rotonde was pulled back for any mid-October sun, and chestnut trees were dropping leaves on the tables. She spotted a tattered portfolio propped against a table where four men talked and gesticulated. She sat at the closest free table. Fanny would talk to them if she were here.

Fanny. In their last moments there had been words of counsel and praise, bolstering each other for struggles ahead, well wishes, promises to write. Already she felt a hole in her heart, as though she'd left behind a part of her and would never be able to recover it.

She ordered a *plat du jour*—half a pullet and *asperges d'Argenteuil*. Fanny loved asparagus. It was more expensive here than in the student restaurants on St-Michel where waiters wrote the amount with grease pencils on butcher-paper table covers.

A russet leaf fell on her wrist. She twirled it between her thumb and forefinger and glanced at the men. One was natty in dress, but the others were shabby, with worn shoes. A smear of cadmium yellow screamed from a frayed sleeve. One wore a rumpled felt hat tilted forward. She understood a few words of their conversation— *perspectif multiplex, peinture a l'huile, coup de pinceau*—and occasionally a name—Henri, Georges. Even if she could speak French, what would she say? My name is Emily, I'm an artist and I've run out of money so I'm going home?

Still, it gave her keen pleasure to take sidelong glances at the portfolio not five feet from her foot. Maybe one of the men would pull out something to show the others. The tone of their conversation changed as they counted out francs, bickering like old women over a few centimes, even the well-dressed one. The man in the rumpled hat left in a huff. The man with paint on his sleeve grumbled and then finished off the wine of the man who had left. They'd probably have the same squabble the next day. She finished her *café* and put the leaf in her handbag, a *souvenir de Paris*.

• • •

The next day, she paused at the pont Alexandre. Under a cloudy sky, the water lost its full range of hues and glinted only in greens. Was she ready for that submergence into the dark, cool tones of home after a year of warm ones? Ready to paint totems without fussing over details, but with Fanny's sweeping strokes, Gibb's distortion for personal vision, Laffont's modeling of shapes with hue changes, Fergusson's rhythm through repetition, Fauve and Impressionist coloring, but her own vision? She smacked the stone bridge wall. Like Sophie with her native belief and Christianity, she would take what she wanted.

She joined the horde going into the Grand Palais. Room after room shouted hundreds of names. She looked for Fanny's work, Gibb's, Fergusson's. Nothing. Instead, Léger, Vlaminck, Duchamp—names she didn't know and would soon forget, maybe the work of yesterday's arguers.

In one room the range of color was subdued and objects were fragmented. Figures were sliced apart, opened, and rearranged, showing all sides of the object at once, like laying flat an orange peel. The bird panel in Chief Wakias's house and Eagle on her drum had done this to a lesser degree. These took the idea further. One thread of connection between Paris and British Columbia—was this what Gibb was so insistent that she see?

She walked into another room and gasped. *La Colline!* Her hill painting with the patch of red poppies she'd left with Gibb. She clamped her hand over her mouth. Next to it, *Le Paysage.* Hers. Gibb's French title but her name. Her choice to outline the foreground trees in the Indian red she'd used for the trunks. Her vision of the blue roof reflecting the sky. She hadn't allowed herself to imagine why he'd wanted them. Her knees went weak.

No one to tell it to. No one to be with her here and recognize what this meant. Not Fanny or Gibb or Fergusson. Not Alice. Not Jessica, but especially not Fanny. Even though this wasn't juried, to her it was no small thing. Fanny would know that. So would Jessica. Dede would never know. Emily felt for a bench behind her and sat, planting the moment in her mind to pull out later when she would need it, telling herself that now she could face anything—scorn, loneliness, anything. She had been well hung in the Grand Palais, in the center of the world. And now she was going back to the edge of nowhere with only Gibb to know her paintings were here, Gibb who thought that someday she'd be a fine painter—for a woman.

Her paintings sparkled before her, then blurred. She waved air at her cheeks. A gallery floor guard bent over her, offering her a paper cone of water.

"I'm all right. It's just that—" She pointed, her voice tightening. "They're mine."

His eyebrows raised. *"Ah! Formidable. Brava, madame."*

Formidable, Claude's word. And eyebrows too.

She nodded her thanks, smiling as she wiped her eyes.

"Vous êtes américaine, non?"

"No. Canadian!"

Part III

20: Huckleberry

Emily found Sophie digging in her potato patch on a foggy November morning the day after she arrived back in Vancouver. "Sophie, Sophie, I've missed my good friend Sophie," she sang out.

Slowly Sophie stood up, her hand pressing against the small of her back. She was hugely pregnant. "Em'ly!" A clash of emotions streaked across her face. "Annie died."

A roaring rose in her. "No, Sophie, no." She opened her arms and, for the briefest of moments, Sophie's hard round belly pressed into hers before Sophie drew back. She saw Sophie's lips move but didn't hear a sound.

How could God . . . ? No one could say that was a full life—only seven or eight years, only a beginning. Had Annie Marie ever known how much her being mattered? How Annie had loved to ask questions. *You like painting or trees?* she'd asked. *They are the same.* As though she'd known it already. Dede didn't know. Are they the same? No, Dede and Annie are not the same.

She'd felt like Annie Marie's auntie. How could Sophie keep breathing, in and out, in and out? She wanted to shoulder some of Sophie's grief, to carry it for her until time dulled its sharpness. Why was it she couldn't keep a child alive?

"What do you think it was? Pneumonia? Tuberculosis?"

"I don't know the name. Just sick with coughing." Sophie held the door open for Emily, as if to avoid that question.

How hard it was to enter a house where a child has died. She was afraid it would be unbearably spare, but inside there was the basket cradle hanging expectantly.

"I got lots of baskets to sell." Sophie held up a huge rectangular one with her church coiled in darker strips, and on the roof, two tall triangles. "See? Our church house has two steeples now." She grinned. "Two steeples are better than one. And it has electric lights too."

How could she change the subject so blithely? Where did she store her pain?

149

"Do you have electricity here too? And water?"

"No. A tap on Third Street, same as before. But streets have names now." She opened her eyes wide and mocking. "Just like a white lady. Now I have an address."

As Sophie rummaged through piles of baskets, Emily noticed a new hooked rug on the floor. It had two figures in full skirts, large and small, both with braids, holding hands—Sophie's grief in every knot of fabric.

Sophie handed her a round basket big enough for apples. "For you."

"Really? It's lovely. What are these?" She pointed to a row of animals running around the rim.

"Billy dogs. Frank's idea."

"Ah, no tail. Of course. Thank you."

"Did you learn what you went for?"

"Yes, but it was hard to hear a spirit song away from the big trees. I'm itching to get out woodsing with you, as soon as I pay the sisters a proper visit and get Billy dog."

"You came to see me first? Before your sisters?" Sophie's eyes opened wide in astonishment, and her hands shot up to cover her mouth.

Emily raised her shoulders and smiled. Slowly, they walked to the church.

"See? Two steeples. Twice as Christian as before." Sophie laughed at her own joke. "Named for Saint Paul now."

Inside, a new Gothic rose window cast colored shapes across the pews, and dust motes floated in the still air. Emily leaned forward until her head touched the pew in front of her. An ant shouldering a burden twice its size paused in its jagged course across the floorboards. She felt helpless in giving Sophie any comfort. She wondered whether Sophie had saved Annie Marie's clothes, if she'd kept a lock of Annie's hair.

She closed her eyes and saw Annie drawing in the dirt, saw Dede thrusting open the windows in November—for character-building. Annie, with only the character of simple happiness, would be harder for her to get over.

At the cemetery they walked past the oversized marker for Margaret Dan's son, past the grave of Casamin, Sophie's first son, where Sophie straightened the stick, to Tommy's. Emily lingered there but

Sophie urged her onward to a new little grave where the wooden marker read, *Annie Marie Frank 1903–1911.*

"She lived longer than Tommy. I'm going to buy her a big white gravestone with a cross carved in like Joseph Dan's. For Tommy and Casamin too. God will be happy when they all have Christian headstones and then He won't take them more. I almost have enough for Tommy's, the graveman said."

She imagined Sophie walking among her graves, her back plumb straight, listening for her children's babble working its way upward through grains of earth, happier babble if the child had a headstone. What could a person say about that logic?

"Another baby's coming by and by," Sophie said jauntily, her nose in the air, her eyes looking sideways for a reaction.

Emily took a noisy, exaggerated breath. "I'd never have guessed it."

Sophie's hand went to her belly. "Big, huh?" The corners of her mouth, her cheeks, eyebrows, all her features lifted in a smile generated by something beyond belief, a smile that gathered Emily into it.

• • •

"No, Lizzie, I really don't want to visit Dede's grave on the way home. I just got here."

Lizzie snapped the buggy reins and they lurched away from the ferry landing in Victoria. Emily watched a hardness slide across Lizzie's face to fester as an internal wound which would, she knew, work itself to the surface and, at some unexpected moment, erupt.

The reunion with Billy was more joyful, full of welcome-home barks, drooling excitement, a rousing game of roll-the-rubber-ball, and a little mutual tousling on the dining room floor. Even Lizzie laughed at his antics. It seemed to break the pall from her refusal to visit Dede's grave.

After supper, Emily and Lizzie carried her bags upstairs. "You can sleep in Dede's room," Lizzie said at the landing. "She left a note for you on the top of the dresser. Maybe after you read it, you'll be more reasonable about paying proper respects at her grave."

"When did she write it?"

"The night before . . ." Her chin quivered.

"I'm sorry. You don't have to say." Emily held her until Lizzie pushed away, and then she entered Dede's pale blue bedroom alone, closing the door softly behind her.

A hairbrush, talcum sprinkler, toilet water, and pewter-backed hand mirror were marshaled in a row equidistant from one another, and in front of them, an envelope positioned squarely on the dresser scarf. She took off her shoes and lay down, hoping to doze, but five minutes later, she tore open the envelope and read Dede's upright handwriting.

Emily,

I suppose you'll be happy to hear that there are some few things I'm sorry for, but only a few. You have to recognize that our dear parents worried about leaving you. "You see to it that Millie minds you," Mother told me often. She trusted the others to act respectably but not you, so you see, since you were so intractable, I had to force you into obedience. Perhaps now you can spend some time reflecting on the grief you caused and the heavy responsibility placed on me. I have put my family first in all things, to my own self-denial. You have done everything you wanted. We shall both have to answer for our actions in the hereafter.

Dede

A wallop as precisely aimed and full of ire as that first kick under the dining room table. Hadn't Dede had her say in life, but she had to speak from the grave as well? How pathetic that the bagful of life Dede had collected was so limp that she was still hoping to stir up a pot of guilt in her last dying breaths. She put the letter in her carpetbag to read again later, and crawled into bed under Dede's ice blue coverlet.

• • •

Hoping Lizzie wouldn't demand that she visit Dede's grave, Emily went tiptoe around the house for the next four days. She made Dede's bed first thing in the morning, smoked only on the back porch while she painted, kept her turpentine outside because it nauseated Lizzie, and made a point to be prompt at mealtimes and not skip afternoon tea even if she was in the heat of painting. On the fourth morning, a delivery truck came into the gravel driveway.

"My crates! My French paintings!"

"Just in time," Alice said. "You can unpack them at teatime. We invited a few friends. It was going to be a surprise."

Talkative and expectant, the women took seats in the parlor, balanced their teacups and waited while Emily pried open the crate. The first canvas happened to be a pensive young girl in a Concarneau wine shop. Bad choice. No wonder no one said anything. She pulled out another, the Brittany kitchen with Héloïse knitting a sock by her fireplace. It was acceptable subject matter, but still no one made a comment.

"That's Héloïse. Her orchard had such sweet peaches."

Alice and one woman nodded.

A landscape with elms and cottages was next. "I remember that place, in Crécy," Alice said. "That long walk we took along the canal." She smiled at the memory. "That's a nice cloud."

The cloud was the only pale thing in the painting.

"Did Gibb tell you to paint the water with red smears?"

"No, Alice. The water told me."

Seeing the canal painting again was like seeing an old friend. She turned to the crate to choose another. The church near St. Efflam should please them, at least the subject matter. She lifted that out. There was dead silence. It could not have hurt more if they'd thrown stones. She thought of Fanny and felt as though she were playing out a scene in Dunedin. When they'd seen them all, a missionary wife said, "I don't know, Emily. You used to paint quite sweetly."

"But she was in the Paris salon," another woman said. Her voice reeked with utter bafflement.

Quickly, Alice changed the subject to French food, a tactic Emily knew was to save her from being argued over, or, worse, to avoid confrontation about something of which she, Alice, had been a part. Emily stacked up a load of canvases and took them upstairs to Dede's bedroom.

She hated herself for doing it as soon as she set them down. She was not ashamed of her paintings. She was ashamed of her sisters. Of their tea parties with art as an excuse to show off baking skills and china patterns, of their narrow lives all ticketty-boo without a doily out of place. Underlying that, and worse, was their disinterest and incapacity. She sprawled onto the bed. What had happened to

Alice? Had France not penetrated, that as soon as she came home, provincialism set in and filmed over her eyes? And Lizzie, bare-nerved, Bible-breathing Lizzie hadn't said a word. It slid into her thought like creeping ice, while regarding the cross on St. Efflam's church, that nothing she would ever do would seem important to Lizzie. And nothing Lizzie would ever do would seem important to her. Fine. They wouldn't have to look at her paintings.

. . .

She went to Vancouver and rented a studio flat on West Broadway in a low-rent district, one light room large enough to hold a class, with a basic kitchen in one corner. Over the next several weeks, she moved her paintings and clothes from Victoria, got her furniture and easels out of storage, and hung her new work edge to edge all the way to the ceiling, like the Salon d'Automne. She would have covered the ceiling too, if she could have figured out how. And she placed two ads—one advertising children's art classes, and the other announcing a studio show. She collected Joseph at Jessica's, and Jessica had to come see everything right then.

"They're marvelous! Your colors shout to be noticed." She put her hands on her head and squeezed hanks of hair. "It's like you're not afraid of anything. Now aren't you glad I made you go?" Jessica said smugly, teasing.

"You!"

"You!" Joseph squawked. "You. You. You!"

. . .

"Didn't I tell you they'd come?" Jessica said at the studio exhibit behind her tray of cookies. "Forty-eight people so far."

They could hardly fit in the room. Emily whistled softly. Many of them were from the Vancouver Ladies' Art Club, but more were strangers, which was a good sign. She strained to hear individual comments in the noise.

"She paints like a man," one man sputtered.

"But it was done in France," his wife countered.

"Exactly. You can see she was influenced by that madman, van Gogh. You can't tell what anything is. They're the wrong colors."

"Amazing that you know so much about van Gogh," Emily said to him. "I lived there and don't know a bean about him."

"My, France certainly had a ferocious effect on you," a woman said, taking off her gloves, one precise finger at a time, to reach for a cookie from Jessica's tray.

What a sappy smile on that woman. She'd promised Jessica she wouldn't get on her high horse if she heard anything ignorant, but she hadn't promised she wouldn't return their sappy smiles.

A man elbowed his way in front of the woman. "Do you mean to claim that you actually see blue shadows in nature?" he asked.

"Yes, I do. Shadows can be any color, depending upon what's opposite them."

The man grunted and turned away.

Emily whispered to Jessica, "What an old acid drop."

"Sh." Jessica studied an oil of a mackerel vendor on the quay in Concarneau. "I've never in my life seen such innovative color handling," she said in a loud voice and clanked down the tray. "Save that one for me. It takes me beyond surface reality."

All conversation stopped. Necks lengthened. Heads swiveled. People looked at each other dumbfounded as Jessica counted out the money into Emily's palm.

A woman in a fur collar pointed to a canal scene at Crécy-en-Brie. "This is the new French art, then, is it?"

"It's one of many new ways of painting," Emily said.

"Now tell me how to say the place." She made Emily repeat it twice. "Such a pleasant village. So French." The woman reached into her handbag and brought out a checkbook.

By the end of the evening, two other strangers had made fair-sized purchases. "I'm tickled to bits," Emily said after everyone except Jessica left. She kicked off her shoes. "Not a slam-bang frenzy, but it's a start."

· · ·

In the morning, Jessica knocked on her door with two newspapers.

"Bad or not so bad?" Emily asked.

"Bad bad," Joseph muttered.

"Don't make assumptions until you hear, either of you."

Jessica read aloud. *"The riot of color exhibited by seventy paintings was no less than startling. The blues were so very blue, the yellows unmitigated, the reds aggressive, yet the exhibit was interesting as an indication of the French distaste for detail."*

"Sounds like he's writing about jelly beans," Emily said.

"Just listen. *Since Miss Carr is said to have had two paintings in the Paris Salon, we can only assume her work to be similar to what is being shown on the continent. Still, for a lady painter who had once shown promise to have thrown reason to the winds, it is perhaps not incorrect to say that she has outraged nature with her colors."*

"Snivel and rot."

"Rot. Rot. Don't talk rot," Joseph said.

"What do you know about it, Joseph? Painting is one of those occupations where you have to keep proving your talent to people who have none. Stuffed-shirted critics yakety-yakking that 'We, the educated and refined, will set standards of artistic taste, in the name of the Father and the Son and the Holy Spirit.' "

"It's not all bad, Em. You sold four."

"Only because they were painted in France, not because the buyers knew a smidgen about art. Except for you."

"Never satisfied. You're impossible. Angry if you're not praised, suspicious if you are." Jessica slapped down the review.

Emily screamed, "It's on the women's page!" She crumpled it, then flattened it. Above it was a gossipy account of the affairs of English aristocracy and a fashion editorial. Emily mimicked a prissy voice: *"Any woman swashbuckling alongside her husband in trousers is an outrage and a threat to all good women of the province.* So is excluding women's art from the arts page! Show me the other one."

Jessica winced. "It's not a review. It's an editorial in the *Province*. Anonymous." She slid it across the table.

Emily read it to herself.

Before going abroad, this Miss Carr showed no small talent in depicting local scenery, but now she exhibits only the work of an agitated imagination. The arrogance to assume she can improve on nature by outlandish colors without delineating properly a single leaf shows in her sorry attempt to eclipse the Almighty by producing bizarre work she in her misguided mind considers more satisfactory than nature itself.

"I've been called a wild beast! A Fauve!" She laughed from the root of her throat. "Now that's a badge of honor!" She tacked the clipping to the wall.

Jessica laughed too, in relief.

Just like Fanny, she was an outsider—too different for Vancouver, not different enough for Paris. Always on the edge, allowed in for a time if she promised to behave, but ridiculed or ignored if she gave an inappropriate peep.

What would Fanny do? Abandon her home, and escape to France where she could take comfort in others being ridiculed too. And if she did the same? It would be a grand reunion at Gare du Nord with lunch at La Rotonde. They'd show each other their new work.

No. It was inconceivable to leave. British Columbia was her heart's home.

"This blather can't go unanswered."

"That's the spirit, Em. Let 'em have it!"

She found some letter paper and fired back a response.

March 20, 1912

Your unnamed editor who states that I claim to "eclipse the work of the Almighty" has not grasped the smallest principle of the new art movement. Paintings are inspired by nature, true, but made in the artist's soul. That's why no two individuals see the same thing and express it alike. To attempt to reproduce France or Canada without filtering it through one's sensibilities is mere copy work, done by people worried over the number of leaves on a tree. Though they may have harmonized their colors, they have not plumbed for the feel. The new ideas are big and they fit this big glorious West. I do not say mine is the only way to paint. I only say it's the way that appeals to me. To people lacking imagination, lacking even the integrity to sign their names, it could not appeal.

Emily Carr

She read it to Jessica who clapped and then held out her hand. "Give it to me. I'll make sure it gets mailed."

Emily licked the envelope and smacked it down with her fist. Jessica snatched it and darted out the door.

Emily cackled. Fanny and Gibb would be proud.

"Come on, Billy. I can tell you've been thinking about a walk. Let's go to the reserve. I bet we'll find a new baby."

. . .

The cool sea breeze at the reserve invigorated her. Buds on the cherry trees were about to burst into waxy cups sized for a doll. Spring would be early this year, and that meant summer was coming. She had a journey to plan, research to do in the museum library, Chinook to study, letters to write to William Halliday and the Halls.

She found Sophie's door ajar, the air full of steaming clams, and poked her head in. "Yoo-hoo."

"Look, Em'ly. Babies!" Sophie's face glowed. "Baptized!"

"Two?"

"Twins are plenty luck," Aunt Sarah said, one baby in her lap. "Like two church steeples."

Sophie handed Emily a baby. "This one's Em'ly Marie Frank."

"No, she isn't," Sarah said.

Sophie lifted the blanket. "Oh!" She giggled. "No. That one's Molly Theresa. Emmie has straight eyes."

Looking closer, Emily saw that the baby in her arms had slightly crossed eyes.

Sophie lifted the other one from Sarah's arms. "This one's Em'ly Marie." She puckered her lips and made kissing sounds.

"They're both beautiful, Sophie." She felt the satin skin of Molly's cheek.

Sophie's delirium of happiness made her rock. "Emmie's named for you."

"That's dear of you, Sophie. Nothing could please me more."

"If you want, when she's older I'll give her to you."

"Sophie! That's absurd. She's yours! People don't give babies. They're human beings."

Sophie's shoulders drooped and she turned away.

Sarah took one look at Sophie and signaled Emily with her eyes that she'd hurt her. "Some Indian women do, when another woman don't have a baby of her own."

"I'm sorry. I didn't know."

Had Sophie been thinking this ever since Tommy's funeral when she offered to share a baby? Sophie must have misunderstood when she'd told her that people don't share babies.

"Did you think, all these years, that I didn't consider sharing enough? That's not what I meant at all." The thought that she'd sounded ungrateful with mere sharing thudded in her chest. "I didn't expect—"

"Not for keeps," Sophie said, playing with Emily Marie's hand. "An Indian gift, like white people say." She sputtered a sheepish laugh as if to cover embarrassment for again having offered something unacceptable to white people, but it rang false. She had meant what she'd said, a gift of what she most cherished. What agonies she must have gone through all these years to arrive at this.

Ashamed, Emily watched Molly's tiny lips, moist and moving with a will of their own. "Who's Molly Theresa named for?"

"For a Squamish woman long time ago tipped over in a canoe off Raccoon Island. She took a big baby in each arm and little baby in her teeth and kicked and kicked to a logging camp. Little baby dead. Big babies live. She got the Royal Humane Society Medal from Queen Victoria. I name one Molly and one Emmie so they both grow up strong."

Sophie smiled with her whole being, her face fluid with joy. It was that quality of hopefulness, that belief that at any moment life could offer a reversal, that made Sophie so dear.

Emily held Molly while Sophie nursed Emmie, and then they switched. Emily put her finger behind the curve in Emmie's toes lined up like a row of corn kernels. Emmie's foot pushed back.

Sophie cooed some Squamish words and Sarah joined.

"What are you singing?" Emily asked.

"A sleep song. I learned it from my grandmother."

"More old," Sarah said. "I learned it from my grandmother."

"Can you sing it in English?"

Sophie's voice was low, her words halting. "Sleep, baby of huckleberry eyes. Sleep, baby of salmonberry lips. Rest soft till the morning come. If you die before moon rises, I will weave a cedar ladder, I will follow you to sunset."

21: Loon

Emily grasped the wooden gunwale of William Halliday's govern-ment boat, one hand chilled by wind and spray, the other buried under Billy's thick neck to keep it warm, her feet cramped under her bedroll, her eyes taking it all in. Shoreline firs along Johnstone Strait between Vancouver Island and the mainland leaned toward the water glistening like polished pewter. Gulls lined a narrow beach, their reflections cast on the shiny raw umber mud, each one a whisk of gray brush stroke mirrored by its opposite shape.

Tillie James, the Kwakiutl girl from Alert Bay whom Halliday had brought along, gestured to a pod of whales gliding in arcs, then diving deep. Emily sat up straighter, hoping to get another look at them.

"It mean something when you see whales," Tillie said above the engine.

"What?" she asked, but Tillie didn't answer.

She'd have to imagine. To her it meant casting off, diving into new waters, facing solitude in the wilderness, feeling the greatness of Canada in the raw. This year, 1912, would be her year of discov-ery. Before she'd left, Lizzie's pious tongue had spit venom about idolatry and foolhardy schemes with aborigines, as if she felt she had to fill in for Dede. She was casting off from that too.

After half a year of teaching, she had earned enough to take six weeks of summer to paint as many totems as she could, on the is-lands in the straits and up the Inside Passage and the Skeena River into the bosom of British Columbia. Her mind reeled with what she might encounter. Wind lifted the feathers on the backs of the gulls and numbed her face. She leaned into its salty bite. Good clean wind to blow away doubt.

By late afternoon, she peered through light fog at the veiled vil-lage of Guyasdoms, eighteen miles from where they'd started in Alert Bay. She felt as though she were looking through finely spun ashen silk teasing her with only a glimpse of a building and its frontal pole. Halliday nosed the boat toward the beach and Tillie lowered herself into knee-deep water to pull it in. Billy jumped out, splashing them all.

"Billy, stay close," Emily shouted.

"I'll be back the day after tomorrow around ten," Halliday said after they had unloaded everything. "Mind ye, be ready. Tides don't wait."

Nodding, she checked her gear on the shore—bedroll, food box, easel, folding camp stool, large sketch sack containing two paint-boxes, drawing board, sketch pad, brushes, pencils, charcoal; and her portfolio with tall canvas-covered boards for oils and card panels for watercolors. How the devil would she manage all of this when she didn't have Halliday to take her places?

"Just don't forget us," Emily called out.

After the whine of the engine dulled and the slap-slap of the boat's waves diminished, utter aloneness set in. No canoes, no people, not a single human sound to give her comfort. Swirls of vapor made the place ghostly and secretive.

"Isn't anyone here?" she asked Tillie.

"All gone to a summer fishing camp. That's why he told me to stay with you."

Emily looked at Tillie, slight and trembling. "To protect me? You? How old are you?"

"Fourteen."

"You ever been here before?"

"Maybe, when I was little. To a potlatch."

"You aren't so big now." Emily looked at the speck of the boat in the V of its widening wake, the shrouded expanse of gray trees and grayer water. "Neither of us is."

A shivering double cry cut through the silver-gray vapor, stretching in a long, penetrating arc, and descending to a mournful yodel. A loon. She didn't move. It came again, those two short notes releasing that unearthly call and then the half-laughing, half-crazed finish, chilling in its beauty.

She hoisted her bedroll, food basket, and easel. Log steps smeared with velvety green algae led from the clamshell beach to a raised plank walkway overgrown by bushes so tall she couldn't see above them. The damp planks had been overtaken by an army of reddish-brown slugs trailing thick slime. Two steps onto the planks sent her slipping sideways. She dropped her bedroll and her arm shot out to steady herself against the bushes. Their sting attacked her hand and wrist. "Don't touch, Tillie. They're nettles. Billy, stay." She lunged to grab him and her hand brushed against them again. The itching began immediately.

Holding his collar, she followed the wooden walkway down a row of bighouses. Not houses. Creatures. Enormous, blocky fantasy creatures as big as houses. One house front was painted with gigantic eyes and a leering grin. The whitewashed double doors were two front teeth. A beaver. A diving whale was attached vertically to the next house. The whale's open upper jaw jutted forward ten feet as a porch roof, and the door was a tongue inside the red mouth—as inventive a design as Chief Wakias's Raven's beak. On the whale's back rode a sprightly little man with curling frog-like legs, and Raven was caught between the tail flukes. On the roofline next to it stretched a sleepy, gray, two-headed sea serpent. She stepped backward to take it all in, slid on a slug, tumbled into the nettles, and let out a yelp that made Billy bark.

She beat back the nettles with her easel and caught a glimpse of the far end of the village. What was *that?* She scrambled to her feet and thrashed through undergrowth toward a towering colossus, a single elongated figure, not a stack of totem animals, not carved onto the front of a pole, but a statue by itself, probably twenty feet tall. The red torso and round cedar belly were clearly human. Clearly a woman! An ogress. Block-like wooden breasts hung downward, with nipples that had been carved into, what? Eagles' heads? With eyes and beaks? Arms fashioned from added wood extended forward at the shoulder, reaching. A terrifying sight. High nettles prevented her from seeing the woman's face.

"What *is* she? A witch?" Emily murmured.

No answer. Tillie had gone back to the shore for a second load. Wind whistled, and it started to rain.

Separate from the bighouses, across an open space, stood a small white clapboard house with windows and a peaked roof, the mission house. "Come on, Billy. This way."

In a minute, he said with his nose in a puddle scummed over with algae.

"Billy! Now!"

When Tillie turned Halliday's key in the lock, something scuttled inside. In the damp, dim interior smelling of mildew, Emily dug into her food box for a candle and matches. Tillie found some wood and built a fire.

"Won't the missionaries expect that wood to be here when they come back?"

"We only use a little. I'll get some new tomorrow. It will dry by and by they come back."

They baked potatoes at the fire's edge which they ate with smoked salmon and apples. Tillie handed her a shiny brown something spread with what looked like congealed tapioca pudding. "Herring eggs on kelp," Tillie said. "It's good."

Emily bit down on the cool, rubbery surface which squeaked in her mouth but was relatively tasteless. She scratched her face. It was impossible to ignore the tingling, and rubbing her cheek on her sleeve had only made the irritation worse.

"I saw you fall into the *jumjumclum*," Tillie said. "Alder bark's the Kwakwaka'wakw way to get rid of the sting, but I didn't see any. Use, you know, from your nose. Not as good, but always with you."

"Kwakwak . . . ?"

"Our tribe. We say Kwakwaka'wakw. You say Kwakiutl. More easy for you."

Tillie pantomimed blowing her nose into her hands and spreading it on her face. Emily followed her instruction. It helped a little.

"You remember me from a time ago? You made pictures on the beach."

"Did I draw you too?"

Tillie nodded. "I kept it for long time. My little brother Toby ripped it. It made him sad."

"I'll do another now." She took out a small sketch pad, and penciled in the shape of Tillie's face, as round and brown as an earthenware plate. A braid hung forward over her shoulder.

"What's that woman? That big carving?" Emily asked.

"Dzunukwa."

"What's Dzunukwa?" Her tongue struggled with the deep buzz that launched the name.

"She lives in the forest." Tillie's voice became husky. "When mothers hear her call, *huu, huu,* they so afraid they act like trees. Arms out but they can't move."

Emily remembered Sophie telling Tommy about a Wild Woman of the Woods, but Sophie had used another name, Kak-something.

"What does she do?"

"She carries off children in her basket and smokes them to eat them."

"Why does she have eagles' beaks on her nipples?"

Tillie was silent in her pose.

"If she's bad, why do people put her in their village?"

"Not always bad. Sometimes she gives good things." Her voice was soft with awe. "If you chase her she turn to smoke."

Emily sketched Tillie's hair. Where it was pulled tight from a center part, she rubbed in highlights with her India rubber.

The fire crackled, her pencil scratched, Billy snored, and the wind moaned, but still she heard another sound, like an owl hooting only lasting longer. "What's that?"

"Dzunukwa," Tillie said.

"Is she crying?"

"No. She doesn't cry. Mothers with dead babies cry. She of the Woods, she just calls, *huu, huu,* and takes the babies."

A harpy! She thought of Annie Marie, Tommy, and the un-named one, a mere fluttering, short-lived as a moth. "Do many babies die in Alert Bay?"

"Some. My brother did. Not Toby. And two cousins too."

"Were you afraid of Dzunukwa when you were little?"

Tillie nodded minutely. "When I went too far away, Mama told me Dzunukwa will get me."

Emily shaded under Tillie's brows to get that intensity and fear into her eyes so pinched together.

"Is Dzunukwa still alive?"

"Yes. She dead hundreds of times, but she can put herself together again. She always comes back and sings, 'I have the spirit power.' "

"What's her spirit power?"

Tillie lifted her shoulders. "Many stories." She ate a strip of kelp with tiny, thoughtful chews. "Only some people can tell them. Not me."

Emily put down her pencil and gave the drawing to Tillie. Her eyes glowed and her wide smile expressed her thanks.

They let the fire die down. Cold night crept in through the window that had become a square black hole. Tillie pulled her blanket over her. Billy was restless. Emily sympathized, but the sound of his nails tappety-tapping on the wooden floor was annoying. "Billy. Lie down." She pointed to the floor by her bed. Tillie's breathing took on a gentle rhythm. Maybe that would give Billy the idea.

The call of a loon pierced the light thrum of rain, asking and asking, urgent in the darkness, otherworldly, the loneliest sound she'd ever heard.

Emily felt the ogress with her fierce beak breasts staring in at them with whatever eyes she had. Tomorrow, she'd stand before that Wild Crone until her every feature was seared into her memory, and she'd make of her a thing of terrible beauty.

· · ·

By morning the rain had stopped. She walked around the nettles to the rocky bluff above the sea which gave her a fine view of Dzunukwa, as if this Forest Fury had just stepped out from the trees behind her. Wisps of vapor floated above her head. Tense stillness engulfed Emily and the figure. Emily stared. Dzunukwa stared back. This hideous, mighty Queen of Dark Places stared back. She had to wrench her eyes away from the clutch of Dzunukwa's empty sockets in order to study the other features of her face. Wide whitish circles around her eye holes. Thick black brows over them. Round ears sticking out. Gruesome cheek cavities in scooped-out red ovals. The mouth—that garish, ghoulish mouth with red bulging lips pushed out in an O as if she were howling that low *huu*, like the sound made by blowing across a bottle, a chill, keening hoot.

And those eagle breasts. Those beady black eagle eyes. That sharp hook of a beak on each nipple ready to snatch and tear. What did it mean? In spite of what Tillie had said, this Hellhag was pure savage.

She could see this Wild Cedar Woman wasn't afraid of anything— suffocating forest, lightning, torrential rain, cougars, isolation, vastness. She was of it. She could see in the dark, stride through bogs, race wolves, fight bears, penetrate the impenetrable, be alone. The only one of her kind, having no mate, she could look upon raw life or death and not shrink from either one. She could even rise from the dead and put herself back together again. If only an ounce of that raw power could become hers. She felt the pull of Dzunukwa's extended arms. Were they itching to steal a child, or were they reaching for her, taking her to her bosom?

Dzunukwa's mystery deepened along with the darkening sky. Rain threatened. She'd have to work fast. That meant watercolor, not oil. She pulled out two large sheets and placed them vertically to accommodate the tall figure. Before such a ferocious creature, she had to talk herself through the process. Simplify the shapes. Use Fanny's long, loose strokes in burnt sienna for the torso. Exaggerate to express. Build up a chromium oxide shadow on her arms to take on the forest colors behind her. Highlight her breasts with a smear of cadmium red medium for expression, like Gibb would do. Make it lurid, like his nudes. Lay another smear on her cheek. Surround the black hole of a mouth with a thick, pale Indian yellow ring for lips. Outline the ring in cadmium red deep. Outline the eyes, the ears, the arms in black.

What about the nipples? A momentary pause. A catch in her rhythm. Later. Keep the rhythm going. Do the surroundings now. Make the nettles lick Dzunukwa's legs like green flames. Use Fanny's long strokes in Prussian green and viridian. Highlight with shorter, narrower strokes of yellow ochre. Do shadows in ultramarine. Outline in indigo and black. Simplify the trees in the background into overlapping triangles.

The beak nipples. She stopped to think it out. How could she paint what she couldn't understand? But if she didn't paint them, no one would know that they were there. And if she did, Fanny's prediction would be right—her own expression would vanish in her awe of the totem, and the eagle faces would be wrong, too tight considering the broad, sweeping lines of the rest of the painting.

Dzunukwa's lowing came again. *Huu, ah, huu. Who are you?* she seemed to be hooting. *Recorder, or artist?*

It had been easier to simplify in France because she didn't care about preserving the details there. They didn't mean anything to her. But here, whatever they meant to the Kwakiutl, to her those beak breasts suggested a Beldame Nature not benign. The nipple that fed could also scratch and tear. She slashed a thick dark line, curved outward and downward toward the nipple, like a scythe. She painted the reverse shape on the other side of the nipple to make a point at the bottom. She did the same for the other breast and added two black dabs on each pointed nipple. Let them suggest what they may.

The haunting call of the loon resounded, as though it were the lowing Dark Forest Goddess herself. Emily unleashed her own unearthly call, yodeling and hooting, back to the wilderness.

22: Raven

"A secret," Tillie's mother, Beatrice James, said softly on the beach at Alert Bay where Emily was painting. A full-bosomed woman wearing large abalone-shell earrings, Beatrice carried herself with authority. "Chief Wakias got an invitation for you to Chief Tlii-Tlaalaadzi's potlatch."

"A potlatch! Me?"

"Sh!" Tillie scowled in exaggerated seriousness. "You can't tell them at the mission house." Then she grinned.

"Tell Mrs. Hall that my husband, Mac James, is taking you to paint at Quatsino. Then they go wrong way to find us."

What would Claude think of this? Would he be there? He'd be surprised to see her. His eyebrows would pop up.

Lizzie would be starched silly if she knew, but Victoria was more than two hundred miles south. Emily imagined a missionary society meeting in the family parlor and Lizzie announcing crisply, As long as those Indians still do their cannibal dances at pagan revels and then go to church afterwards, there's plenty of the Lord's work left to do. We're not finished until we've rooted out all heathen practices and backsliding.

Whatever they did at potlatches, it had to do with totems, Claude had told her. If she was ever to paint the poles with expression or understanding, she had to find out what they meant to the people who created them. Whether potlatches were illegal or not, she'd be a fool not to go.

"What's the chief's name again?"

"Chief Tlii-Tlaalaadzi."

"That's quite a name."

"Means great big bonfire," Beatrice said. "What do you do if you are too close to a bonfire?"

"Back away."

"That's what other chiefs do too if they want to give a potlatch. They know they can't give one big like he can. You will see. Many things he will give."

. . .

At each tide, family by family left, as if they were going fishing, or to their summer berry-picking lands. On Sunday Reverend Hall would look across empty pews and see only the infirm and the residential school children from St. Michael's. His beard would tremble in anger when he gave the invocation. If William Halliday happened to be here, he'd bolt out of the church, head south in his gas boat to the BC Provincial Police. Without knowing where this potlatch was among dozens of islands, it was unlikely that the BCPP would arrive in time to stop it—she hoped.

Only after Tillie's father pushed off their canoe two days later and they were well out into Johnstone Strait did anyone mention the name of the place—Mimkwamlis on Village Island up Knight's Inlet.

Toby arched his back and said, "Mimkwamlis mean Village with Rocks and Islands in Front," a slight tone of showing off in his voice. He giggled at Emily's expression and added, "The Mamalilikala Band of the Kwakwaka'wakw people live there."

Emily whistled at the words. "Thank you, Toby. Now I understand. But aren't most potlatches in winter?" Emily asked.

Toby turned to his mother. "One year ago the chief at Mimkwamlis died," Beatrice said. "A disgrace if the new chief does not raise a pole for him now. He can't have old chief's rights until he does."

"The police won't expect one now," Mac added.

Emily looked at the two boys nestled asleep against Billy in the canoe, Jack, maybe four years old, and Alphonse, a little older, Tillie's cousins. "Are their parents already there?"

"No. They were arrested for potlatching so they can't come."

"You mean they're in jail?"

"No, just can't go to potlatches. No worry. They don't put white people in jail. Yet."

Something in Emily's look made them all laugh. Worry crept up her spine.

The family sang the paddling song, "*Si-whwa-kwa, si-whwa-kwa,*" to keep the rhythm across open water until they entered a narrower waterway. Mac tipped his head in the direction of a great blue heron feeding in the shallows. He let the canoe glide toward shore, small waves licking its sides. "We camp here tonight."

Emily looked at the sliver of beach frilled with foam and scattered with dried sea lettuce, a rough-textured rocky outcropping at one end, a snag rippling the current at the other. Drooping folds of hemlock sheltered this long-necked bird balanced gracefully on legs delicate as fern stems. When the canoe touched the shore, it flew off with a loud *grak*.

"A blue heron always does a person good," Emily said.

Mac smiled. "A good sign."

· · ·

They approached Mimkwamlis late the next morning. Boats came from all directions. "Won't they know it's a potlatch with all these boats?" Emily asked.

"They'll hide some, and we have lookouts," Mac said. "Meanwhile, everybody has plenty good time." He looked at his son. "And Toby sees his first pole raising."

Sixteen poles, one in front of each bighouse, reached above the rooflines, facing the beach. One house had an enormous raven, bigger than Halliday's gas boat, sitting on the roof peak. A single male figure with outstretched arms, and an oversized head, wearing a tall, tapered hat, stood separate, close to the shore.

"Is that the new pole?" Emily asked.

"No. It's a speaker's figure," Beatrice said. "You'll see."

The minute their canoe touched the white clamshell beach, she heard words chanted in Kwakwala coming through the figure's wooden mouth. Billy barked back at it and they all laughed.

Tillie put her arms around Billy's neck. "It's only to welcome us, Billy."

On shore, two lines of men formed to carry the thirty-foot canoe into the woods. Emily kept Billy on a short leash so he wouldn't get in the way. She lifted his chin to face her. "Now don't go putting your nose into everything. We're guests."

He blinked, struggling to be patient.

"I can hold on to him if you want to draw," Tillie offered.

"Thank you. He thinks everyone is gathered here for him."

She set to work on a watercolor sketch of the welcome figure, then found another one, without a hat, standing near a crazily crooked staircase up to the bighouses. "This place is spectacular. Everywhere I look, I see another painting subject."

They climbed the stairs and dodged some boys playing games to get to the new pole resting on blocks and covered by tarps. That was disappointing. She would have loved to get a close look. It lay flat on the ground, the base overhanging a fifteen-foot slanted trench. Ropes were draped loosely over a temporary scaffolding erected near its base. She couldn't think how such a heavy weight could be brought upright.

In front of Chief Tlii-Tlaalaadzi's bighouse, hundreds of folded blankets were stacked as high as the roof. Next to fifty-pound sacks of flour and sugar, there were crates of china, pillars of buckets and wash basins, twined and painted spruce-root rain hats, carved and painted bentwood boxes, baskets, gramophones, even treadle sewing machines. Apparently, if the police boats came this far, no amount of hiding goods would help. There was food too—baskets of dried salmon and halibut, five-gallon cans of oolichan grease, baskets of bannock and berries.

"Blackberries, Saskatoons, black gooseberries, and stink currants," Tillie said, gesturing to each proudly.

In front of the stacked goods, men wearing bowler hats and suspenders, some with gold watch chains, and women in colorful print dresses faced two men and a third who had some function between them. "It's *haana-aa*, I Will Change Your Mind. A game. They bet about where are the bones."

The players were stoic, but the people watching, urging one choice over another and giving warnings, were laughing. No one was trying to hide what he or she was doing. That did not make Emily relax.

A matron whose jacket buttons were ready to pop served whipped soapberries from a two-foot canoe. The girl standing beside her handed out small paddles that people used as spoons. A toothless man wearing suspenders slurped up the froth and grinned. "Indian ice cream. Easy to eat," he said. Emily dipped her paddle into the canoe for a dollop of the soft pink foam. It tasted bitter and sweet at the same time. Toby and Alphonse and Jack came running to get their share.

Tillie laughed. "Afraid they'll run out?"

Emily stood at the edge of a crowd surrounding several chiefs whose headdresses were carved animal faces. They wore elaborate blue and green blankets edged in red and decorated with hundreds of mother-of-pearl buttons in Raven and Eagle patterns. She recognized Chief Wakias, and wished she could ask him to pose, but he seemed unapproachable wearing the regalia.

Beatrice pointed out Chief Tlii-Tlaalaadzi, a wide-faced older man whose Eagle headdress had ermine tails hanging from the sides. His speaker stood beside him wearing a bark head ring and button blanket. Holding a heavy carved staff with Eagle at the top, he spoke in Kwakwala, and the crowd of men and women opened around the pole to be raised. Men sitting behind a hollowed-log drum began to beat a rhythm, slowly at first, then faster and louder. With great ceremony, men lifted the tarps. The crowd murmured approval and then sang their joy at seeing the carving. Although Emily couldn't see the top of the pole because of the crowd, the Raven, Bear, Killerwhale and Wolf that she did see were magnificent. The carving was surprisingly sharp-edged, the wood smooth, the figures heroic, full of meanings she could not grasp.

Toby nodded toward a man moving through the crowd, speaking to everyone as he passed. His skin was furrowed by time like the great old poles at Alert Bay. "My uncle," Toby said. "Hayward James. He carved that pole." Toby did a proud little hop.

She realized with a flush of excitement—the toddler at Alert Bay years ago who knew he'd be an artist because one of his eyelashes was put in his uncle's paintbrush, that was the same Toby.

"I can't see," he said.

"You will," Beatrice said, lifting Alphonse to see while Tillie lifted Jack. "You'll remember this for a long time."

Suddenly it was essential that Toby see everything. Emily spotted an empty crate and fetched it for the boys to stand on. "Try not to hop," she cautioned.

Lines of men, Mac among them, squatted by the pole to shoulder it from underneath. A hush spread through the crowd. Ropes creaked and the pole raised several inches. She knew she was witnessing something few white people understood. Halliday would call it a senseless tug-of-war with a dead tree, yet the rapt attention of every person here showed that in that tree lived history and pride and ancestry and love.

Hayward James crouched beside Toby and whispered. His gestures spoke lovingly of the wood, its grain and texture, its fragrance. He'd lived with the cedar, studied its character, responded to its spirit. Here, at this moment, art was being transmitted. She hoped Toby understood the responsibility.

Raw energy pushed up the column inch by inch until pairs of smaller supporting poles crossing like scissors could be propped under it. Children who'd never seen this before and old people who'd seen it many times all stood still and silent, as though they all were holding their breath. The men rested four times, while the chief's speaker recounted events in the lives of the dead chief and his ancestors. Raven, Bear, Killerwhale, Wolf, and the top figure, Eagle, rose higher and higher against the sky. The line of men pulled ropes over the scaffolding, and in ten minutes, start to finish, it was up. Incredibly, it was up—Eagle, wings outspread, soaring. A sigh whooshed like wind through the crowd.

Men filled in the hole with boulders and tamped down dirt. No shout of hurrah went up when the ropes were released. It was an occasion deeper than cheers, a moment of reverence. Toby tipped his head back. Emily put her cheek close to his. "Someday you'll make a fine work of art like that."

The chief's speaker announced that they would give out the blankets right then. Mac and Beatrice exchanged serious glances. Emily asked what it meant.

"Most times they don't give out anything this soon," Beatrice said.

One by one, the blankets were presented to people whose names were called. This, she guessed, was the beginning of the potlatch. Emily looked over her shoulder to see if BCPP boats were bearing down on them.

Drummers carried the log drum into the bighouse, and drumming started again as people filed in. Emily tied Billy's leash to a tree, and gave him water and food. Hemlock bows decorating the doorway brushed her cheek when she entered with Tillie, and wood smoke stung her eyes. A quavering hollow rattle startled her. Raven, all beak and tarred bark feathers, swooped across the room on a cord. A man poured grease onto the fire, which crackled more and lit up the room.

Emily and Tillie's family sat where they were directed to. She felt the bench vibrating beneath her. A whistle hooted like a ship's horn. Panic seized her. Was it the BCPP? She whirled around. No. Only Dzunukwa carved on an interior house post, her cavernous cheeks familiar yet fearsome. Somehow the whistle sounded as though it were coming right through her fat, open mouth. Then the room grew ominously quiet, like the silent tension before the rising of a theater curtain.

Chief Tlii-Tlaalaadzi walked once around the floor, his arm a steady scythe through smoky air. White down and feathers floated out of his headdress like swirling snow. With statuesque grace, he saluted Chief Wakias, the thirteen other chiefs and dignitaries, the guests from other bands, and finally the Mamalilikala people. His speaker planted his staff into the ground and gave the welcome, accentuating certain words by gesticulating with both hands, tilting his head, raising his eyebrows, bobbing up and down, bending his knees, shaking his clenched fist. It was a ritualistic world, foreign, forbidden, and utterly fascinating.

The chief sat with a man wearing a bear-claw headdress shaped like a candelabra. Beaks hung from his robe. Emily thought he must be a shaman. She visualized him rattling his bear claws over a sick woman's stomach, chanting syllables linking her with earth and seasons, breathing down her throat the steam of herbs and skunk cabbage roots.

Silhouetted against the open door, a man decorated entirely in hemlock branches crouched. He wore a head ring of branches, a skirt of branches. Branches crisscrossed his chest and hung from his shoulders. Except for circles around his eyes, his face was blackened with charcoal which, together with his expression, made him look possessed.

"He's a Haa'maatsa, a cannibal dancer," Beatrice explained. "Don't be afraid. It's not real."

He danced into the room to staccato drumbeats, squatting as if he were carrying something large in his empty arms. In spite of the imagined weight of the thing, he rose up frequently, stepping lightly to the drumbeat. No one could carry a real dead body the way he was pantomiming. Drums pounded in Emily's chest, tensing her shoulders. This was one of the dances that caused such Christian outrage. She shouldn't watch, but she couldn't look away.

The dancer's movements conveyed both attraction and repulsion toward the body. Forces of good and evil unleashed themselves in his movements. He hurled the body down but couldn't wrench himself away. He lunged closer, circling the empty air in which he saw the body. Chants joined the pulse of drums, louder, faster, halting abruptly, and breaking into rapid broken-rhythmed tapping. He bent down and it did appear that he bit, then leapt, then bit again, tortured by his urge, until at a resounding boom, he flung himself away from what he saw and disappeared behind a wooden screen, spent, the demon exorcised. Good had reigned. Or so she chose to think.

They had trusted her with this, a grisly pantomime of a morality play shrouded in secrecy, and she would tell no one. She had crossed a line. A chasm lay behind her, separating her from most other white people. Yet this didn't make her Indian. She dangled in a middle ether. She wondered if Claude had ever seen a Haa'maatsa dance. He hadn't mentioned it. Maybe he'd been trusted with it too, and was keeping the secret.

Six men carried in a carved wooden feast dish, eight feet long. It tore her breath away. It was Dzunukwa reclining, her calves and arms supporting her. Her trunk, breasts, kneecaps, and navel were cavities steaming with food. The bearers set the giantess directly in front of the chiefs. Ceremoniously, Chief Tlii-Tlaalaadzi touched each of the cavities with a staff as if blessing them.

Tillie whispered, "See? Dzunukwa is the Wealth Giver too."

Bestower and Plunderer, all one. Maybe all people had need of such beings to account for lack and plenty, good and evil.

Stewards using three-foot carved ladles served the chief from Dzunukwa's cheeks and eyes. They presented food from the breasts to the visiting chiefs, from the navel to the shaman. Seeing these men, their robes heavy with bird beaks and animal teeth, eat as if eating Dzunukwa's entrails struck Emily with awe. She envisaged Hayward James carving such a dish, and Beatrice sewing teeth and abalone shells in heraldic patterns on robes, using her grandmother's awl to punch holes in the puffin beaks and attaching them as fringe to a shaman's apron to rattle when he walked. Then she imagined herself doing the same thing.

Women presented the kneecap bowls to clan leaders, who served their families. Others brought in three-foot alder serving dishes shaped like canoes and filled with fish, and smaller Wolf and Frog bowls, all to be distributed around the room.

At some signal from the drummers, Dzunukwa crept in. With lustrous white eyes, blood red cheek cavities, wild black hair, a basket on her back, the masked ogress danced, calling, "Huu, huu." Children in the front rows recoiled.

A Raven dancer clad in feathers leapt in through the door and swirled around the room, cedar bark strands flying behind him as a tail. Giant wings flapped, the wingspan ten feet across, creating a great wind. Jack shrank back against her legs.

The mask the Raven dancer wore was a handsome work of sculpture, painted in blue and red and black, the cedar grain showing satiny in unpainted places. A terrifying three-foot beak opened to reveal another mask inside, a placid child's face—Annie Marie's face, Emily thought—then clamped shut. Raven, the Trickster offering a child, then shutting her away, showing his catch, then hiding her. Another dancer wore a crescent moon mask which opened to show the sun. Nothing was as it seemed. The masks changed right before her eyes. In wavering firelight, birds transformed into boys and then changed back into birds. Big wooden crabs, untouched by dancers, scuttled across the dirt floor. Little canoes with tiny wooden paddlers moving their paddles slid after them. Eagle with flailed bark tail feathers dove down from the rafters at a young man sitting near the chief. The young man pretended to be afraid and the crowd loved it.

Emily was dizzy following it all. Drumbeats pounded in her chest. Her ears throbbed, but she succumbed willingly to the drums, the smoke, the phantasmagoria of lunging, swooping creatures. It was theater and spectacle and carnival and religion and living, moving art, and she was breathless to take it all in.

A group of men burst in the door wearing officers' uniforms. "By the authority vested in me as captain in the British Columbia Provincial Police—"

Laughter drowned him out, as if this were a skit. Emily froze. He tried again. The laughter was weaker this time. A few dancers slipped out the door carrying their masks. Older children ran out after them. One of the officers raised his pistol to the ceiling, ready to shoot. The people quieted. The captain spoke. "By order of the premier of the Province of British Columbia, Dominion of Canada, and under the auspices of William Ditchburn, regional superintendent for the Department of Indian Affairs, I order you to cease the activities of this potlatch."

"Bunch of bullies strutting in here creating a foofaraw," Emily muttered.

William Halliday strode in, his feet spread wide as if he were a general. Behind him came Reverend Hall, his roving scrutiny accounting for who was here. For an instant, his eyes met hers, filling her with dread. Maybe white people could be arrested for potlatching. A law's a law. She clasped her sketch sack, just in case. But no. She was part of this. She would stand her ground, even though it meant she'd never be invited to stay at the mission house again.

The drumming began softly, slowly—the shared pulse of the whole room. An officer fired his pistol at the ceiling. She heard Billy bark outside. All drumming stopped. The little regiment marched into the center of the bighouse. All the chiefs rose in unison. The captain consulted William Halliday, then shouted rudely right at Chief Tlii-Tlaalaadzi, not at his speaker. "I order you to stop this potlatch immediately. You know well the potlatch ban in the Indian Act. 'Anyone who engages in or assists in celebrating the Indian festival known as the potlatch or in the native dance known as the *tamananawas* shall be liable to imprisonment.'"

Pompous zealot. Oh, wouldn't she like to heap a tower of scorn on him, right here in front of everybody.

Chief Tlii-Tlaalaadzi stepped forward. His voice rolled out deep and solid. "We are doing what our laws command us to do, what we have always done. It is an ancient law that bids us dance, older than your Canadian law."

"It's a savage practice and a deplorable custom which will never advance your people in the scale of civilization. Furthermore, it's against the statutes of the Dominion of Canada," the captain said.

"It's no different than Christmas," someone shouted back.

That unleashed hot speeches shooting back and forth across the room while the men of Mimkwamlis carried the Dzunukwa feast dish out of view. People hid masks and birds under blankets, and carried off the dance paraphernalia.

"Chief, order that this potlatch be stopped or you must come with me."

It seemed an impasse. The air was charged. Everyone rose.

"I will never order my people to stop what their ancestors have told them to do. It is not harming you, and it is not harming Canada. Let it be known that we, the Mamalilikala Qwe'Qwa'Sot'Enox' of Mimkwamlis, will never stop potlatching."

He swept right through the group of BCPP who parted for him to pass, his button blanket flaring. White down billowed out of his headdress. Men in the regiment raised their rifles as a signal that no one should follow them out. One of the BCPP carried something large wrapped in a blanket.

Everyone was stunned into silence. Emily was petrified with worry that people would think she had let out the location to the Halls or to Halliday. Eventually, elders passed from group to group to account for the children of each family.

"Why did so many children run?" Emily asked.

"If they belonged in St. Mike's School, they'd be beaten and locked in," Beatrice explained.

People found sleeping places for the night, some in the bighouse, some in the forest. Emily brought Billy inside, and settled on a wide sleeping platform, cradling Jack like a lost kitten. Hearing the crooning of mothers and the various rhythms of sleep sighs from young and old felt strangely comforting.

Toby banged a stick on the platform below until Tillie made him stop. He pulled away from her and drew his knees to his chest. It was a hard time to be Kwakiutl.

Mac offered her his new blanket.

"Thank you, Mac. You're a kind man." She draped it over herself and Jack. "They knew it might happen, didn't they? That's why they gave out the blankets first, to hide the masks."

He managed a nod.

"I'm glad I came."

"We are too."

· · ·

In the morning, the atmosphere was leaden. People moved slowly, murmuring instead of talking. Chief Wakias spoke privately to a group at the far end of the room. No one brought out any masks. No one danced. Drummers slumped behind the drum. Still, there was a kind of victory in just being there together.

Word flew through the bighouse. The Raven mask was missing. "They took it for their court case," Beatrice said. "After that, a museum will get it. If not a mask, then a child, for St. Mike's. We were lucky this time."

By mid-morning, the business of the potlatch went on quietly. The chief's speaker held in one hand the carved talking staff; in the other, a black Dzunukwa mask gleaming silver at the forehead. Not once did he do the bobbing movement to accentuate his words.

"What did he say?"

"The Mamalilikala will never stop potlatching."

"Nothing about the raid?"

"No."

She was stunned. Was it too common to be worthy of note?

Holding the Dzunukwa mask before him, the speaker and his assistants began the distribution of goods. Maybe that was the response—in the face of theft, the giving, an aggressive act, to go right on, Dzunukwa leading them to put themselves back together again.

Relief washed over Emily when she was called to receive a share of smoked salmon and a small dish stamped with *Royal Albert—Bone China—England* on the bottom. If they suspected her, they surely would not have made this presentation.

Her final gift was a twined spruce-root rain hat in the same graceful, curved shape as on the welcome figure. "I will wear this with pride that I received it at a Mamalilikala potlatch," she said solemnly.

Mac chuckled. "You say you're going up the Skeena River?"

She nodded.

"You'll need it."

People laughed, and Tillie held up her arms, fingers down, wiggling them, signifying rain. Emily put on the hat and grinned. People smiled back and she grinned more broadly.

23: Willow

"Not many women take passage on the Skeena River."

Emily turned from the sternwheeler's railing to face a man with an exceptionally narrow head and a mustache that perched on his upper lip.

"Especially white women traveling alone," he added, leaning with too-casual familiarity on the railing close to her, baring brown-stained teeth to chew his cigar.

She moved back a step.

"What might your business be in Indian territory?" He emphasized the last two words as if he were speaking to a child.

She looked at the willows along the bank. Her business? To become big, like the Mamalilikala spirit was big. To find in herself the Wild Forest Woman alive and fearless.

"I want to see all the poles I can," she said.

"You working for the government?"

"No."

"Railway?" His lower left eyelid twitched.

"No."

"Museum?"

"No. I'm working for myself. I'm an artist."

"You collecting artifacts?"

"I most certainly am not!"

"Where've you been?"

"Most of the villages off the Skeena River. Kitwanga, Kispiox. Kitsegukla. I've been here two weeks. I'm on my way back down river now."

"How did you know where to go?"

"I read and I asked questions."

He folded his arms. "So ask. Alfred Poole's the name."

His cockiness infuriated her, but he might know of a village she didn't. "Where in your opinion are the finest poles?"

"No question. Kitwancool."

"How do you get there?"

"Sixteen miles up a tributary from Kitwanga, but you can't go there, lady. Gitksans are a fierce people. That's why there's poles left. They don't want to see you. They don't want to see anybody ain't Gitksan."

"I haven't had any trouble in other Gitksan villages."

"Pff." A bit of tobacco flew out of his mouth. "Kitwancool's different. You won't find a place to stay. The missionaries been run out."

"I have a tent."

"You'd better have a revolver too, unless you expect that dog to defend you."

She stood up straighter. Her hand pressed Billy's head to her thigh. Lizzie had told her the same thing, and had taken her upstairs and opened Father's bureau drawer where his pistol lay wedged between monogrammed handkerchiefs. "If you must go, in the name of God, take this with you."

She'd picked off a handkerchief and said, "You're right, Lizzie. I do tend to get the sniffles on trips." The memory of Lizzie slamming shut the drawer made her smile.

"I'm dead serious." The man opened his jacket enough to show the handle of a gun. "Indian unrest is heating up."

"Are you offering your services or just trying to scare me out of sport? I'm more afraid of a gun than a Gitksan."

"How 'bout an axe? They went after a party of surveyors with axes last spring."

"I'm not coming for their land."

"Maybe you won't find what you're looking for and you'll go back to wherever you came from. Maybe you'll see you made a mistake. The poles are all cracked or fallen or sold anyway."

That word, *sold*, struck her as unctuous. The way it slid off his tongue told her why he was here, and that he wanted no competition.

"It's a dying culture anyway." He spit over the rail, as if to dismiss her and her purpose and the poles.

"No, it's being killed. Hacked to pieces. There's a difference," she retorted.

She took hold of Billy's collar and moved to the opposite railing. "Sometimes men are three parts beast to one part human," she muttered. "Present company excluded."

· · ·

Encumbered by gear, she disembarked at Kitwanga, carefully stepping down the gangplank so as not to lose her balance.

"Hey, lady!" Alfred Poole called from the steamer. "Just remember, you can't say I didn't warn you."

She turned to see him hawk and spit again over the ship's rail.
She went back up for Billy and another load, ignoring him.

What a waste of good blood.

With only a glance at the forest of poles facing the wharf, she
and Billy went into the Hudson's Bay post to buy provisions, and
overheard that a Gitksan teamster and hunting guide named Luther
Moody was taking a load of planks and grain to Kitwancool that
day and would return three days later.

"Where can I find him?" she asked the clerk.

"Turn around is all you got to do." He nodded, pointing his
beaked nose at a man examining a pair of long johns.

Emily approached the lean, long-haired teamster and asked if he
would take a passenger. Grooves from the corners of his mouth
and on his forehead all converged at the bridge of his nose, forming
a permanent squint.

"Just you?"

"And my dog. And my gear."

His tongue was industrious in digging food out of uncomfortable
places in his mouth. "What's it worth to you?"

She reached into her pocket for a five-dollar bill and held it out
to him. He made a sucking noise and took it.

"Got no seats. Got to ride on a sack of oats."

"That's fine."

He pointed out the window toward a horse and wagon under a
tamarack near the narrow wooden wharf.

"When are you leaving?"

"By and by."

She bought some mosquito repellent, apples, smoked salmon,
and dog biscuits, and went out to the wagon. The lumber was
shoulder high. "Now isn't this a pickle. Got any ideas, Billy?"

She found some crates and buckets and an empty oil drum, and
arranged them, the buckets upside down, in an ascending pile.
"There now. A proper stairway." Glad for her split skirt, she hoisted
her gear, one item at a time, and came down for Billy.

"Now are you going to cooperate or am I going to have to shame you into obedience?" She planted his front legs on the lowest crate and pushed his rump. "Up. Up! Get up there!" He whined. "Yes, all the way. *Allez-oop!*" She gave one mighty shove. He barked and scrambled up, tipping over the bucket. "Good boy. I knew you could.

"But I'm not so sure about me. Not a soul here I'd want to give my plump rump a push." How could she return the things to where she'd found them once she was up? She took back the buckets and oil drum, and kept one skeleton of a crate. Gingerly she stepped up, wedged her foot onto a protruding plank, did a few little hops which turned out to be false starts, and hauled herself up by her fingernails.

Bald eagles circled in the gray sky above the olive green river, while miners hurried to load their boats with supplies. An hour passed. If she went looking for Luther, she'd have to execute the as-cent a second time. Nothing to do but stay put on her perch. Were they laughing at her in the Hudson's Bay post, seeing how long she'd sit up here?

Actually it was a fine vantage point to draw the poles eye to eye instead of from the ground, the way she'd painted them when she'd come up river. It solved the problem of foreshortening, but did nothing about the bigger difficulty of Gitksan poles. Gitksan carving wrapped around the sides so neither a frontal view nor a profile showed the entire figure. She tried a three-quarter view.

A rattling, sputtering engine noise caught her attention and she looked up. The prow of a boat rounded the curve, chugging against the current, its crooked stovepipe topped by a coolie hat. A French flag snapped in the breeze. *La Renarde Rouge!*

"Claude du Bois!"

She stood up without thinking and smacked the top of her head on a branch. The horse lurched and jostled the wagon. She fell back onto Billy and the oat sack. Billy barked.

"Mademoiselle Courageuse!" he called, flinging his arms wide. "And the dog of no eyes!"

He secured the boat, turned off the deafening racket, and swung his legs over the side onto the wharf.

"*La reine de la forêt* on her cedar throne!"

With a flourish of the dock line, he executed a courtier's bow and came over to stand by the wagon beneath her. "What are you doing up there?"

"Waiting, it seems."

"For me? *Quel changement!* If I remember right, it was I who was left waiting for you."

She could feel herself blush. All that running out of his tent. She'd been a damned fool. She wanted to heap kisses on him, he looked so good, but her position on the lumber prevented that.

"You certainly took a long time coming," he said.

"I went to France."

"*Mon Dieu!* A long way to find a Frenchman such as I." He grinned.

"To study painting."

"Not to look for me?" He pounded his fist over his chest. Dust billowed from the buckskin. "Oh, don't break my heart the second time. Come down from there."

"No. I had a devil of a time getting up." She felt herself slipping into the spell of him. "I'm going to Kitwancool."

"Ho-ho!" He blew air out his mouth in bursts. "You certainly are *une dame courageuse.*"

"Yes, and I've been to a potlatch too. At Mimkwamlis."

"Sh!" He held his finger to his lips and made a show of checking for spies. "Unbelievable."

"And I've been to Alert Bay and Guyasdoms too. And Kispiox and Kitsegukla. Now I'm going to Kitwancool, any minute in fact. Have you been there?"

"No. They don't . . ." His forehead tightened into a scowl. "The Kitwancool River is too narrow. Too many rocks. These poles aren't good enough?" He waved his arm toward the ones along the bank, then rested his hand on her ankle.

"The best ones are in Kitwancool. I'm told." Just the way he held on to her ankle, naturally, with familiarity, melted her resolve.

Luther Moody and two young men came out of the Hudson's Bay post and loaded two small oil drums and a crate onto the front of the wagon to use as seats, and climbed up. Rats! Of all times for him to come.

Claude squeezed her ankle. "I can't talk you out of going?" His voice was serious. "*La Renarde Rouge* would welcome you."

His rugged smile peeking over his beard made her feel wanted. There he was, so close below her, a man of the moment, able to meet the elements with a song, full-hearted and free as a breeze.

"No." Her voice sounded paper-thin.

"You can have the captain's quarters." He hugged his arms to his chest and rotated his shoulders. "It's warm when you're wrapped in furs. I'll sleep in the skiff, yes?" His eyebrows popped up in hopeful anticipation.

His funny face and antics—she felt affection for him in spite of everything.

"No," she said more firmly.

His pout pushed its way out of the shag of his beard. He scrutinized Luther, and said a few serious words to him in Chinook.

Claude looked up at her. "How long will you be gone?"

"Three days."

"Attention, mademoiselle." He lowered his voice. "Trust only dogs with no tail." He shook her ankle gently until she nodded. "I'll be here when you come back."

He smacked the horse's rump and the wagon lurched forward. She grabbed hold of Billy.

Claude took off his hat and waved it in an arc high in the air. *"Adieu,"* he called.

She raised her arm in salute, abandoning herself now to his exuberance.

• • •

The road became a path, then a braid of gullies. She had nothing to hold on to except the corner of the grain sack, and she lost hold of that with every jolt. The ride would have been far more pleasant if she'd been able to ride the horse instead of the wagon. She hugged Billy to her side, tickled by Claude's surprise in seeing her here.

"Will it be all right if I set up a tent at the edge of Kitwancool?" she asked the driver.

"Not for me to say." Luther spit tobacco juice and the breeze blew it onto her skirt.

One thing was certain. Luther Moody and his two young friends didn't care whether she was going to Kitwancool or not. That narrow-headed shyster on the steamer was exaggerating. And Claude? What lay behind his urging her not to go?

Whatever it was, she would stay on guard.

"Are there poles in Kitwancool?"

"Some."

So much for thinking Luther Moody would tell her anything. His surname suited his temperament.

They joggled in silence under the shade of aspens and tamaracks. When they passed a tall waterfall with bursts of silver-white spume trailing comet tails, she said, "Beautiful, eh?"

He only grunted. A few minutes later he added, "There are some poles in Kitwancool."

Long after lunch of an apple and some smoked salmon, the wagon got stuck in a stretch of deep mud. The men climbed down. She took off her boots and stockings, hiked up her skirt, and slid down into swarms of mosquitoes. Her legs had fallen asleep and she almost dropped to the ground. The brown mud oozed up between her toes, and the suction resisted her at every step.

Two on a side, they placed planks, length by length, in front of the wheels and managed to get across onto drier ground where Luther gave her a boost back up onto the wagon. Dull thunder rolled in the distance and wind whipped the aspen leaves to a frenzy.

"Might rain, eh?" Emily said to Luther.

Apparently he preferred not to waste words on the obvious.

If the sky decided to crack open soon, the road to Kitwancool would turn into slippery muck. She wondered how rain would sound inside *La Renarde Rouge*.

Six hours later, when they arrived at Kitwancool, she found she'd scratched her bitten ankles raw. The bruise-colored sky pressed down on roofs and bent the tops of hemlocks. A woman took down flapping laundry and disappeared inside a closed-up house.

"Who should I ask to—?"

Wind howled louder than her words. The men on the wagon ignored her and hurried indoors.

She unloaded and looked around. Billy bleated a high, trembling whine. "Oh, stop sniveling. Help me think what to do."

There appeared to be two Kitwancools a distance of some three hundred yards apart. The new village of small houses, each with a single window, was situated in a high meadow set far back from the river by a bluff. Judging from the woodpiles, clotheslines, pails, and trampled earth, everyone lived on the higher meadow. It wasn't dangerous-looking, just poor and unfriendly. Nothing encouraged her to knock on a door. The old Kitwancool lay sunken and deserted along a riverbank. Down among the ruins of a pair of bighouses were more than twenty tipping poles—what she had come for.

She strapped her tent and bedroll onto Billy's back, hoisted the rest of her gear, and trudged across the meadow. She lost her balance going down the bluff, and landed on her rump. Under the totems, she tipped her head back and let out a long sigh. Such a gallery of beings, human and animal, alive in the wood. These had none of that Alert Bay fierceness. No teeth. No claws. Only gentleness. An old man on one pole gazed at a sad-eyed bird, thin and anxious, with a drooping beak on another pole. The man's wan smile was sympathetic toward the bird's dismay. He had grown parental. They had a language beyond words. Alfred Poole was right. These were marvelous.

Across a grassy area overhung by willows along the bank she saw a group of curious houses no higher than four feet, surrounded by bedraggled gardens and enclosed by short picket or spindle fences. Were they raised tombs? Memorials? Grave houses? Some had windows and doors. One even had a chimney. She peeked through one window and could barely make out dishes scattered around a sewing machine. A woman's grave.

Wind bearing the mineral smell of rain-to-come lashed willow branches against the grave houses and tore through her wool sweater. "All right," she said. "You proved your point."

A raindrop splatted on her hand. She ignored it. Then another, and another. She put on her potlatch hat. It blew right off. She chased after it. If she didn't get her portfolio under cover soon, her work would be ruined. She unrolled the used tent she'd bought from a Klondike outfitter who had assured her she could set it up herself. "It's only a one-man tent, ma'am. Easy as pie," he'd said.

Wind flapped the canvas toward her, then yanked it away. She seized a corner, threaded a stake through a grommet and stamped it into the earth. A gust tore it right out. "Easy as pie," she muttered, and tried again. Same thing. It had seemed simple, setting it up in the yard in Victoria, but it wasn't now, not with rain pouring off her nose. Lizzie had watched her and declared that if the Lord intended women to sleep outdoors, He would have given them fur. Fur! She could be nestled in fur in Claude's boat right this minute. She yanked the canvas angrily, wrestled with its stiffness, found the opening, and shoved everything inside. If she had to, she could crawl in too.

The abandoned bighouses offered nothing. One had no roof, the other only a few planks under which horses huddled. She looked at the new village through robes of rain. Closed up tight, and far away. She looked at the sodden graveyard. Close by.

She took hold of two corners of the tent and began to drag. "Come on, Billy." He barked and skittered away. "Come!" Lightning cracked, trailing an electric hiss, and he charged toward her. She dragged the bundle to the largest of the grave houses, in through the picket fence, and opened the little door. It broke off its hinges. Billy growled. "Get over here." She shoved the bundle through the door, yanked Billy by his collar, and backed in on her knees. He barked. Lightning made him jerk away. She caught him by the front leg, dragged him whining through the doorway, and blocked it using the door propped sideways inside.

"It's all right, Billy. Calm down." She put her arm around him. "I'm sorry, pooch."

The blackness smelled of rotted wood, mildew, and the ooze of maggots. Her pulse pounded at the root of her throat. Rain battered the roof inches above her head, and willow branches scraped and rattled like skeletons knocking for entrance. Billy shook his wet coat at her. It made no difference. She was already soaked.

Slowly, the darkness grayed. Barely discernible, a man sat on a chair. She screamed. Billy barked. Rain swallowed their sounds. She clutched Billy's neck. The outline of a hat touched the roof. He wore a shirt and pants, but on his face, when lightning flashed again, she saw the rough grain of wood. She let out her breath in one great gush.

"It's only a carving of a man, Billy. A man whose son or grandson may have ridden on the wagon with us today."

Mice scuttled around her feet, poles creaked in the wind, willows slapped the roof, thunder rolled like drums, rain roared like a freight train. She hugged Billy and cried into the lanolin smell of his wet coat. It wasn't mink, but it was something.

Who did she think she was that she could march in here and do what she wanted? It was the question Father had asked whenever her imagination prompted some action she hadn't thought through. Nympholept. Damn. Why did he have to be right?

She thought of Claude holding her ankle, trying to talk her out of coming here. Why had he let her?

Respect. For her. It had to be. He knew what she wanted most.

Lightning burned the outline of the figure of the Gitksan man into the blackness. She swallowed the lump in her throat and addressed him silently: Maybe you lived so long ago that you won't recoil at the thought of a white woman who loves the poles here entering your grave house. I will not violate you, or the sacredness of your resting place. A temporary sharing of roof is all I want. I will leave you untouched.

She listened for a response, but the figure seated before her was silent.

24: Mosquito

It wasn't sleep that got her through the night so much as exhaustion. When she crawled out of the grave house, dawn spilled over the eastern peaks. Mercifully, the rain had stopped, but it felt as though mold had grown in her hair, her ears, her mouth. She went to relieve herself near a skunk cabbage muskeg by the river gushing in a brown torrent. Teeth-cleaning had to consist of a dry brush. She heard wood being chopped in the upper village, and saw Luther and his team and wagon leaving.

Crossing the meadow, she looked up at the wet poles. On one, a frog peeked out of a beaver's mouth. A small human face was tucked into a bear's ear. Some of the humans were holding children, one just as gently holding a frog. A few animals held their paws together as though they were praying. If Lizzie saw this, it would melt even her Christian heart.

On one, a frog mother faced downward, and smaller frogs were lined up ready to leapfrog down the column. The pupils of Frog Woman's eyes were carved into childlike human faces, and tiny human hands curved over her bottom lids as if babies were peeking out each eye. Was it meant to suggest a mother watching her children? Gibb would see that as the expression of an idea in the carver's mind. And to think, if she'd let that slimy toadfish, Alfred Poole, scare her off, she would have missed it.

A man strode toward her on the bluff waving his arms angrily. "Get away, woman. Go away."

Billy growled.

"I'd like to draw the poles. May I?"

"Museum?"

"No."

"We don't sell here. Get."

He hurled a rock. It hit Billy in the haunch, a loud crack, like a stick breaking. "Hey!" she yelled. Billy barked and jumped in a frenzy. The man threw another that came close to her ankle.

She grabbed Billy by the collar and ran behind the nearest big-house. She checked him over while he licked his haunch. Apparently nothing was broken.

"I'm sorry, Billy. He's a mean old unhappy man. He meant to hurt me, not you."

She sat with him awhile and gave him a good scratching under his chin where he liked it.

It was strange. None of the poles here fit the fierce Kitwancool reputation. What had happened to turn these people hard? One thing was certain—she and Billy wouldn't be sleeping in any friendly Gitksan house. There was no alternative. She had to master the tent. She bloody well wouldn't spend another night in that grave house.

It was relatively dry right here, and hidden from the village by a bighouse. She waited awhile but no one came, so she started. Erecting the tent wasn't half as difficult with no wind.

"There we are, Billy boy. Our Kitwancool mansion."

She dove into the smoked salmon and gave Billy his doggie hardtack. He gobbled it down. "That good, eh?" She bit off a piece. "Not entirely bad."

It was already mid-morning and only an occasional sound came from the village. She didn't see any children to befriend and win a welcome through them. Halliday had said most of the people would be gone to their summer fishing camps.

Ignoring her clammy hands, she began to sketch the bear pole, but to get the best angle, she had to expose herself to view. Before long, shouts blasted from the meadow above.

"Stop, white lady. Get away. You can't steal that pole."

A large man, not the same one, stood on the bluff, his feet planted widely, hands on hips in a threatening posture. She gulped. He could have an axe tucked behind his back. And axes could be thrown.

"Steal it? How could I? I'm only drawing it."

"Draw now. Steal later."

"Not at all. I'm drawing them now to paint them later."

"Who told you to?"

"No one." But plenty of people had told her not to.

He came down the bluff in a side-to-side rolling sway, his stomach bulging over his pants. His large fingers curled inward. His shoulders, belly, cheeks, chin were all round, even his nostrils, but in his eyes, she saw spikes that could gore steel.

"Why didn't you ask?"

"I— Who? I didn't know who to ask."

His entire bulk became a scowl. "You from the government?"

"No. I'm just from me. I want to paint all the poles in the province. Just where they are. Before . . ."

"Before what?" He scowled.

She wondered if Alfred Poole had been here.

"Before they disappear. White people need to know how beautiful they are right here where they were meant to be."

"You should have ask."

"You weren't here. How could I ask you? If you were here, I would have asked. Do you own this pole?"

He looked at it, not at her.

"You must be a great man to have so many crests in your family. What's your name?"

"Henry."

"Only Henry for a pole this tall?"

He pushed out his chest. "Henry Albert Douse. I like Henry Jumbo is better."

"Henry Jumbo, I'm Emily Carr. You speak such good English."

"I worked in white man logging company."

"This is a noble pole, but there's one figure I don't understand. That little person is coming out of the ear of a bear. Can you tell me the story of that?"

His shoulders jerked and the scowl returned. She had him. If it wasn't his pole, he couldn't tell the story. She'd read that in the museum library, and hoped right now that it was true.

"Go ahead." He waved his hand. "You have permission." She offered him the drawing from her sketch pad. He shook his head and walked away without it, and she relaxed into her work.

· · ·

It rained again during the night, and the tent dripped in several places. Billy kept squirming toward her to avoid them until they were both huddled on the dry side of the tent. When she poked her head out in the morning, she disturbed a puddle on the canvas and a deluge of cold water poured down her neck. "Aye, Billy, what I would give to be a furred species like you."

She wanted to paint the pole she'd seen farthest up river near the muskeg thick with mosquitoes and fetid with skunk cabbage where she'd gone to relieve herself. She oiled her skin with mosquito repellent, wound a scarf around her neck, and put on two pairs of socks and her potlatch hat. Was she going to let a few teensie weensie man-eating jaws scare her? Spunk up! she told herself, marched toward the muskeg, and opened her stool.

She lit a cigarette to ward them off, and studied the totem. An indecipherable creature with a long uplifted protruberance perched on the top. Under it, as she looked down the pole, there was a band of children playing, then Eagle with a crack through his right eye, another band of children, and, at ground level, the most moving figure, a man or woman, possibly a mother. The broad face had a shoulder-to-shoulder smile, the mouth not turned up, just stretched wide. The mother, if it was a mother, held a child facing forward, showing him with pride. The baby's face had the same wide smile, as though feeling the love that surrounded him. She'd call the painting *Totem Mother, Kitwancool*.

A ticklesome image entered her mind—Lizzie seeing this as a

painting. She'd think it a sacrilege, an Indian madonna. Her face would explode in outrage, her mouth dropping open the moment the thought occurred to her that heathens had dared to appropriate a Christian motif.

Emily suddenly realized her hands were burning, covered with the gray fur of a hundred mosquitoes. "Hellfire," she shouted and shook her hands. No mosquito oil in the world was obnoxious enough to fend off these demons. What she'd used had just glued them to her skin. Blowing on flesh she'd unconsciously been scraping raw, she ran to the river to dip them for relief.

Dzunukwa wouldn't be run off by a mere mosquito. She'd put herself back together again. Emily took off one pair of socks, plastered mud over her hands, put the socks on over the mud, and went back to the totem mother, steeling herself to concentrate.

To render motherhood in wood, the carver had exaggerated the mouth, the source of lullaby and love, into a smile that pushed up the cheeks above it. In reality a smile couldn't stretch the width of a face, but the exaggeration dramatized the figure's joy. The hands resting lightly on top of the child's head and cupping him from below were out of proportion, smaller than the width of her smile, as if to suggest gentleness. All that she'd seen in France was here in Kitwancool. Distortion for expression—she'd almost lost sight of it.

Think of everything as shapes, she told herself. The heads of mother and child were squarish, the mother's mouth a round-ended rectangle, her thighs elongated ovals. Now make those shapes express something personal. She thought of Sophie's smile when she presented her twins. Such a smile could illumine a house, could turn a world. She stretched the smile even wider. She enlarged the mother's right shoulder and left forearm, made them club-shaped and strong to enclose the child. She wasn't an anthropologist. She was an artist.

Mosquitoes hovered above her watercolor. When they landed on wet areas they stuck, but tried to fly anyway, trailing color in threadlike paths across her paper. When she tried to lift them off with her brush, they came apart, wings and legs spread across the page. They gummed up her brushes, landed in her paints and writhed, distracting her from her rhythm.

Henry lumbered toward her. "Why did you choose this pole?"

She pulled down her scarf. "Because it speaks family to me."

He looked at her unfinished work. Her stomach cramped. He'd be critical. When critical eyes crept in judgment across half-born work, the heartbeat of it always died. It was an invasion she'd have to endure. She had invaded first. She braced herself while he scrutinized the painting. He'd expect factual recording. He might even hate it.

"You are a crazy woman—"

"I most certainly am not. It's what I feel about this pole."

"To stand by this pole all day, you are. Nobody with a brain in his head come near this pole this time of year."

"Why?"

He tipped his head toward the bog. " 'Squitoes."

"I know." She pointed to the curious top figure. Instead of a beak, it had an unwieldy encumbrance, a long narrow prong, long enough to bite through thick clothing. "A monster mosquito."

Henry's laugh bubbled up from his belly. "That's not a mosquito. That's a woodpecker. Mosquito has only long . . ." He touched his mouth and then extended his arm. "No body. Just . . ." He made his hand look like a jaw opening and clamping shut.

She laughed until thunder rumbled.

"Why you want to make pictures of poles?"

It wasn't an idle question. The wrong answer might cost his permission and she'd have to leave. His cocked head conveyed genuine curiosity.

"Because I love even what I don't understand. Because they show a connection. Trees and animals and people. I want white people and your grandchildren's children to see this greatness."

He seemed to be considering his reply. "Tonight you stay in my house. It will rain again."

Warmth rushed over her. "Thank you."

He shook his hand, blurry with mosquitoes, and reached out to pet Billy behind his ears before he left.

. . .

Hours later, Henry stood in his doorway waiting. "This is my wife, Mrs. Douse. A Nisga'a chief."

"Hello. And thank you," Emily said.

Mrs. Douse was a mountain of a woman whose arms barely crossed over her bosom. The skin at her throat hung like a turkey and her hair was plaited into a single braid. But it was her strong nose and no-nonsense eyes framed by crow's feet that proclaimed her the matriarch, a native Queen Victoria. She spoke no English, or didn't choose to, gave orders from a carved settee piled with blankets, and followed Emily with her eyes.

"You sleep here," Henry said as he brought Emily into a separate room, bare but for a white-style open coffin in the center. "No worry. Empty. It's for me someday. See?" He climbed in, lay down, bent his elbows out to measure the width. "A little tight. I think I'm getting too fat. I had another, but my friend died, and so I gave him it."

Emily didn't know whether to laugh or commend his generosity. "Well, I won't bother it. I'll sleep over here against the wall." In the corner she found her tent and bedroll folded neatly next to her food box.

"No worry about my wife either. She doesn't like men come to take poles to museums. Last year men from Ottawa bought her father's pole from her brother. Paid cheap. Her brother went to Hazelton and spent it all. One big drunk and that was that."

"So she sent you out to . . . ?" His scowl told her not to ask, told her she'd been argued about. Being linked with the likes of that oily buyer on the riverboat made her face burn. Somehow, she'd won Henry's trust. "Thank you," she whispered.

• • •

Luther didn't come on the third day, or the fourth, which worried her about getting back. The hope of Claude waiting faded into disappointment. By mid-morning of the fifth day, she'd eaten everything in her food box, and had shared her last apple with Henry's small grandson. She was sitting on a stump in front of the house eating Billy's biscuits when Luther drove up.

"I thought you'd forgotten me," she said.

Apparently he didn't think an apology was necessary.

Mrs. Douse came to the doorway and spoke rapidly to Henry.

"She wants to see all the pictures," Henry said.

"Now?"

"Luther will wait." He turned to Luther. "She makes pictures with her hands, not with a box." He pantomimed looking through a camera.

"All right. A show! Dandy."

Then she remembered. The distortion. They'd think she made mistakes. Apprehensively, she tacked them all to trees, more than twenty of them. The few people left in the village came out to see. They touched the sketches, smelled the watercolors.

"*Hailat*," they murmured. "*Hailat*."

"What's that mean?" she asked Henry.

He held up his hands and wiggled his chubby fingers. "Person with spirit power in the hands."

She could hardly swallow. "That's a generous thing to say."

Luther examined each painting, turning them over to see if the backs of the poles were on the back of the paper.

Emily laughed. "I was afraid I would run out of paint if I painted the backs too."

"You need to go to Haida Gwaii," Henry said. "Far islands. You call them the Queen Charlottes. Poles are different there."

"How are they different?"

"You go see. If you spoke truth about painting poles before they're gone, you'll go to Haida Gwaii." He gave her a steady look. "Here we live with our poles. Some of us always stay in fishing season. We guard them. They don't on Haida Gwaii." He turned away from his wife. "Tanu, Skedans, some of the best villages have nobody left. Nobody to watch the poles."

"Nobody living there? Why?"

"Because what the *Pasisiuks* brought."

"*Pasisiuks?*"

"White people. Measles here. Some other thing there."

Having to be told this made her feel ignorant.

"Haida poles need you. Now."

That struck her with the force of a solemn drumbeat. No one had ever said that she or her work was needed.

"They can teach you something."

Looking at the watercolor of Frog Woman, Mrs. Douse spoke several sharp words to Henry in Gitksan.

"That pole belongs to my wife's family," he said.

"It's a wonderful pole, so full of humor and life."

"My wife wants that you leave the painting with her."

Emily stifled a groan. She'd only done one of Frog Woman.

Mrs. Douse squinted at Frog Woman's eyes, which Emily had enlarged to show the babies' faces in the mother's pupils. Mrs. Douse's expression softened, as though she were seeing herself looking at her children. Henry turned from his wife to give her time with the painting. Mosquitoes swarmed around all of them. No one moved to brush them away.

Luther looked at Emily and tipped his head toward Mrs. Douse, as if to give Emily a sign. Right here in Kitwancool was perhaps the most important person ever to want one of her paintings.

"It's not a good one. Tell her I will paint a bigger, better one on a board with paint that will last. I will send it to her at the Hudson's Bay post in Kitwanga."

She knew that was asking more than mere permission to paint in the village. It was asking for trust.

Mrs. Douse aimed her eyes with their dark eye pouches at her. Layer by layer, as though peeling an onion, Mrs. Douse was judging her character, right down to her vitals. Emily wanted to scratch her neck where a mosquito had feasted, but no one else moved. She stood still until Mrs. Douse turned to her and nodded, shaking decisively the loose skin under her chin.

Emily nodded back, a ceremony of agreement, and then nodded to Henry, with another meaning. Haida Gwaii. She would try.

25: Mink

Emily offered a five-dollar bill to Luther for the ride back.

He shook his head. "One five-dollah, two ways."

He let her ride with him on a plank resting on empty oil drums. It slid whenever they went around a bend, and once she fell off. After that she sat in the wagon bed facing into the sun, holding on to Billy, scratching through her blouse. She waved away mosquitoes until her arms ached and she gave up. Billy scratched too.

"Mean little devils, eh?"

Billy scratched harder in agreement.

At every lurch of the wagon her head throbbed. Seven hours and nothing to support her back. She felt achy, thirsty, feverish. Watching ruts in the dirt road stream out from under the wagon bed, she entered Kitwanga backward. Billy leapt off the wagon as soon as it stopped.

"Mademoiselle Courageuse!" she heard behind her, and turned to see Claude with his arms raised, wagging his head.

"I'm no more courageous than a bowl of jelly. I've just been jostled to kingdom come."

"But you've been to Kitwancool and back."

"Did you turn to stone right here in the road? This is exactly where I left you."

"I went to Hazelton." He rested his hand on the laces of her men's hunting boot. "If you hadn't come back today, I would have set out to find you."

"If I hadn't come back today, you wouldn't have recognized me. I've been attacked by an army of carnivores. Every mosquito in Kitwancool cut its teeth on my flesh."

"Your face is pocked like a giant strawberry." He reached up with both hands and helped her down. Her legs buckled under her, but he kept her from falling.

She thanked Luther, who nodded an acknowledgment while Claude unloaded her gear.

"What you need is a hot bath and a steaming fish dinner, but *La Renarde Rouge* only has enough fuel right now to take care of one thing. Which will it be?"

Bath? Her hair was matted and dirty, but on the deck? The mere thought—

"Supper. I'm already a blazing furnace."

"Ah, you're hot, mademoiselle?" His eyebrows popped up.

"I mean, from the sun, the mosquitoes." She fanned her face. "Supper."

"Then you're hungry, *oui?*"

His grin told her he knew he'd trapped her again.

She grinned back. "Painting hard requires food. I worked hard. The carvings were marvelous."

"It's you who is marvelous."

They carried her gear to his boat. She landed on the deck with an "Oof," off balance, arms flailing, dropping her gear. Far from a marvelous maneuver. Billy whined on the riverbank.

"Convince yourself, Billy. I can't carry you across."

"Does he like mush?"

"After a week of doggie hardtack, mush would be caviar. To both of us."

Claude produced a pot of leftover mush from the top of the boiler, waved it in front of Billy's nose, grasped his collar and urged him across. "See? Monsieur Bill likes *La Renarde Rouge*." He poured water from a skin bag, set the pot down for Billy, and arranged some pelts for her on deck.

"Tonight we put them below deck for you, with mink too, yes? For me, the skiff. A promise. But now, take a little nap. I'll be right back." He kissed her on both cheeks, his beard smelling of tobacco, his brown eyes bright with anticipation.

She lay down with a groan, positioning her face in the shade cast by the tin hat on the stovepipe. Every joint creaked. Now if she could only stop scratching. She closed her eyes and let the boat's motion lull her. Did she really know what sort of a man Claude was? What he had in mind ought to make her nervous, but it didn't. She had no energy for nerves. If he mentioned her running out of his tent in Vancouver, should she tell him that she'd come back that next morning after he'd left?

No.

He'd called her marvelous. How could this man be attracted to her? She was graceless, fat around the middle, not dainty like Alice, or statuesque like Clara. Apparently there weren't many beauties of the two-legged variety in the wilderness. Was what she'd eliminated from her life, with acceptance, suddenly plopping into her lap?

His heavy foot jostled the boat and she jerked upright. One by one, he lifted his purchases out of a gunny sack—two fish, a cauliflower, potatoes, bannock bread, an Indian squash, and two large, dark, unlabled bottles. "Indian brown ale. The finest in the wilderness. Don't move. I cook for you."

She leaned back against the furs with a sigh. She must have been holding her back and shoulders tense for five days. Having someone—

him—cook for her, take care of her, melted her stiffness. The trip was harder than she had anticipated.

"Thank you." The words came out in a mere squeak.

He lit the boiler, picked up the pot Billy had been drinking from, poured in more water, and dumped in the vegetables in big chunks. He gutted the fish and lay them in a pan, poured some ale for her into a tin cup, and drank from the bottle.

She choked on it. "Tastes wheaty. Kind of bitter, but good. Anything's good." She drank in large gulps, feeling relief as the river of liquid coated her dry throat. She rolled a cigarette and offered it to him. He took it, and she rolled another for herself. After the first drag, she relaxed in the pile of furs and gazed at the trees along the bank.

"Look at all the different kinds of trees here. Will there ever come a day when I'll know everything there is to know about green?"

Claude seemed amused and poured her more ale.

"If God is good, no," she said, rubbing Billy behind his ears as he lay next to her. "If I had the energy, I'd sing a hymn to green."

"Green, all the time green. Enough to make a person scream. If God is good, He'd make some trees purple or blue. Or even gray."

"He does. At least that's the way they see them in France."

"Who?"

"Les Fauves."

"Ah, tu parles français maintenant, oui?"

"Non." She tried to say it in the French way, through her nose. "See that spruce? It's blue-green."

Claude thrust out his bottom lip. "Green."

"See there, along the shore, those firs streaked with purple shadows. That aspen flecked with yellow light. See in the distance, those mountains. They're milky gray-blue."

"That's mist."

"Mist veiling a forest. There are shy greens that retreat behind mist. Dull greens that lie down and sleep. Young greens that are frisky as a puppy. Spring greens that dazzle the eye."

"Solid green that drives a man mad." He looked at her and laughed softly. "Take off those gum boots and wiggle your toes. It will make you feel better. No mosquitoes here."

"Some Gitksan carver must have been bitten to smithereens once. He put a giant mosquito on top of a pole, with a prong long enough to bite through boards. A man told me it was a woodpecker, but I swear it was a mosquito."

She pulled off her boots, keeping her brown wool stockings on, and told him about the Mother-and-Child pole, the Frog Woman pole, and Mrs. Douse wanting to keep a painting. "That meant heaps more than a passel of Vancouver society matrons buying the whole lot."

He turned the fish in the pan. "Where do you go now? Up the Nass? Alaska?"

She gazed at the sun's glow behind the highest firs, the golden ribbon of river gleaming in the west, going out to sea, mixing with the waters of Haida Gwaii. The poles are different there, Henry had said. What would she be missing if she didn't go?

But she was an artist, not a researcher. What did it matter if she brought back an incomplete impression of native art?

To Henry Albert Douse, it mattered, even though he wasn't Haida. There had been that sad, soft tone in his voice when he'd said, *Nobody to watch the poles.* They had named her something. *Hailat.* Person with spirit power in her hands. Maybe that wasn't just a compliment about her paintings. Maybe it acknowledged her power to do something. She had imposed herself on them, and now, with as much gentleness as the Kitwancool totems, he was asking for something back.

Claude put his hands on his knees and his face inches from hers. "I said, where do you go now? Up the Nass? Alaska?" His eyebrows lifted hopefully. "I can take you."

To go with him? Now? Her old dream—painting and Claude together. She looked at his funny, dirty face, his cheeks puffed in a smile above his beard all crinked and cranked every which way, his eyes glistening, pulling her into them, waiting for an answer. The possibility that they might yet become lovers pulsed in her like a drumbeat.

Wherever you're going, she almost said.

"A man in Kitwancool said I should go to Haida Gwaii."

Claude straightened up and let out a wolf growl that made Billy perk up. "Haida Gwaii. The Queen Charlottes, eighty miles out to sea." He scowled at the fish.

"Some of the poles there are in empty villages, unprotected from thieves. They're not going to last, and I don't know when I can come north again."

"Hecate Strait is a hell hole of treacherous water for small boats. Fog thick as thunderclouds. Fog that sneaks up and suffocates you, turns you crazy in circles. I have no instruments to navigate in fog."

"I didn't mean you should take me."

He turned the fish, all buoyancy gone from his features. In a few wordless minutes that seemed like an hour, he put a tin plate of food and a fork before her. *"Voilà."*

She ate. "As fine as any restaurant I went to in Paris."

He smiled, a wan, disappointed sort of smile, held his fish by the head and tail, and tore into it with his teeth.

"Do you think it's right, what I'm doing?"

He pulled two fish bones from his mouth. "It brought you north, so it's right."

"I mean—"

"I know what you mean. It's right, and it's important."

"Do you know a man named Alfred Poole?"

"Gitksan?"

"White."

"No."

"I think he's some kind of scout or dealer in poles to museums or collectors. He's one notch lower than a mosquito, sucking the lifeblood out of villages. He's speeding up what nature will do in her own good time."

"You need to go." He tipped his head back to finish the ale. "A steamer leaves Prince Rupert every Monday at noon and puts in at Skidegate on Graham Island of the Charlottes." He slapped the gunwale. "*Renarde* can take you to Rupert. It's a hundred eighty miles to the coast, but the river's with us. From there Rupert is only a short way up the sound." He tipped his head back and closed his eyes. "What day is it?"

"I honestly don't know. Friday?"

"I thought it was Wednesday." They laughed until Billy barked. "Monsieur Bill, do you know?"

"No. He never knows."

"I'll find out." Claude heaved four black oil drums onto the dock. They sounded empty when he set them down. He rolled one of them toward the landing house.

"I'll pay you, of course," she shouted to him, ahead of her.

He turned back and grinned. "Maybe yes. Maybe no."

A tingle traveled through her. She couldn't be so naïve to think he was doing this just for friendship. For whatever reason—Haida Gwaii or Claude du Bois—she felt excruciatingly alive. She put her boots back on, leashed Billy to the boat's wheel, and stumbled after Claude, rolling another oil drum. Out of breath, the buzz of the ale in her head, she caught up with him as he was coming out of the landing house.

"It's Sunday!" he shouted. "We leave at dawn. Four-thirty."

She worked alongside him, loading supplies, his and hers, from the Hudson's Bay post. By the time they finished, she could hardly stand. He lit a small lantern and hung it over the hatch, tossed a blanket into the skiff, and came back to arrange a bed of furs below deck. He invited her in. It wasn't much to speak of, just a crawl space really. Billy settled right in the middle, sniffing the furs.

"*Non!* Not for you!" Claude pushed and slapped but Billy didn't move.

"Billy, here!" Emily snapped her fingers and pointed to a place in the bow. Begrudgingly, Billy obeyed, but not without a whimper. Emily stretched out on the furs, exhausted and weak.

On his knees beside her, Claude whistled a descending note and his eyes shone in the lamplight. "Here, at last, you sleep in mink, *oui?*"

"*Oui*, in the queen's pajamas."

He scrunched up his face. "*Non. Rien.* Sleep in nothing."

She fanned her hand over the fur and chuckled. "One day an MP's wife in Ottawa or London will wear this fur to the theater, never knowing."

To pick up where they left off, nothing in the world prevented her, now. Right here, tonight, it might happen—to love without hesitation or fear. At Rupert they would part. No claims. Just two people coming together on a river.

"The virgin in a man's boots." He unlaced them and took them off, then reached for her wool stockings.

She tensed and tucked her toeless foot behind the other knee.

"Now don't be coy with me." He held her other ankle, waiting.

She closed her eyes and saw Fanny bending over her foot, knowing all. She stretched out her leg, an offering of trust. He began to peel off her stocking. She felt it go, inch by inch, down to her ankles, over her heel.

"Ach!"

She froze.

"*Les petits démons!* A million of bites! Poor girl."

"Yes, but I painted the Mother-and-Child pole." She smiled. "It was in a swarming bog."

He crawled toward her face, and she opened her arms to him. "You don't tease me this time," he said. Smelling of fuel oil, he kissed the mosquito bites on her neck, her ears, her eyelids. He lay next to her and kissed her mouth, opening it with his tongue, his hard desire surprising against her thigh, making her squeeze inside in small involuntary waves. Heat surged through her. Her whole body felt feverish, nauseous. His beard chafed her cheek and she winced.

"You hear the potlatch drums?" He covered his heart with his open hand. "The beat of passion, *oui?*" One eyebrow arched and his mouth formed an uneven, amorous smile.

She tried to muster the sound of drums within her, that pulsing she'd felt before supper, but only the sadness of the ruined potlatch at Mimkwamlis came to mind. She felt an almost imperceptible slackening, any drums too faint to be felt. She couldn't answer him.

Sweat trickled down her temple. She raised her hand to wipe it off. Her fingers and wrists were swollen. He seemed alarmed at the sight of them. Her head, neck, everything felt swollen and hot. She couldn't lie still. The tingle from within merged with the tingle on her skin, making it almost unbearable. She wished she had chosen the bath. A cool one. The supper and the beer hadn't settled well.

"Too hot, *oui?*" He unfastened the top two buttons on her blouse. His fumbling concentration was amusing. Letting him was easy now, because of Fanny.

"*Mon Dieu!*" he cried, and backed away. "Your skin!"

She opened her blouse to her waistband and looked down at the red and bumpy flesh of her breasts and midriff, inflamed and raw from scratching, dotted with bloodied specks and tiny scabs.

He blew on her skin to cool it. "Émilie. Émilie," he murmured, pain in his voice. He said her name as naturally as though he'd been saying it to himself for years.

"What to do? What to do?" he murmured, shaking his hands, and scrambled up onto the deck. She heard him rummaging in the cabin. "Où est-il? Où est-il? Ah!" He scrambled back down with a tin.

She raised up on her elbows. "What's that?"

"Ointment."

"What kind?"

"Sh. Lie down." He took off his buckskin shirt.

She watched his muscles moving under his skin. Even in the dimness she saw the line on his neck between bronzed and lighter skin. She lay back and threaded her fingers through the hair on his chest.

He smiled wryly at the attention. "Your blouse," he whispered, waving his hand for her to take it off. She did, and spread it under her and on both sides to protect the mink.

He dug his fingers into the tin and placed dots of salve on her cheeks and throat and smoothed it on gently. It was cool and soothing, but smelled oily, maybe slightly fishy.

"Is my face puffy?"

He nodded. "Poor Émilie. Émilie." It was as though once he'd finally said her name, he must say it again and again. He worked the ointment down her neck, over her shoulders, down her arms, over the backs of her hands. She felt herself relax into his sliding caresses, acquiescing to whatever ministrations he would do. He smoothed the salve onto her right breast, onto the side, lifting it, under it, and around again, cupping it in his palm while he massaged. In a hazy thrill of not knowing where his hands were going, a long sigh escaped her, but the thrill receded, as though belonging to another person.

"Alors, comme ça. Doucement, oui?" His voice soft.

He moved to the other breast, and down to her waist, his thoroughness telling her that his tending to her gave him pleasure.

"You have spirit power in your hands," she murmured, amazed at such tenderness in a man so rugged, a man for whom it was important that she paint the Haida totems. If she had an ounce of inclination . . . But somehow, in spite of what she'd once hoped for, it had all drained out of her.

His eyes looked deep, as though seeing beyond her skin, into her soul. "I thought I knew. I thought I understood. That you are *pas-sionné*. That you could be *passionné* for me. *Mais, non.* Only for art. Only for art. *Mon Dieu,* to stay in that mosquito pit—to *paint!*" Slowly, he raised his eyes to hers, dark with anguish and moist with a new recognition. His fingers curled into fists pushing against his chest. "I cannot. I see you are too sick."

Her eyes welled up with the truth of all he said. Only for art. For this moment, probably forever, it had to be enough to know that she had been desirable, and perhaps even loved, in his way, smeared with fish grease.

"One more thing." He clambered up on deck and down again and laid the little French flag, wet and cool, across her breasts.

She laughed softly. "Does this make me French?"

"*Oui, mademoiselle. Une dame héroïque.*" He raised his fist and it hit the roof of the cabin. "*Pour l'art!*"

He kissed the palms of her hands and drew back, looking pitiful. The corners of his lips turned down. "*Bonne nuit, Émilie.*"

"*Bonne nuit, Claude.*" She smiled. "*Monsieur Galant.*"

He took the lantern, climbed up and was gone.

26: Moss

At noon William and Clara Russ, the Haida guides whom the minister on the Queen Charlotte Islands had recommended, arrived at the Skidegate dock in a gas boat towing a small dugout canoe. "Ready?" William asked.

"If I'd known we wouldn't leave until now I could have painted all morning," Emily said.

"Tide wasn't ready." William's look told her she had a lot to learn.

No one could understand the pressure of time pinching her.

Not entirely true. Claude could. He'd cast off well before dawn, navigating by lamplight, letting her sleep. How he'd fought the big swells, pulling levers, straining the little engine, swearing, sounding the steam whistle in a jolly rhythm as they chugged into the harbor at Prince Rupert, then rushed her to the steamship dock, flailing his arms, shouting, "*Vite! Vite!*" when she didn't walk fast enough. At the gangplank, he gave her a long succulent kiss, tipping her head back, using up the few minutes left, until the ship's horn hooted and he said, "*Bonne chance, chérie.* Don't scratch. Paint."

. . .

In the brisk breeze, William's hair lifted like thick black thatch and Clara tightened her head scarf. She looked at Emily's men's shoes, said something in Haida, and lifted her own skirt to show men's shoes. Her high, wide cheekbones squeezed the skin above them into crow's feet, and laughter rolled up from her belly. Emily laughed too.

They circled a sandbar on the east of the archipelago and turned south.

"Look," William said, and nodded toward sea otters lying on their backs on kelp beds.

They were cracking open clamshells between two rocks on their chests. One threw a clam right near another one sleeping on a rock so the splash woke him up.

"They so funny," Clara said with an all-over, crinkly smile. In a moment her smile vanished. "When they sad, they show it too. I watched one carry her dead baby around, howling for days."

"Scrape scales off a fish, feathers off a bird, skin off a man and you get the same thing underneath," William said.

There was something about both of them she liked very much.

All afternoon they saw no boats, no docks, no sign of man. "Are we going to Tanu first?" Emily asked.

"Yes," Clara said through a dreamy smile. "Village of my *naani*, my grandmother."

"It's a place of lappings of water, whispers of sea grass, cryings of ravens," William said.

When they nosed between islands, the sea flattened to a sheet of gunmetal, and she got a closer look at the rain forest, far more jungle-like than any she'd seen—tangled and impenetrable, a single, ancient being tentacled in wet green and teeming with moist life. In a double bay divided by a forested point, poles spiked the low vapors hanging over both beaches. William cut the engine and Clara let down an anchor made of a jagged rock enclosed in a net of twine.

"Tanu," she said. "Many people lived here. Seven generations. Raven families this beach. Eagle families there."

William took Emily, Billy, and her equipment ashore in the canoe, saying he'd go back for Clara. Emily stepped out and looked around. Long wisps of sea grass pulled flat against the sand by the retreating tide looked like lime green brush strokes. Storms had battered the village, ripping planks, collapsing roofs, blowing down poles. Skeletons of houses huddled against the rain forest and it seemed that eyes peered out of openings in the ruins. A raven flapped by, croaking a warning.

"An eerie-queery place, eh, Billy?" she murmured.

He felt it too, staying close to her legs, ears cocked.

She stopped at a fallen pole and passed her hand over the moss-covered paw of Bear holding Beaver. Frog peeked out from the crook of Bear's leg. Out of Killerwhale's mouth squirmed Seal. She loved how smaller space-filling figures sprang out from the wood, their faces sprightly while the larger ones were austere and aristocratic. Without human figures, these totems were more otherworldly than the Gitksan poles.

Three roofless house fronts, flush against each other, leaned precariously, each with a magnificent frontal pole of nine or ten stacked figures, the lowest ones with openings serving as entries. Fireweed and ferns grew within the ruins, and moss softened everything, making the surrounding air glow greenly.

"*Eeyaa aa mee,*" Clara whispered. "There used to be two rows of houses. Gone. All gone. Only forty years. House of the Long Potlatch, here. And there, Sound of Clouds Rolling. Gone."

"It's too bad," Emily said.

Someday what she saw would be gone too, swallowed up by rain forest. And she, gone as well. The ruins and looming forest made for melancholy thoughts. She was overcome with the need to leave proof that she had been here, had seen the touch of man on this far-flung place. She climbed onto an overhanging rock to position herself to paint the three ruins.

"No, no!" Clara waved her off. "Don't sit there."

Emily jumped off. "Why not?"

"Killerwhale spirit lives under that rock."

Of all the rocks on the island! She hadn't expected she'd have to accommodate spirits. The minister had said Clara and William were among the first to convert. Apparently Clara swung between contrary beliefs as easily as Sophie did. Emily moved to another vantage point.

William took Clara's hand and led her away from where Emily was working. She watched them step into a mossy house pit and sit together where a family fire might have been. Clara tipped her head onto his shoulder. Emily imagined them ministering to each other through sickness. She'd felt that exquisite pleasure herself, with Claude, and was happy for them.

Her painting of the houses would be a memorial to loving families, done with Impressionist colors—dove gray for the house planks, with washes of aqua, rose, and lavender. Their softness would express what she'd never experienced—that home could be the center of the affections, the dearest spot on earth for those who had been born there, had shared and grown large and unselfish with love, had worked together and rested from storms together, had wept with loss and died there.

· · ·

When Emily finished, Clara led her to the forested promontory dividing the beaches of the two clans. The carpet of moss was so thick that she had the sensation of stepping on a wet sponge. Her footfall squeezed out diamond dewdrops. Trailing lichen hung from boughs like torn veils, yellow-green berries with maroon speckles grew thick and plump, and pungent skunk cabbages brooded over puddles stained brown from rotting cedar. Water trickled unseen— the underground drinking, no, slurping of clear milk. Frogs croaked in different pitches, a chorus going at it hard and happy.

"Oh, the glory of living things!" Emily said.

"No. Not always living." Clara drew back a branch of pink salal blossoms hanging like tiny church bells. A sunken headstone stared back, walleyed. Fine moss filled the letters of the inscription, *In Memory of Charlie.*

"Oh. I'm sorry." Her own remark embarrassed her.

"My *naani's* brother," Clara whispered.

"May I ask why he doesn't have a coffin pole?"

"God doesn't like totem poles. The Christian way is in the ground. Charlie was the first Christian to get smallpox in Tanu.

After that, they died so fast they couldn't bury them all. The live ones left Tanu to save themselves. At night you can hear the dead ones wail."

No words of healing came to mind. She stared at the encroaching moss, the headstone—and saw the stones of Sophie's graveyard.

. . .

For supper Clara boiled bracken shoots and an octopus she'd clubbed in a tide pool. It was sweet but tough. While they ate by the fire, Clara told stories about totems that walked into the sea, drums that beat by themselves, a chieftainess whose potions made fiery men humble and frightened men brave.

Lavender twilight fell over the water. When it deepened to purple, Clara sang a mournful song in Haida.

"What does it mean?" Emily asked.

"How white people took our fine young boys and girls to Victoria," William said, "took them to school. They got flu there and died, all of them."

Clara rose and picked up her blanket. "Keep a little fire burning. Maybe bears come here."

"Where are you going?"

"To the gas boat. William won't sleep here with ghosts," she said, but it was Clara who hurried off first.

Baffled, Emily watched their lantern wink out in the blue-black sea. She lit her oil lamp, carried it into the tent, and saw slugs everywhere, crawling on the tent walls. "Ach!" Her stomach convulsed. One the size of a dill pickle was nosing into her bedroll. She grabbed a piece of driftwood and a pan to scrape them off. Moist flesh crept over her wrist. She knocked it off, and flung the driftwood toward the sea.

She yanked out her bedroll and shook it, inspected it by the oil lamp, turned it inside out, carried it far away, made Billy get in with her, rolled up in it so tightly nothing could get in, and let the light run out. Sand fleas tickled her face so she drew her head in like a snail. She listened, alert for anything. The forest creaked and groaned and the sea grass swishing in the wind whispered back, sh, sh. Tanu was not a dead village.

. . .

As they were leaving the next day, Clara leaned toward her in the canoe. "My *naani* said when everyone left Tanu for good, the ravens cried, but the people were quiet, even the babies."

Emily sat very still. Ravens keened against the distant sound of clouds rolling. She felt her chest expand to take in the enormity of sadness. When Tanu was far behind them, she asked Clara, "Did you have babies?"

"Two boys. Two girls. The girls married now."

"Grandchildren?"

"Six from one daughter, once. Now four and two."

"What do you mean?"

"One daughter had no babies and the other many babies, so she gave her sister two, the oldest girl and the baby."

"Gave them? How could she?"

"She cried for months and couldn't eat, she was so sick, but she was a good sister."

Awed again by the generosity of Sophie's offer, Emily whispered, "I have such a sister."

. . .

"Today I'll show you a hero pole at Cumshewa, my village," William said cheerfully. But when they entered Cumshewa Inlet and William peered through vapor hanging like gauze drapery, his forehead knotted into grooves of confusion.

"Gone."

He dropped to his knees on shore and passed his hand over a spread of bluish green sea asparagus. "It was here, the pole for Great Splashing of Waves, my father's chief. In front of House of the Stormy Sea." Bewildered, he looked around, as if the pole might have moved. "It took five tries to build that house. Every time he made the house beams, a storm came and washed them away. Later, Chicago men bought the house to show at a big fair. Now his pole is gone too." Slowly he sat back on his heels. Clara placed her hand on his shoulder. "It was my favorite," he said.

Her throat pinched shut. She was too late. Henry Douse had known how little time was left. She watched the shadow of a cloud darken William's woeful face.

"Missionaries told us that people who love graven images will be thrown into a burning lake forever," William said.

"Then they'd have to throw me too," she said softly.

He turned away and his words came with a struggle. "My father was one of those new-style Indians who wanted to get out of the blanket. He earned money packing up totems at Yan and Skidegate. Cut them in pieces to ship to museums. A dollar a foot." His voice became faint and high. "When I was old enough and the missionary got a job for me, I did the same." He stroked the sea asparagus.

She could offer him no words of comfort. She didn't even know if she could touch him.

Quietly they walked up a rise and came upon a huge cedar Raven with wings folded to his sides, beak raised, sitting on a thick, low stump overlooking a meadow. It was not a pole, but a full-bodied sculpture, the bird, head-to-tail, longer than the height of the stump he sat on. Moss had grown on his head, his back, the tops of his wings, and the hollows of his eyes.

"There was a house here called Where Raven Makes Strong Talk. Our people died here. Piles of them. Anyone who went in did not come out." He told her how Raven on one corner of the house had a mate on the opposite corner, with the dead piled up between. "Now she's all broke, and he's alone."

"How did smallpox get on the island?"

"On all of Haida Gwaii. Our people got it in Victoria, brought it home with them in trading canoes, dying on the way. In twenty years, only one in ten Haida lived."

She tried to pin down exactly what that meant to families, children, sisters. Her thoughts scattered like fitful moths.

"Raven still makes strong talk. See how his beak points upward? This is the hero totem I will paint."

The gap between her sympathy and her skill felt as wide as a sea. It seemed that the native carver saw the inner essence of his subject first, in this case that solemn strength, the spiritual aspect of Raven, and, chip by chip, the carver revealed the shape that embodied his thought. She'd been taught to see from the outside, but the times when she had approached a subject from its inner essence, as she had with Dzunukwa and *Totem Mother,* she was able to get closer to its true nature.

The vapor turned to mist, then drizzle. She tried to shelter her paper with her slicker. Water trickled through her paints. William erected a canopy over her using a piece of sail. It flapped in the wind and kept coming untied so he held it above her all afternoon. The rain falling on his face was without consequence to him. His arms must have ached horribly.

Water slicked off Raven's beak in sheets, soaked the moss of his eye until it could hold no more and fell like tears. She lifted the upward swoop of the beak to make it more defiant. Her brushes and paper, her hands, the back of her neck all felt damp. Even her bones ached from dampness. Paint that dampness. Get it into the work. Paint the struggle, the bite of raw wind, the iodine tang of the sea, its briny feel on her skin. Paint the queer raven noises in purple-black nights, the dark juiciness of earth, the smell of people dying, the village abandoned, unguarded except by a regal, rotting bird as alone as God, Cumshewa's relic of remembrance.

27: Salal

Emily heard a sharp, I-mean-business knock. It wasn't Sophie's soft knock. Who besides Jessica and her sisters knew she'd moved to this smaller studio-flat on West Broadway? She stepped over Joseph's cage, and Joseph protested with an "Awk!" She opened the door to a gray-suited, gray-mustached, gray-haired man. At least he was consistent.

"Miss Carr? I'm Dr. Charles Newcombe, from Victoria, representing the Provincial Parliament."

"Yes."

"You did write them about the new museum gallery and legislative library of the Provincial Parliament, didn't you?"

"Yes, I offered my paintings of native villages and totem poles as a collection," she said at the doorway.

"As somewhat of an expert in Northwest Coast cultures, I've been sent to assess your work."

"Come in. You'll have to ignore the mess." She kicked Billy's blanket under a wicker chair, and moved Joseph's cage to the sink to be out of the way. "I didn't expect anyone so soon. I'm not actually ready. I'm preparing a show for spring."

She dragged out the canvases stacked under her worktable and leaned them against walls. She moved paint rags, palettes, jars of brushes aside on her worktable and laid out drawings. She spread watercolors on the floor. "I came home with twenty oils and sixty watercolors. There's no space to show them here."

He looked up at the seven wet canvases hanging on wires from ceiling hooks. "I can see that."

"There's more." She stepped over Billy to haul out the canvas boards leaning in the bathtub, and laid them on the unmade bed.

"Why don't you come to my exhibition? It'll be the largest art exhibit Vancouver has ever had. No single artist has ever hired a hall in Vancouver and mounted a one-person show, large or small. Once I work up these studies, there'll be two hundred works, more than half of them large oils."

"When?"

"In two months, March eighteenth, in Dominion Hall."

She'd scrimped to the bone on heating oil, wore two sweaters indoors, went clamming with Sophie on weekends to make a chowder that would last until midweek, gave up chops and evening tea and jam, and cut her own hair in order to afford the rental fee.

"I can see enough right here to report to the committee."

"Have the committee come."

He squinted, tipped his gray head, stroked his mustache which drooped like hemlock branches. He seemed preoccupied with digesting his lunch.

"They certainly show the mystique of native iconography."

"Thank you."

"This one is faithfully drawn. Similar to one I purchased."

"An oil? By whom?" She expected him to say Ted Richardson, the American she'd met in Sitka.

"No. A totem."

"You *bought* a totem pole?"

"For the Field Museum in Chicago."

She dropped into a chair, thinking of William weeping at Cumshewa, stroking the sea asparagus as if searching for a lost button.

"These might be useful to the museum staff in illustrating monographs on clan legends," he said, "but you've used no standard of comparative size. Your Kwakiutl potlatch welcoming figure, which everyone knows is short, is depicted the same size as this much taller Haida pole."

"But they're different paintings. They're not photographs."

"Precisely. Your daubs are laid on with such a heavy hand you have to stand across the street before the colors blend."

He gazed at them both until some thought snapped him out of reverie and he continued examining others.

"Too bad they're so brilliant. They're not true to the conditions of the coast villages. If you'd tone down your colors and if your inaccuracies were corrected under proper supervision, then the museum might want to hire you to do a wall panel."

"Inaccuracies corrected! That's personal expression." She heard Fanny. *You can't have it both ways.* "I'll starve and call it joy before I paint under the supervision of a committee, Dr. Newcombe."

"It's a shame that you've mixed art and science. They may not like that, but I'll make a report and see what they say."

She stood up to usher him out. "Fine."

"However, this one and this one and that, I'll take."

"But you just said—"

"Never mind." He smiled. "I like them. They're for me."

One was the Kwakiutl welcome figure. She was baffled.

"I was hoping to keep the collection intact, to be seen by all people in the province. They say something important when viewed together."

She watched him write a check. The money would buy frames. She could rework those subjects from her sketches, and not diminish her collection.

He noticed her drum on the wall. "A fine example of Tlingit craft. You have a keen eye. How much will you take for it?"

"Not for sale."

He glanced sideways at it as he left, as if to say he didn't believe her.

Billy licked her hand that held the bank check.

"Oh, for God's sake, Billy. Stop slobbering."

She didn't know what to think. Her totem paintings had been

bought! Someone liked them enough to pay hard-earned money. She whooped a little and got down on all fours to tussle with Billy. But Dr. Gray Eyes had bought an actual totem too. And what kind of a report would he take back to the almighty committee? Still, the prospects sent her into a fever of joyous work.

· · ·

Several weeks later, a letter arrived:

> We regret that we cannot consider your work appropriate either for the legislative library or for the gallery. The liberties you took damage their use for the anthropologist. Although we recognize the efforts behind your work, we cannot put ourselves in a position to imply that your illustrations are accurate representations of the Northwest Coast native villages.

She snapped the letter in the air. "Signed by a committee that hasn't seen a single painting, hasn't felt their cumulative effect, probably hasn't ever seen a pole in its proper setting."

It was too sobering for anger.

But they hadn't seen Dzunukwa either, Dzunukwa who could stride through bogs, make mincemeat of committees.

"We'll see what the people think, won't we, Billy?"

· · ·

Choosing apples from the grocer's outdoor display, Emily heard a commotion up the street. The grocer ran out to see. Emily followed, holding tight to Billy's leash.

Police were rounding up Squamish from their waterfront village on Kitsilano Point and herding them to the dock and onto a barge. Everyone was carrying something—chests, gunny sacks, baskets, blankets tied into bulging bundles. Policemen shouted for them to keep moving. Men loaded their canoes and gas boats.

"Do you think it's an evacuation against sickness?" she asked the grocer.

"Worse."

They hurried to the bank to get a better look. A crowd of onlookers was gathering. At the gangplank to the barge, a man was recording names while another handed out money. Some men accepted it. Others passed, heads high, silent. It seemed a repeat of pushing out the Songhees from Victoria's Inner Harbor.

She smelled smoke and gasoline, saw white men running with torches. Billy's ears went back. In a few minutes, one house and then another went up in flames. Billy backed away and yanked her off balance. Flames leapt to houses, barns, fruit trees, their little cemetery and its sacred places. Rage seethed in her.

"Awful," the grocer said. "This has been brewing for years. Eliminate the eyesore, the politicians kept saying. Clear out any native vestiges so those rich folks of Fairview will be spared the sight. That half-mile stretch of waterfront property's too valuable to waste on Indians." He shook his head. "They were honest neighbors."

The ragtag families looked pitiful crowded on the barge—children frightened and crying, women pressing their faces into their husbands' shoulders. Some old people wailed. Others were mute, expressionless, stiff as statues.

Amid the din of the fire roaring and the shouting of orders, she tugged Billy toward a policeman and asked, "Where are they taking them?"

"Get back, lady. Get the dog out of here."

"Tell me where—"

"Mission Reserve. North Vancouver."

Sophie's reserve.

"But there's been no treaty. Who ordered this?"

"McBride." He waved her away with his stick.

The provincial premier. A Conservative and a colonial. She gripped Billy's collar and moved back, choking in the smoke and muttering, "Oh, what I'd give to tell him to his face to go to the devil."

· · ·

For a month she painted in a burst of energy, several canvases going at a time, and then confessed to Jessica, "I'm worried. It was wealthy Vancouver citizens who made the government round up the Squamish. How can I expect those same people to understand or even care about what I paint?"

"Then educate them. Give a talk in the exhibit hall."

"Explain what ought to be plainly visible in the work?"

"Tell your experiences, like you told me. Dzunukwa and Tillie. Things like that."

Emily snorted. "I have no stomach for those know-it-all speechifiers talking your hind leg off just to glorify themselves."

"People don't know what you know, Emily. A lecture on totems and native cultures would do something. Don't you owe it to those people who helped you?"

She thought of Mac and Beatrice taking her to the potlatch, Chief Wakias, Henry Douse. She'd sent Mrs. Douse her painting. She hoped she liked it. But that wasn't enough.

She sighed. "Yes, my little Miss Conscience. I do."

• • •

To commit herself, she wrote to her sisters.

March 2, 1913

Dear Alice and Lizzie,

I know it's not easy for you to get to Vancouver, but I've rented Dominion Hall on Pender Street for an exhibit of my Indian work, all the way back to my first trip to Hitats'uu. I think you'll see I've learned a great deal in fourteen years. Even though I detest all those vapory tabby cats who meow out their thoughts, I'm going to give a talk on March 18 at 8:00 in the evening. If you would come it might help you understand why, as you say, your sister persists in painting pagan artifacts, or why she paints at all.

Affectionately on this soggy morn, Millie

She folded a silent prayer into the envelope and sealed it. Three cents' worth of hope to sail across the Strait of Georgia.

• • •

Wearing her blue gabardine dress that cinched her waist, she felt like a lamb dressed for slaughter. Her handwritten speech with last-minute changes stuffed into her handbag, she paused at the stairs to Dominion Hall—she'd walked fifteen blocks and didn't want to arrive flushed and out of breath. The gray façade seemed to lean forward at her like a courthouse. She grasped the handrail and pulled herself up the steps. Jessica was waiting for her inside, all smiles.

Miraculously, people came. The ads in the newspaper had worked. She and Jessica moved quietly in the gallery, listening.

"It's all very well to see it at an exhibition, but one doesn't hang this sort of ... of whatever"—the woman waved her glove at a mortuary pole—"in one's home."

Emily humphed to herself. Sneerer at sacred things. What did she expect from a glove flipper?

"Grotesque. Gloomy," another woman said.

"Isn't it more stimulating to feel uncomfortable than to feel nothing at all?" she said to Jessica, loudly.

"They're done too quickly," one man said.

"Perhaps you looked at them too quickly," Emily said.

Resentment choked her. "Fossils," she whispered, adding in a loud voice, "A Nisga'a chieftainess wanted a pole painting so much she wouldn't let me leave until I promised her one."

"Quiet," Jessica said under her breath. "These people were good enough to come. You have to support yourself. Now get up there and set them straight!"

She stepped up to the dais. When she heard herself begin the lecture, her voice sounded thin and distant, as if her ears were plugged with wax.

"My object in making this collection of totem pole pictures has been to depict these striking, monumental relics in their original settings. I wish to make a tribute to the inventiveness of the art and the dignity of the way of life of the province's first people. What you see here represents only a fraction of the great native societies of British Columbia. . . ."

She made clear the size of the poles, some sixty feet, and their sheer numbers, sometimes two dozen in a village. Except for Jessica beaming in the front row, she couldn't read the faces in the audience. Her dry throat itched.

"Most westerners transplanted their ideas about art from the time of European migration and haven't changed them, yet our landscape demands a new style. Our isolation from art centers should make it easier for us to be ourselves, to derive our inspiration from the land and the art of its first peoples. . . ."

Gibb's idea. Oh, for an hour with him now.

"However, there's one style that does belong—"

The rear door to the exhibit hall creaked open. Maybe it would be Alice and Lizzie.

It was Sophie! Dear Sophie, with her back so straight, in her good plaid skirt, her head wrapped in a yellow scarf. And shoes. And behind her, Sarah in her purple shawl, her bearing aristocratic. They kept their eyes fastened on her, ignoring the rustle in the room. And a few steps later, hesitating, Margaret Dan. She couldn't believe it. What had Sophie done to get her to come?

Emily could hardly contain her happiness. She welcomed them with a huge smile, and looked down to find her place.

"There's one style that does belong, and that's the original art of Canada's West Coast done by tribal carvers. The oldest art in Canada and it's the most modern in character. For the native artist, the principles of exaggeration and distortion are methods to express the inner nature of animal and human figures, to find the spirit of a thing. And it is these principles that I am exploring in my current work."

The three women stayed right inside the door. Sophie stood square-shouldered, lips a firm line declaring her right by friendship to be here. Sarah was calm and observant, but Margaret, looking stealthily to the sides of the room where the paintings hung, seemed uncomfortable. Bless them for coming.

Emily recounted some experiences on her travels, and told of the complex culture the totems represent, explaining that the animal crests indicate kinship and ancestry, not so different from a coat of arms, and serve as reminders of legends. She explained the burial practices, as far as she understood them, and spoke of the terrible dignity of the coffin trees.

"I love these places with all my being, and the art, and the fine people I met. They can teach us many things." She saw several heads turn and some scowls in the audience.

"If I might digress, perhaps you're wondering why there are so few people in my paintings. Some villages were never reinhabited after devastating epidemics, and only ruins are left to tell of tragedy. Most were just temporarily empty because of fishing season outside the villages . . ."

She paused, deciding whether to go on.

". . . on lands their ancestors have fished before European arrival, lands necessary to their survival."

She paused again, scanning the audience for a reaction. Her underarms felt moist.

"This absence of people should not be construed as agreement with policies to remove native peoples from their lands."

With that, she may have nailed the last nail on the coffin of any possible Vancouver art career. Some people whispered, but nobody left.

"I glory in our magnificent West, and want to celebrate and preserve the memorials of its first greatness. These poles, so full of dignity, should be as important to Canadians as ancient Celtic relics are to the English. In only a few more years, they will be gone forever, which is why I want to complete my collection while there is still time."

Polite applause. People stood up to see the paintings. With only the strength of her stare at Sophie at the far end of the exhibition hall, Emily tried to send her a message. Look at *Totem Mother, Kitwancool.* That's you! Emily tipped her head sideways toward it. Sophie walked right to it and smiled.

Emily's waistband squeezed her like a python. As she stepped down from the dais, she felt a sudden urgency and fled to the women's washroom, afraid of fainting or some worse humiliation.

On the way she heard a man say, "I don't understand what's so interesting to her about Indian art."

Blind to any beauty not imported. Had he slept through all she'd said? She leaned against the washroom mirror, cooling her forehead on the glass. She had seen no sign of agreement on anyone's face. Not one nod.

She rinsed her face and went out. She worked her way across the hall, giving explanations of totems to those who asked and telling more stories, looking for Sophie and Sarah and Margaret. Apparently, they had already left—the three people whose approval she longed for most.

• • •

After six agonizing days, Jessica helped her dismantle the show. Emily looked at *Cumshewa Raven.* Its defiant posture made strong talk. She pulled in her chin and said in a husky voice, *"Miss Carr's vision suffers from a distortion which renders these Indian idols incomprehensible."* She took down the painting. "There you have it, in the *Province*, for all the world to read."

"You memorized that?"

"It just wormed its way in." She gestured toward the painting as though delivering a judgment in a courtroom. *"Her coloring is in a higher key than is vouchsafed to ordinary mortals to perceive. It is hoped that she will soon recover from this attack of neo-Impressionism.*

"If there's any attacking to be done, it would be me gouging out the eyes of the philistine who wrote that!"

"Vancouver just isn't ready. You overwhelmed them with things they've never seen. Give them time."

"They'll never be ready. It was stupid of me to hope. All those Vancouver land developers don't want people to see the vitality and dignity of native culture. They're profiting from breaking the Indians, and I . . . What am I doing?"

"You're honoring them," Jessica said sternly.

"But without a positive reception from whites, I've done nothing by these paintings to counter the tragedy of Cumshewa and other ruined villages. Nothing to counter the torched village just a few blocks from here. Nothing to counter any loss, not only of Sophie's babies, but all those up the coast."

Jessica looked at her in shock, her eyes tearing up.

"I can't paint what people with pocketbooks want and feed my passion, and I can't paint for Indians and make a living, or a difference. Where does that leave me?"

"Just wait, Em. The creaky old world will come around."

Sometimes her simple nature got on her nerves.

"The issue cuts deeper than that. It's who I am." Her words came out in a high crackle. "Don't you see? A Gitksan man said I had spirit power in my hands, and yet I held out that same hand for money from a white man who's buying up totems for museums. What do you think that does to me? It tears me apart."

"You're both working to preserve them, so what's the point?"

"Jessica, stop! I know what I know. This show was do or die, and it died. Family, love, and now art—they've all failed me, but that's something you who have everything just can't grasp."

Emily grabbed her handbag and dashed out the door. Cold air smacked her in the face as she hurried toward the Burrard Inlet ferry. That was an awful thing she said to Jessica. She hated herself for it all the way across to Sophie's house.

• • •

"I don't think the exhibit is going to make any difference," she told Sophie.

"To who? They didn't like it? Who are they?" Sophie asked in her clipped manner, nursing one of the twins. "Who?"

"Buyers. People with power. People with votes."

"Why do they have the right? I know baskets. I decide good and bad. You know painting. You decide."

"But only if the government or individuals *buy* can people—Indians or whites—*see* your handsome Ancestor and all the other poles."

That stopped Sophie, but only for a moment. "A few fat men don't like them? So? You still have them."

"Sophie, what I've done—all those years. I'm afraid it might not mean a thing."

"You afraid? Everybody's afraid. Two villages now in one. What next?" Anger blazed in Sophie's eyes as she looked at Emily, and softened as she unwrapped the twin she'd been holding. "Everybody's afraid," she said, a low murmur.

The baby was thin, with a fever rash and a rattle in her breath. Bewilderment swam in Sophie's clouded eyes.

The other twin, hanging in the basket cradle, began to fuss. Emily lifted her out. "Poor little darling." She raised her to her shoulder. "Little darling Molly."

"That's not Molly. That's Emmie," Sophie said sharply.

Emily looked again. The eyes were crossed. Before, it had been Molly with crossed eyes.

Sophie held up the twin she was nursing, her hard stare fending off any contradiction. "This one's Molly. Emmie's the strongest baby. Named after you."

What Sophie had done! Switched the names so it would be an Emmie who would live. Live but with a different vision, distorted by anyone else's standard, but natural to her.

And Sophie would go right on producing baby after baby just to have them wilt. Infinitely worse than producing painting after painting to have them blasted or ignored. What was a painting after all? What could a painting do?

She bit her lip. "I can't stay in Vancouver. I have to go home."

"Puh! To Victoria? Giving up?"

"No. Just to live with my sisters for a while. No rent to pay. Plenty of food. The oddball sister who doesn't belong. Like stuffing a whale into a teacup. But it'll be near the provincial government. Maybe there'll be other opportunities."

"You can live with us."

The look of simplicity in Sophie's face told her that she meant it. She would not doubt her generosity this time.

"Thank you. That's good of you. But, no. I have to go."

Sophie gave the sick twin to Emily and brought the healthy, cross-eyed twin to her other breast. At the moment, none of the glory of the Kitwancool mother shone in Sophie's tired face. "Sophie, we can do something for Molly. We can take her to a doctor, or get some medicine."

Sophie's eyes flashed. "White doctor?"

"Yes. In Vancouver."

"Your doctor? Someone you know?"

"No. I don't know a doctor, but I'm sure I can find a good one."

Sophie snorted. "No white doctor anywhere did anything for our people in smallpox time long time ago. Let them all die. Babies. Grandmothers. All die."

Her throat felt scorched. Tanu and Cumshewa came home to her. "It's different now."

"Maybe white doctor do something bad to Molly. One less Indian."

"Sophie, no!"

Sophie's arms clutched Emmie to her breast, and her head moved slowly side to side.

"All right. But if you ever change your mind, write me. I'll be here the next day."

"Auntie will miss you too."

"Tell her I appreciated her coming. And Margaret Dan too. I want to say good-bye to Jimmy but I know he's working hard."

"Some days he works. Some days he only at the taverns."

Emily watched Sophie hold Emmie to her breast as she stared out the open doorway into the night, at the spot where Annie Marie had drawn in the dirt under the salal bush, and at the glinting black inlet and the city that was swallowing her husband.

Part IV

28: Eagle

Angry banging on her door made her jump. Mr. Pixley charged right in and shook an old shoe at her. "What is the meaning of this? I found this under the maple tree with this filthy rag inside."

"You left it in the basement kindling box. That means it's a castoff."

Before he could sit down, she pulled the rope attached to a pulley that hauled a chair to the ceiling.

"No it isn't. I just misplaced them somewhere. Where's the other one?"

She yanked up the second chair, feeling smug about using her space-saving invention against this sorehead. "Under the lilac bush. They're mouse houses. Poor suffering little creatures. All snow and frozen ground outside and them with no place to keep warm."

"Warm!" His face grew red. "Warm! You're worried about the vermin keeping warm? Better you should worry about your tenants freezing. Or the war. Worry about soldiers freezing. Worry about anything but mice."

"I do, but mice I can do something about."

He glanced at a painting. "Monstrosity," he muttered on his way out.

"That's my mother," she yelled. "Ethel Dzunukwa. She eats people she doesn't like. Would you like to meet her?"

All the decent young men were dying in the trenches in France and only sniveling no-goods were left to rent rooms. Croakers who demanded more heat for the same money, who complained of a wobbly table when they could just as easily fix it themselves, who counted into her palm every dollar of their rent so slowly they were halfway into the next month before they finished. She stormed down to the basement and turned down the valve that sent heat into Mr. Pixley's apartment. She had a mind to let Susie, her white rat, loose in the hall to terrorize him.

She grabbed the mail on the way back upstairs. A letter had

been forwarded from the Island Arts and Crafts Society. Maybe, against all odds, a painting had sold and it was a check. She went inside and ripped it open. The paper had been torn raggedly from a tablet, the handwriting jerky and uncontrolled.

> *December 16, 1916.*
>
> *Dear Mrs. Emily Carr.*
> *I saw your pictures at the Island Arts and Crafts Exhibit. They are so mighty so true. I looked and in my head I was in my illahee. Kitwanga wind cold lonely sad and Kispiox totem poles like tall men talking and Kitsegukla eyes and eyes and eyes. I would like to buy them all. I think you must be a* hailat. *Do you have more. I would like to see them. Very much I would like to. May I come. Where. Please you can write to me in Victoria Hospital.*
>
> > *Yours sincerely and respectfully Harold Cook.*
> > *The end.*

A lump formed in her throat. *Hailat.* It had been four years since she'd heard that word—what they'd called her in Kitwancool. Who was this man? A Gitksan? Someone in Victoria had seen her own deep feelings in the paintings, someone in a hospital. She wondered which ward this Harold Cook was on. She noticed what looked like a child's smeared pencil drawing of a totem on the back of the letter. The eyes were enormous.

"What do you think about this?" Emily said, waving it in front of Billy.

He followed it with his eyes and then struggled to shift positions on the rug, as if he were saying, Make an effort.

"That's what I thought. I shouldn't ignore it."

Even if Harold Cook was a child, she wrote him back, and saw eyes and eyes and eyes on totems. She squeezed her own eyes shut to *be* in those wild, bewitching places. Her head dipped onto the table. Where had the years gone?

Into endless arguments with Alice and Lizzie about her "inordinate love of rodents," about taking in André and any other stray cat who meowed pitifully, about the hair net she wore with the black velvet band across her forehead, about missionaries who aided their Indian communities in governmental disputes over hereditary land claims. And, always, they argued tooth and nail over native art as their collective Canadian heritage, which Lizzie customarily dismissed with, "Pooh. They're a dying people."

At least her apartment house put two neighbors' yards, a narrow lane, and Alice's schoolhouse between them, thanks to Alice's loan allowing her to build it on her portion of what was left of Father's nine acres. Theoretically, the plan was dandy—one big upstairs room serving as studio, living room, and kitchen, with good north light and a sleeping attic above it for her and Billy, and three apartments—one upstairs next to hers and two downstairs. She'd live off rents so she could paint. But when the recession hit, rents had plummeted. The Hooked Rug Period and Clay Pot Period followed, dribbles of income that kept her from painting. Her front yard bore two wooden signs: *House of All Sorts—Apartments to Let* and *Vegetables, Chickens and Eggs for Sale.* She'd squeezed onto the bottom of that one, in smaller letters, *Paintings too.*

André padded across the letter. His white and yellow-ochre fur looked like splotches of oil paint on the floor at Colarossi. She picked up a drawing pencil to play with him. It felt foreign, heavy. Art was another life, a continent away.

And now this letter stirred it all up again.

· · ·

A few weeks later, the buzzer sounded. Tantrum barked his high, yipping, griffon puppy bark. A large man with drooping shoulders, in his early thirties perhaps, shifted from foot to foot at the doorway. His pale face with sparse blond whiskers seemed anxious. For politeness' sake she tried not to look at his pasty white forehead, scarred and dented. A tuft of blond hair stood up on the top of his head like a feather.

"I'm Harold Cook."

How could a person smile so seriously? "Yes?"

"Are you Mrs. Emily Carr, the artist?"

No, she wasn't. Not anymore. "Miss Carr."

"I'm Mr. Cook."

He reached into his jacket pocket and drew out an envelope. A newspaper clipping fell out and he yelped, then lunged to catch it. One ankle and foot turned in and made it awkward for him. He unfolded a crumpled paper and cleared his throat.

"*Dear Mr. Cook.* That's me. Mr. Harold Cook. *Thank you for your kind letter appreciating my work at the Island Arts and Crafts Exhibit. You seem to have the capacity to understand the places and the totem subjects. Yes, I do have more. You can view them at my studio, 646 Simcoe Street, if you don't intend to give me an earful of art claptrap. Sincerely.*" His voice went up an octave. "*Sincerely, Emily Carr. The end.*

"You're Emily Carr. I'm Harold Cook."

No, he wasn't Gitksan. And he wasn't a child. "Come in."

He lurched through the doorway and his shoulder slammed against the doorjamb. The moment he saw the totem paintings, his face flushed. "Oh! Oh!"

She pulled out several others. He sidestepped in front of them, teetering, murmuring indecipherable sounds. His head bobbed irregularly. "Kitwanga," he sputtered and pointed to one. It *was* from Kitwanga. "Kitsegukla," he said and pointed. "Where Salmon First Wake." Right again. "Kispiox." A sigh leaked out all the way up from his toes.

"You've been there? You know these places?"

He gazed at her with watery eyes. She soaked up the sight of him in order to fill her mind for future days with the reminder that someone had looked at her paintings with appreciation.

He slumped onto the floor over his turned-in foot in front of *Kispiox Village.* "I lived in Kispiox." Agony deepened his voice. "My *illahee.*" His chin quivered. "I thought I'd never see it again. That totem pole is Eagle Who Knows Sorrow." He rocked forward, tugging absently at his rumpled socks. "It made a long shadow creep across the village. I played under it. I saw it with snow in the cracks."

"A white boy in a Gitksan village? When?"

"Before they sent me away."

His face, twisted by memory, stopped her from asking more.

"That pole cracked as soon as they put it up. It made a big sound." A violent shudder shook his shoulders. He raised his arms in a circle. "Big potlatch. I didn't get to go. Big beating."

"What's *illahee?*"

He tugged at his rumpled clothing. His misshapen forehead,

scarred and dented on one side, knotted even more under the quivering spray of straw-colored hair. With his gaze riveted on *Kispiox Village,* he answered, "Land that gives comfort."

He jerked to his feet as if the sight were too much for him. "I have to go now." He backed out the door, looking as long as he could, then turned and stumbled down the stairs.

She was stunned by his intensity. Was this the only kind of person who could love her paintings, the sort you'd quickly look away from on the street? She looked back at them. They were beautiful—to Dr. Newcombe, and now, after four years, to one other person. They seemed to stir to life something deep in him, and dormant in her. Seeing him transfixed, as if the totems were speaking to him, practically melted her and made her want to hear that strong talk herself.

She went down to the basement and squeezed a thick rope of cadmium red extra deep into some leftover tan wall paint, black into another can, and stirred until her arm ached. In her attic bedroom, she lay on her back and studied the raw underside of the roof, deciding where the wings should go, how the heads should face. Not an Italian fresco, just her secret ceiling. She sketched with a fervor she hadn't known in years—their wide shoulders, their curved beaks, the stylized native rendering of overlapping feathers as U shapes—and then charcoaled it on the slanted wooden ceiling. With slow, delicious strokes, working all night, she painted two big eagles on the wood, face to face. *Two Eagles Who Know Sorrow.*

· · ·

A few days later, Harold stood at the door again. He held out an eagle feather. "It's for you. Miss Emily Carr."

She noticed his pale blue eyes fastened on her, adoring. It was amusing, but a bit embarrassing too.

"Why, thank you, Harold. It's a perfect one." It pleased her that he didn't think she would consider it worthless.

"Please may I see the paintings?"

"Of course."

He sat cross-legged in front of *Totem Mother, Kitwancool* most of the afternoon, rocking, rapt, absently petting André, lost in the mother's smile. "You are a hailat. Person with spirit power in your hands."

Elation filled her. Then, swift as a brush stroke, guilt killed it. Power to do what?

Harold lifted his shoulders unevenly, took out a clipping from his shirt pocket, and began to read aloud. She had the distinct impression that he had practiced. It was the review of a group Island Arts and Crafts show.

"Miss Carr's work is of a decidedly different character. I doubt that even the most patriotic of Irishmen have seen grass as green as in her pictures of Brittany. The blues and reds of Alert Bay are just as blinding, but one picture of a canal in France shows the artist's Post-Impressionist style in its least aggressive form. As for the grotesques she stooped to elevate as art, the less said the better."

He stumbled over *Impressionist* and *grotesque*, saying it in three syllables, *gro-tes-ques*, but read it proudly, as if it were solid compliment. She had to laugh.

"That show was a year ago. Why didn't you come sooner?"

"Couldn't."

He seemed to be holding in some horrific secret. His fear of telling it met her fear of hearing it. Yet, she wanted to know what moved him about the paintings. She invited him to supper. While she fried up two chops, he picked off a book from a stack on her worktable and read. He ate with his hands more than polite society would tolerate. She pretended not to notice.

"How did you come to live in Kispiox?"

"My parents were missionaries." He stared at his bowl, his face blank. "I have to go now." He stood up so quickly his chair tipped backward. "They'll be angry with me."

"Your parents?" She wondered if Lizzie knew them.

"No."

"Come upstairs first, Harold. I have something to show you."

She took the oil lamp and led him up the ladder stairs to her attic. When he saw the Eagles hovering above them in flickering light, wings outspread, their feathers outlined in U shapes, his mouth dropped open. He noticed the Eagle drum she'd bought in Alaska hanging on the wall.

"A tom-tom," he whispered in awe.

She placed it in his hands. He took hold as though it would shatter. The vein leading to the dent in his forehead pulsed. What horrible thing had happened to him?

She moved his hand to the crossed thongs in the open back and put the drumstick in his other hand. "Go ahead."

Gently he let the drumstick fall. A warm, rich tone filled the attic. He shot her a look tortured with memories, and handed it back to her, as if afraid of its power.

"You may have it. Take it with you."

His blue eyes widened, lit with a wild fire.

29: Grass

Emily turned over the newspaper next to her morning toast, not wanting to see those dear haggard men in Belgian trenches, not wanting to remember an unshaven face and wonder how his Saskatchewan farm was struggling along without him, whether he got through another day, or died grotesquely in some stinking trench, his lungs scorched by mustard gas. Did birds die too at Verdun? How was Fanny managing? And Gibb? Her dog-eared letters to them straggled back months later, undeliverable. Who could concentrate enough to create art when armies inched closer?

Outside, Mrs. Pixley in her robe and slippers snatched up her newspaper in a halting motion, as if afraid to know, afraid not to know. A few minutes later, Agnes Smythe did the same. Then, all sounds in the apartment house stopped. No conversation, not even footsteps or a tap running. The tenants met the roar of Europe with silence. Her knife scraping the palest film of grape jelly on toast sounded monumental.

She slid her breakfast plate aside, tucked her feet under Billy lying like a tousled lump of black and white rug, and began a letter.

Feb. 20, 1917

Dear Jessica,

I miss you fiercely. Has it been a year since I saw you last? Oh, weepy days. Not a body here to talk art with. Hardly a single decent canvas. I feel like a damned fool for so many things. The little apartment house has only one long-standing tenant: Loneliness. To make ends meet I had to cut up the apartment next to mine into three rooms without kitchens, so now I'm a boardinghouse cook. One step forward, two steps back. I'm flabbed to death with tiredness. Please come for a painting lesson or a critique or just a plain, old-fashioned good talk, but let's promise not to talk of war news. We'll paint in Beacon Hill Park. Be prepared to see a barrel with a hair net. Come soon.

Yr flappy old friend, Emily

Two weeks later Jessica stood in the doorway smiling, her red hair heathered by strands of gray, her eyes as green as ever, thrusting out a bouquet of jonquils. "Fresh from the ferry dock."

"A sight for sore eyes. You, I mean. The flowers are dazzling too." Emily brought tea and Lizzie's biscuits and jam to the long table that served as dining and drawing table. "Just shove those books aside."

Jessica looked at them as she moved them—cultural anthropology of Northwest Coast villages, the Bible, Emily's journals, Whitman's *Leaves of Grass*, Emerson's essays with a paintbrush marking "Self-Reliance." "Curious combination," she said.

"Aren't there whole kingdoms of fine thoughts to discover?"

"Have you been happy here?" Jessica asked.

Emily pulled her mouth to one side. "I get dreadful hankery for wild places, and the people. They're outsiders, like me, so they have something to tell me. I won't be happy down to my bones until I know what it is."

"Why don't you go north again?"

"Oh, Jess, I feel like a snail with this monstrous apartment house on my back. Tell me about your girls instead."

"You wouldn't recognize them. Megan's engaged to a soldier." Jessica's perfect fingernails tapped the table in a nervous little rhythm. "More than two months since his last letter."

"A long time when you're waiting." Emily covered Jessica's hand with hers and was quiet a moment. "How's Megan taking it?"

"She cries at odd moments. Can't concentrate. I want to buy them a painting as a wedding present."

"You don't have to."

"I want to! It will mean a lot to her that it's yours."

"If she sees you've bought a painting as a wedding gift, it'll tell her you know he's coming home."

"Yes, that's good. Let me see your latest. Show me what's wet." Her voice, her smile, her eyes shouted expectation.

"Nothing. Not a tittle of painting, good painting, lately."

Emily winced at Jessica's expression, clearly a reprimand. She played idly with dried brushes in a jar, breaking their stiffness. "Sometimes I exhibit in the Island Arts and Crafts shows. That bunch of caterwauling old tabbies hang me so high only a giraffe could see a totem eye to eye, or else in the dark hallway by the washrooms. They get embarrassed when the press calls my work grotesques that I stoop to elevate as art. They say I have a diseased mind. It does me up purple."

"Burble," Joseph muttered. "Awk."

"You mean to say I've come across the strait just to find you've abandoned the only thing that ever mattered to you?"

"It's not what I planned. I can't seem to teach the floors to mop themselves, and I can't afford help." She saw Jessica check for paint under her nails. She curled her fingers under. "Don't make it sound so permanent."

"How long since you've had a painting spree? A year? Two?"

"More. What do you expect if I'm the only one who thinks I'm any good?" Shame burned. What about Harold? "Without work I'm not whole. Without friends I could be whole if I was working."

"Well, then. Isn't the solution obvious? Is it the war, Em?"

"Don't you have times when life bears down on you so that you can't paint?"

"No. I have times when I'm so exquisitely happy I can't paint. I don't have the detachment. And it doesn't matter. If I stopped painting, it wouldn't make any difference to the world, but you . . . Doesn't talent come with an obligation to use it? Do you want to dry up?"

She already had. Like a river during a summer drought.

"Maybe creativity has cycles. Bears hibernate. Tides ebb before they flow. Even the moon disappears. Dzunukwa dies for a while too."

"But she rouses herself."

"When she's ready. I'm not. I haven't resolved something."

"What?" Jessica's voice was softer.

"I don't know how to say it."

Jessica traced the lip of a teacup with her fingertip. "Don't you have to keep your work before the public eye?"

"I hate this scratching after recognition. It's a curse."

"Exactly, and the result of it is written all over your face—the

pain of the unexpressed. And you know why? Because you're peevish. Because you nurse your injuries, letting them paralyze you.
Letting ignorant people you loathe squeeze you dry while the ones
you care about, you forget."

"You came here to tell me that?"

"No. I came here to paint with you! Forget recognition!"

"The one thing necessary for my work to do its job?"

"Oh, Em, let go of that. Paint because you love it, because *you*
know your work is vibrant and strong and meaningful."

Emily took a tired breath. "Someone said so the other day, not in
those words. A strange sweet man-boy, but something's not quite
right about him." She touched her temple. "That's the kind who
like my work. Not parliamentary committees, but misfits, like me."

Jessica gave her a sympathetic smile. "What does that make me?"
she said, teasing. "Now will you let me choose a painting?"

"Go through that stack of watercolors, and those oils leaning
against the wall."

Jessica moved slowly about the room, taking in everything, including Tantrum's bed box, the cages for Joseph, Susie, and the
finches. "Starting a zoo?" She chuckled, and touched a ceramic frog.
"I didn't know the tribes here made pottery."

"They don't, but I do. A dribble of income. A former tenant sells
them at the Empress Hotel and in Banff. Tourist trade."

"They're marvelous."

"No, Jessica. They're stupid. False."

Jessica looked at a totem-shaped Raven vase and then picked up a
round pot with Sophie's salmon design across the belly. It slipped from
her hands and crashed to the floor. Shards and beach pebbles flew
across the room. Jessica gasped. Tantrum barked. Joseph squawked.
André ran upstairs. Billy just blinked.

"I'm so sorry. I didn't know it was heavy."

The salmon head lay in one piece. "It's only dirt," Emily managed to say, picking it up. "I'm ashamed of making them in the first
place."

Jessica looked up at her. "Why?"

"You know."

Jessica shook her head.

Emily grabbed a broom and swept vigorously. "They come from the wrong place in me. They make me feel I'm no better than a totem thief."

"That's only an excuse for not painting."

She dumped the shards and pebbles into a metal trash can, liking the tumultuous, decisive racket they made.

"Pick out another one you like. For Megan, from me."

"After I broke one?"

"Forget it. I wouldn't give a barleycorn for the lot."

Jessica stood in the middle of the room and turned in a circle, looking for something.

Emily laughed. "You look like you're in a puddle and don't know how to get out."

"What happened to that Haida one with two guardian birds?"

"Sold," Emily said sheepishly. "To Dr. Newcombe. And six others."

"Then what have you been grumbling about?" Jessica shrieked, and Joseph shrieked after her.

"He's taught me a great deal about native cultures."

"Yes! A collector! An educated man. Sometimes you're the most petulant, temperamental, perverse—"

"Cantankerous. Don't forget that. And cussed." Emily pointed to a leaning stack of paintings. "Pick."

"Ugh!" Jessica threw up her arms.

She chose the Raven vase, and an unframed oil on board of Alert Bay with a canoe in the foreground. "Megan will love this. Remember how you wanted to take the children to paint canoes?" Jessica opened her own portfolio and spread out her watercolors on the floor. "Now will you give me a critique?"

For an hour they deliberated over each one until Emily gathered brushes and watercolors and her cheapest paper. She set out a cold lunch for her boarders, and packed the extras. Downstairs she put everything in a maroon baby carriage, and lifted Tantrum in too.

Jessica laughed. "A pram?"

"I use it to cart clay from the beach cliffs. A disappearing tenant left it here when she couldn't pay. Want any old shoes? Frying pans? Books? There was one that's a treasure. By your own countryman. *Leaves of Grass.* Wait a minute."

She went back to get it and dumped it in the carriage. Billy picked his painful way down the stairs but managed to keep up the few blocks to the park.

They set up their easels on the grass facing the woods. It felt ex-hilarating to be swishing a brush around with a friend, but dear old Beacon Hill Park did nothing for her now. After two studies, she rinsed her brushes and spread out the picnic.

Jessica chewed on the end of her brush. "You're dissatisfied, aren't you?"

"How do you know?"

"If I could paint like you can, I'd be dissatisfied with those."

"I can't seem to tear myself away from needing native motifs. I can't get any spirituality out of the forest on my own, without the help of totem creatures."

"That's really at the bottom of it, why you stopped, isn't it?"

"Partly." She slapped her two watercolors face to face and ripped them right down the middle.

"Em! I didn't mean you should do that!"

"It's not you. It's me. I keep searching, but . . ." She stroked the grass, liking its tingle on her palm.

"Is that why you're reading poetry these days?"

"Oh, such a soul, this Whitman had. Listen." She found her marked page.

"The substantial words are in the ground and sea . . .
Were you thinking that those were the words, those delicious sounds out of
*   your friends' mouths?*
No, the real words are more delicious than they."

"See? You've got to find it somewhere else than in people."

"The masters know the earth's words and use them more than audible
*   words. . . .*
The earth does not argue, . . .
Makes no discriminations, has no conceivable failures,
Closes nothing, refuses nothing, shuts none out."

She bit into an apple, wondering how to listen more to messages from moss and trees and grass. She read the next marked section to herself.

Work on, age after age, nothing is to be lost.
It may have to wait long, but it will certainly come in use.

When?

• • •

They walked home on Dallas Road so they could see the shoreline. Sounds of the sea and gulls mixed with a steady, intensifying drumbeat. Smoke blew inland.

"Maybe Songhees are camping here," Emily said.

They looked at each other, wondering, and walked out to the cliff edge where they could see the beach. A lone figure danced around a fire, swirling, lunging erratically, stumbling over a crippled foot, beating on a drum. Her drum. His now. All he needed was an eagle feather, but he had given it to her.

"A white man. What do you think he's doing?" Jessica asked. "Making fun of Indians?"

"No. Making believe. He's the one who loves my paintings."

Sobered, Emily took Jessica's arm and led her away. Jessica looked at her quizzically.

"Look at those great boughs swing," Emily said to change the subject. "The wind makes everything alive. Look at those green and blue shadows dancing under the trees, the way light and dark chase each other harum-scarum. Without movement a subject is dead. Just look!" She squeezed Jessica's arm.

Jessica squinted in a cunning way. "How do you paint wind?"

"Ah! By making the trees go whiz-bang and whoop it up. By painting in thick, vigorous swirls." She traced curves in the air with her arm. "Wind connects everything in one satisfying whoosh."

A slow, shrewd smile crept over Jessica's face. "You'll get back to work. I know it. I can go home without worrying now."

30: Camas

Emily was sprinkling bread crumbs for a pair of doves that had taken residence in her front yard when Harold came down the sidewalk in his awkward, uneven gait, shaking a small brown bag.

"Hello, Harold. Listen." She pointed to the doves. "I'm joy-crazed with their mellow cooing."

"I am satisfied—I see, dance, laugh, sing," he said.

"That sounds familiar."

"Your book. Grass of Leaves." He grinned his delight at surprising her. "A poem called 'Walt Whitman, an American.' " He shook the bag again. "Seeds for the garden. Garden for the seeds."

In baggy pants and scuffed shoes, his blond cowlick sticking up, he seemed a boy still. They went into the back yard.

She'd been watching spring approach tentatively, a few leaves unfurling here, a pale patch of sun there, as if afraid of giving false cheer. Eventually the plants couldn't help it, and tried their best to make up for other shortcomings in the world. Brilliant lime green shoots made an exuberant fringe along the fence.

"Look at those wild yellow lilies shouting huzzah at just being alive."

He did a little wobbly dance mimicking their movement in the breeze and careening over his turned-in foot. Being with him made the world a shade more innocent, like the doves. She felt his contentment, and hers, on their hands and knees together loosening the soil. Every so often he crawled over to Billy lying under the maple, and petted him.

"That's good. He appreciates that," she said.

She dug holes with her finger, Harold dropped in the seeds, she covered them up. "Now the land will give comfort," she said.

He looked at her with suffering eyes. The defeated slope of his shoulders bore a consuming weight. "Illahee," he breathed.

"If there's anything I believe, Harold, it's that everything can grow. Nothing can kill the force that splits rocks to let a tiny seedling through."

He patted the ground, barely touching it. "The seeds need water."

She unfolded herself to get up at the same moment he did. He lurched in her direction, slamming into her shoulder and knocking her off balance. They both fell, sprawled on the ground in a tangle.

"I'm sorry I'm sorry I'm sorry," he said.

"Oof." She righted herself. "It's all right. I lose my balance too, lots of times."

"You do?"

"Does your foot pain you?"

He just grunted.

"Your ankle?"

He puckered up his lips to one side. If that meant yes, what could possess him to dance on it?

"How did it happen?"

"My father sent his snake spirit out to trip me."

"Tell me really."

He hung his head. "I fell into a deer trap and snapped my ankle. There was no doctor to fix it."

"How long ago?"

He shrugged. "I was only a boy. In Kispiox."

"Didn't your father take you somewhere? To Fort Rupert?"

He shook his head. "How come you lose your balance?"

It was only fair for him to ask.

"I was in a carriage accident. A razor-happy London surgeon decided my big toe had to be amputated."

She took off her shoe and wiggled her other four toes in her stocking. Looking as though he were about to cry, he cupped his toes in both hands and rocked.

"When we don't have something, we have to compensate, that's all. We have to find our balance in other ways."

"I'm sorry for you."

"What about your forehead?" she asked as delicately as she could.

He worked the fingers of both hands into the earth as if to anchor himself, and slowly, barely, he shook his head.

. . .

She'd been up with Billy all night brushing him gently and reminding him of all the villages they'd seen together, of the feel of moss at

Tanu, the smell of the grave house at Kitwancool. His eyes followed her movements until a moth distracted him. Even with her help, Billy had been unable to get up the ladder stairs to the attic bedroom, so she had stayed downstairs in the studio, telling him that she loved him, telling herself that she could manage this. Together they watched the black square of the window lighten to gray.

It was time. Past time. She'd wanted him to have a full summer, but now, the end of June was all she dared.

She couldn't let a veterinarian do it. Impossible to find one on Sunday. It wouldn't be fair to ask Harold. Horror clamped her like jaws. She'd have to do it herself.

The Almighty was testing her. *Let's just see how strong you are,* He said to Himself with a smirk. Of course to Himself. That's one thing she could grasp about God—His aloneness.

She took her handbag and cut through the neighbors' back yards, crossed the lane, passed Alice's schoolhouse and went in the back door of her sisters' house. Upstairs, she opened Father's bureau drawer. Even now, between his handkerchiefs, its blue-black barrel lay. Next to it, a box of cartridges. She took them both.

"What in God's name are you doing?"

She spun around to see Lizzie half dressed for church, her face white with shock. Emily shoved the gun in her handbag.

"It's Billy. Not another day. I have to."

"You can't be serious."

"An awful night. I'm taking him to the woods in the pram."

"And then what?"

Then what? She didn't know.

"Why don't you take him to that Indian's husband?"

"Jimmy Frank! Of course!"

If he'd be there. She hadn't seen Sophie for over a year.

"How'll you get the pram up the steps on the ferry?"

"Drag it, push it, stay below deck, I don't know." If she hurried, she could take the nine o'clock and come home on the overnight run.

"I'll help. I'll go with you."

"No. I'm going to give him mutton for breakfast. You can help me get him downstairs in a little while."

Going back through the yards, she hated herself for waiting so long. The stairs down to the back yard would be excruciating for him. He ate. She was glad of that. When she lifted his rear to help him up, his back legs quivered and collapsed. She waited for Lizzie, who lifted his shoulders while she lifted his hips, and they got him downstairs. Emily brought the pram alongside him. "Backward, so his head's looking out," she said. Billy went limp, as if accommodating them, but his front leg caught the handle which started the pram rolling so they had to chase it, carrying him. It should have been funny, but it wasn't.

With a compassionate, worried smile, Lizzie touched Emily's arm. "The Lord leadeth you beside still waters."

"Thank you." For once she envied Lizzie's faith.

Alice rushed into the yard out of breath. "I wasn't dressed when Lizzie told me. I was hoping you hadn't left yet."

She slowed when she came to the pram, buried her face in Billy's neck, and may have cried a little, softly, into his long hair. She straightened up.

"He's going to look up at you with that sad, knowing look all the way there. Do you want me to go with you?"

"No, Alice. You'll miss church."

"I'm going with you! Let me get my handbag."

"No. I'll be all right. Thank you both."

. . .

Billy revived a little on the ferry, smelling the sea and opening his mouth to gobble the wind. By the second ferry, he seemed to know he was going to the reserve where there'd be more smells. As a child squirming in church, she'd watched colors from the stained-glass window bathe the floor and pews in rainbow magic. She'd thought heaven must be like that, just swimming in colored light. For Billy, heaven must be swimming in smells—dead fish, pines, cedars, skunk cabbage, seaweed, and people.

She stopped the carriage in front of Sophie's open door.

"Ooh, Em'ly! You came again!" Sophie sang out from the doorway. "I prayed you don't forget me."

"Never think it for an instant."

The twins stepped outside. "See? My babies. Emmie"—Sophie touched her shoulder—"and Molly. Four years old."

Emily crouched to speak to each one. Molly was smaller. Emmie's eyes were still crossed. Would that make things blurry? Painterly? When she rose, she saw a quality of weariness in Sophie's face. Furrows from the corners of her mouth were forming, and shadows darkened the skin under her eyes.

Sophie looked at the pram in confusion. A few steps forward and she saw Billy. "Oh, so sad for you, Em'ly. So sad." She petted him on the head. "Poor Billy dog." Her face tightened into sorrow lines, but her fingers stroked the maroon fabric of the pram and lingered on the handle.

"Is Jimmy here?" Emily asked.

"No. He'll be back by and by. He went to see Samuel Dan's new gas boat."

"I was worried he'd be working."

"He don't work so much now, only small jobs on the dock."

Emily glanced toward Billy. "Do you think Jimmy would?"

Sophie nodded. "I'll ask Mrs. Johnson to tell him come to the meadow when he walks by. It's pretty there now, all flowers. Billy will like it."

Emily let the girls wheel the carriage uphill on the walk leading away from the sea. At the end of the planks, the wheels stuck in the soft soil. Carefully, Emily tipped the pram sideways onto the meadow and Billy edged his way out. His nose drew him onward in the swirl of summer scents, but his hind end dragged across the meadow grasses. Eventually he gave up and lay panting.

He maketh me to lie down in green pastures, Emily thought. In her own way, Lizzie had given her something.

Violet blue camas blossoms speckled the meadow, offering comfort. Emily threaded some through Billy's coat behind his left ear. The twins giggled and skipped off to gather more, not knowing it was done in sadness. Molly made a flower chain and looped it around Billy's neck. Emmie threaded the stems through the shaggy hair at his rump so the clump of blossoms looked like a pompon. Emily couldn't decide whether it was an annoyance to Billy, or whether it evoked an ancient sacred rite. Since he had let the girls do it, she thought it must be all right with him.

"Why did you bring him all the way here to Frank?"

"He likes Billy." She scratched Billy under his chin, his favorite spot. "And he knows about dying."

"A dog for a few years is better than no dog at all."

Emily managed a nod.

"I have enough money now for Tommy's gravestone. The grave man is making it with a cross carved on it. Very Christian. Next is Annie Marie so I keep to making baskets."

A good friend would encourage a woman who had that much need, like Jessica encouraged her. But what if the friend thought the endeavor was futile or wrong-headed?

"That's good, Sophie."

"They hard to sell these days. The war probably. It's awful. I feel sorry for the women here their sons are gone to it. Margaret Dan's brother is in France. She waits to hear."

"Waiting. That's all we do."

"You don't come to paint at the reserve anymore."

"I'd like to. Not today, though."

"You painted all the totem poles?"

"No. Some I haven't even seen."

"You quit?" Sophie's voice rose sharply. "Fat men in Victoria don't like them either? Then come live here. Here you learn not to give up."

Sophie's disgust entered her like a hot poker. Jessica's she could take, but Sophie was harder, when one reason she'd started the project in the first place was for Sophie. Or so she'd told herself at the time.

"Frank's brother say up north they cut down a pole for firewood." Her words were barbed.

"No. I can't believe it."

She lay her hand on Billy's side and felt long vacant moments between his breaths, as though he were deciding whether or not to take another one.

Jimmy came, and his girls ran to hold his hands. He saw at once what must be done. With a soft smile he said, "Sophie has missed you. See? Our girls are growing up now."

"They're happy children, I can tell."

Sophie led them away, back toward the village. They skipped

behind the baby carriage. She'd leave it with Sophie. There would be no more carting clay. The salmon pot had leapt out of Jessica's hands like a salmon leaping up river to die. She had truer things to do.

Jimmy petted Billy fondly, his head close to Billy's ear, and spoke to him in Squamish. When he stood up again, Emily opened her handbag and looked up at him. He nodded. Quickly, he shoved the gun in his waistband behind his jacket, took the cartridge box, and walked away about ten steps, his back toward Billy.

Emily lay on her stomach and put her cheek next to Billy's head and let him lick her face. With both hands she stroked his paws, scratched behind his ears, rubbed under his chin, along his neck, his back, his haunch that had taken that hurled rock meant for her. She couldn't stop looking at him, and he looked back in utter trust. With wet brown eyes, he said he was sorry he couldn't get up the stairs any more, sorry he knocked the baby carriage when she lifted him, sorry he had misbehaved at the grave house in Kitwancool, sorry he had wandered off when she was digging clay, sorry he made her frantic searching for him.

"You've been the best friend I've ever had," she said.

He blinked. She took it as an assent. Her hand stroked his head one last time, and she stepped back.

"Thank you, Jimmy. You're a good man."

Jimmy lifted him, cradling him powerfully against his chest, and took him into the forest.

She turned and walked quickly through the village to get to the sea so that waves and wind might out-roar any other sound. The girls were playing with seaweed on the beach. Sophie padded toward her. The distant shot riveted their attention to each other's faces.

"Come in the house," Sophie said. "I got fish soup. Maybe still warm."

Inside, Sophie rekindled the wood burner and Emily sank into a chair. Sophie set the soup before her, and watched with soft eyes each spoonful Emily ate. She ached to cry but was ashamed to in front of Sophie. A dog wasn't a child. Nor was it a man lost in war. "I knew it was inevitable, but . . ."

Sophie's arm came around her awkwardly, the first time ever. The feel of Sophie's palm on her shoulder blade cracked open the hold she had on herself. She sobbed.

"I know, I know," Sophie crooned, bending down to her, her hand steady on Emily's back, her body close, her braid smelling of wood smoke. "Billy was a good boy. A good boy. He loved you. You loved him back. I know."

31: Dzunukwa

Before landlady duties intruded the next day, she found a drawing of Sophie she'd done years before. It was nice, but it wasn't a painting. Portraits didn't have to be stiff and pretentious. They could show feeling and character and love. With only squeezed-flat tubes, she probably had enough paint for a small canvas board, but she'd have to use strange colors—a smudge of cadmium orange for her broad nose, violet for her sharply edged full lips, the upper one a bit fuller. She worked her cheeks in tints of raw sienna and red earth, then dulled it with a touch of violet and Prussian green under her eyes. But Sophie was strong—a streak of vermilion along her jaw—and enduring—viridian green for her cheekbones. The Fauve colors were enough to make her giddy.

Once Lizzie had pleaded with her to paint portraits instead of totem poles. When she finished and was cleaning her brushes, something mischievous ignited in her, and she took the painting across the lane and in the side door. "Look, Lizzie. A portrait."

"Why would you want to paint a siwash woman?"

"Because I love her." Emily looked her dead in the eye. "She was good to me yesterday. So was Jimmy."

Lizzie's expression changed, as though she were seeing some aspect of her sister's life she'd never ventured to think about before. "I'm sorry." Her voice softened. "I prayed for you all day yesterday." Studying Sophie's face, she added, "Maybe my prayers were answered."

· · ·

When Emily returned home with the painting, a young man in olive tweed with longish hair, a stranger, stood at her door. His pant legs were tucked into tall laced boots like the puttees of soldiers in news photos.

"Excuse me, are you Emily Carr, the artist?" He took off his canvas hat. Spots trailing down his green tie looked like rabbit tracks.

"I'm Emily Carr."

"The artist?"

"Depends on which day you come. Today, yes. Tomorrow, landlady, boardinghouse cook, plumber, gardener, poultry farmer."

He nodded toward Sophie's portrait. "I'm sure I have the right person. I'm Dr. Marius Barbeau, cultural anthropologist at the Victoria Memorial Museum in Ottawa. Is it possible you could show me your paintings?"

"I don't wish to show them to people who are unsympathetic. I have no energy to put myself back together again."

"I'm sure I'd be sympathetic, just from what I can see in your hand." His smile made his words seem genuine.

She opened the door. "Come in."

Catching sight of *Dzunukwa*, he puffed out his cheeks. "Yes, indeed! Magnificent."

"How did you learn about me?"

"Does the name Luther Moody mean anything to you?"

"Yes. Mosquitoes and mud."

"He said you painted up the Skeena. Some poles that aren't there anymore."

"Which ones?"

"Aha! I had a hunch you'd care. I've seen Dr. Newcombe's collection."

"He thought they were inaccurate."

"Yes, well, he sees like a scientist," Barbeau said.

"And you?"

"I like to think I see like a . . . a whole man. Art and culture and science all together." He looked at *Dzunukwa*. "You understand poles."

"Not all the crests. And not the histories."

"But the feeling. I trust your interpretation." He noticed *Totem Mother*, stepped back and glanced behind him for a place to sit. The only chair was piled with tenants' curtains to be laundered. She lowered another chair from the ceiling pulley. He looked at the mechanism and chuckled. "Inventive."

"Practical." She propped up paintings until the room was a forest of totems. "Sometimes I don't know why I'm doing them."

His eyebrows pinched together. "Why are you?"

"Once I thought it was to make a record. Now I think it's to be close to some spirit I don't understand—yet. To honor the people who do. And to express my love for the West."

"I can see that." He gave attention to each one, identifying the Skeena ones by place and history, asking about Kwakiutl and Haida poles he hadn't seen.

"What did you do up the Skeena?" she asked.

"I collected poles and artifacts and legends."

Collected! Like teacups or porcelain cats. Taking them away from their people. Her hand squeezed the chair's rope. "For a museum?"

"Yes, and for my anthropological interests. I appreciate things people make with their hands." He hadn't taken his eyes from the paintings. "You have an individuality and strength I haven't seen in other West Coast artists other than carvers."

She brought out *Kispiox Village*, and *Frog Woman*, and the large Tanu oil of three house ruins and their frontal poles.

"That one with the frogs is extraordinary. Where's it from?"

"Kitwancool."

"You've been to Kitwancool? Unbelievable!"

"Why?"

"They don't let anybody in. A constable shot their chief once and they went wild until the BCPP put down the uprising. It turned into a blood bath. Ever since, they've been hostile."

"I didn't know."

"How long were you there?"

"Five days."

"Unbelievable! They knew you were painting poles?"

"Yes."

She brought out more, and pointed to *Totem Mother* on the wall. "These are all from Kitwancool."

He smacked his forehead in amazement. "If I might say so, you a woman."

"Maybe that's an advantage. Threats to their way of life usually come in a male package."

He took an hour enjoying all of them, chatting about the places. Finally he leaned two against a chair, *Kispiox Village* and *Kitsegukla*. "I'd like to buy these two, if they're for sale. Are they?"

Her legs melted like icicles in an unexpected thaw and she sat on the pile of curtains. *I have the spirit power,* she heard, distant but sure, Dzunukwa putting herself together again.

"Yes." The word a tight chirp, not at all like Dzunukwa's low hoot.

He rested his forearms on his knees. His smile expressed a manly kindness. "They're marvelous. They have a strangeness yet a sensitivity."

She blew her nose and wiped her eyes. "Pardon me. I've been an ugly duckling so long I thought I'd been squashed flat forever."

"How much?" he whispered.

"It's been years . . . I don't know how to think in price."

He wrote out a check and held it out to her. It trembled in her hand. More than she'd collected in rents for two months. She leaned a Kitwancool bird and man canvas against the others he'd chosen. "Here, take this one too. You've been looking at it."

"Why, thank you! With your permission, I'd like to keep in touch. Eventually, I think, there will be interest in what you're doing. It's faint now, but there's a growing urge for Canada to find its identity in the landscape, particularly the less trodden places. That has to include the places of our indigenous peoples. I know some folks at the National Gallery—"

"Then you think it's all right, what I'm doing?"

He looked puzzled.

"I mean, using Indian motifs." He was hardly the one to give her an objective answer.

"Miss Carr, what you are doing is of inestimable importance. To native cultures, to Canadian art, to Canada itself."

A breath held too long in some deep part of her gushed out.

She walked with him downstairs and watched him carry her paintings down the street. There they went, *Kispiox* too, Harold's illahee. What would he do without them?

She waved with both arms above her head, wanting to whoop, but felt a twinge, for Harold.

Barbeau turned back to her and shouted, "Don't strap yourself to a dishpan. Paint!"

32: Maple

A soiled white sky pressed against the window. She pressed back, the glass cold on her palms, the fog flecked with snow, dressing the maple branches in the back yard, separating her from the world. She sat down to write her Christmas note to Jessica on a folded sheet of paper. On the front she drew herself, roly-poly, bending down to stoke the coal furnace wearing a Mother Hubbard dress, tall boots, and a Santa Claus cap with an eagle feather. Inside, she wrote:

> *Six months of war since your visit. Life wags on. I'm still waiting to hear from that anthropologist in Ottawa. Everything except the war effort has ground to a halt. The world can't exist this way much longer. I worry about Megan's fiancé.*
>
> *Last summer, I moved my paintings and easels into the basement so I could rent the studio too. I slept in the back yard in my tent which horrified Lizzie. Lovely cricket lullabies and moon gleam but no privacy to paint. I'm back in my studio now that chilly weather has set down its haunches, and Dzunukwa is back on the wall singing her power song. If only I could make out the words. I've learned streams of Whitman by heart. He bucks me up when I need it, telling me that "through anger, losses, ambition, ignorance, ennui, what you are picks its way." Still, I resent not having time for the spiritual in tending to the physical.*
>
> *Are there any paints in Vancouver? Impossible to get any here. If Vancouver had some, it'd be worth the price of the ferry. I'd sit up in my coffin if I could get some viridian or Hooker's green. Let's pray the American forces make 1918 the last horrible year.*
>
> *Oceans of love to you and the girls, Emily*

A week later a small parcel arrived. A crumpled tube rolled most of the way up, viridian, with a note.

> *Better on your canvas than mine. No paint in Vancouver.*
>
> *Love, Jessica*

Emily unscrewed the cap and saw a shiny circle of deep green, a color so gorgeous it practically put her eyes out. But what could a single crust do for a starving woman? Should she ration it like everything else or indulge herself in one luscious green painting? She dug out her box of oils, a few cracked tubes pressed flat and rolled, saved for the hope of squeezing out a brush stroke. She jabbed with her penknife at the promising ones to pry back the metal. One painting's worth. Kispiox. For Harold. He'd wept when he discovered it missing. She'd told him that was the pain of painting. A farewell accompanied every grain of success.

She looked for a roll of canvas, and realized she'd used the last to replace a window shade in an apartment. Cardboard would have to do.

She cupped the tube in her palm, paralyzed by fear of wasting it on mediocre work. *You want green paint? Here's a smear of it. Now what'll you do?* God, leaning over a cloud to watch, testing her spunk. She closed her eyes and squeezed out tears.

You can't do everything you want to, my little nympholept, Father had said. She'd been making a Songhees village of wet sand on the beach, hurrying to repair crumbling bighouses after each wave until, in one violent whoosh, the village was flattened to a few pathetic lumps. Maybe, as he'd watched her sob, he'd seen her tendency to beat her head against a wall trying the impossible. Maybe that was why he discouraged her artistic leanings. Could he have been that insightful?

She supposed she could pray. Dear God, send me a sign, clear enough that I can understand. Am I a landlady or an artist? If Barbeau was the sign, then why do I still feel like a wet rag? Please don't let it all be for naught.

No. That was one prayer she'd just have to swallow. It was a disservice to God to put such strains on Him. He had bigger concerns on His mind right now.

· · ·

"Read me *Leaves of Grass,*" Harold pleaded when he'd put away the rake.

He dropped in frequently to do odd jobs—cleaning out the furnace, painting the porch steps, building a bird feeder. She'd read it to him once, not that he couldn't read it on his own. He just en-

joyed the intimacy of being read to. Afterward he started asking for
it at every visit.

"When I finish serving the boarders their lunch."

Harold sat cross-legged on the floor and waited, reading it himself. After the boarders left he handed it to her and said, "Start with
'Walt Whitman, an American.' You know, *Stop this day and night with
me and you shall possess the origin of all poems.*"

They shared a cigarette while she began reading there and
continued.

> *"I know that the hand of God is the promise of my own,*
> *And I know that the spirit of God is the brother of my own,*
> *And that all the men ever born are also my brothers, and the women my*
> *   sisters and lovers."*

She stopped to think, and looked at him, his eyes dewy, hugging
himself, as if he were being filled to bursting. He was too different
to be accepted by anyone but another living oddity. She had to
pour her love somewhere, or it would dry up as her painting had.
Maybe that's what love was—walking willingly into the unknown
for the sake of the other. The sheen in his eyes told her he absorbed it like a thirsty desert.

· · ·

On the morning of November 12, 1918, Emily went down the outside stairs to light the coal furnace, unfolded the newspaper and
read, "Armistice Signed, World War Ends." She whooped through
the hallway pounding on tenants' doors. Soon she heard people
outside beating on pots and pans. Lizzie rushed into her apartment,
fell into her arms and wept. Emily heated water for tea and let
down all the chairs from their pulleys. Tenants who hadn't spoken
to each other for months hugged and huddled around the newspaper, afraid to believe. Alice brought scones. At eleven o' clock, to
represent the official end of the war in Europe the day before, Mr.
Pixley stood on a chair and read the newspaper:

*"At 5:00 in the morning of November 11, the German delegation at Compiègne
signed the armistice, by which the German army is to retreat and surrender its*

weapons and aircraft, the German navy is to be interned, and the Allied forces are to occupy the Rhineland. By 11:00 a.m., the 1,586th day of the war, all firing stopped."

Emily imagined Megan's fiancé climbing out of a trench to stand upright in unaccustomed safety, stunned by silence, marveling that he had survived. Were Fanny and Gibb celebrating? What about Héloïse and Madame Bagot? Or were they too numb?

At Sunday's supper, Lizzie's grace was simply a Bible verse. "To every thing there is a season. A time to kill, and a time to heal." Lizzie looked up after the Amens. "With God's forgiveness, I've found a greater need than missionary work," she said softly. "After two months of training, I can work as a physical therapist's aide at the veterans' hospital. Maybe I can help those poor damaged men."

Emily saw a yearning for approval in Lizzie's expression she'd never seen before. She wanted to stand up and cheer, but such overwhelming endorsement might crush Lizzie's empathetic leanings. "That's a fine, upright thing to do," she said, patted Lizzie's wrist, and held on.

The whole city seemed to crave lightheartedness. There were rousing concerts in the park again. Alice planted tulip, hyacinth, and daffodil bulbs, not just vegetables, and as soon as they bloomed in the spring, Lizzie took pots of them to the veterans' hospital.

Emily found a new way to earn money. The government offered land to returning soldiers to raise sheep. They'll need sheep dogs, she reasoned. She could breed them. She bought two females, hired a male for breeding, dispensed with boarders, and rented full apartments. No more boarders eating in her studio. She set up easels, stretched canvases, ordered paint, and waited for it. Meanwhile, puppies upon puppies arrived. Harold was beside himself.

"Don't get too attached," she warned. "They're for profit."

She took him with her to the pet shop to advertise her first litter. Smelling of animal urine and feed, the shop was a riot of barks and peeps and screeches. Harold went from cage to cage imitating all the sounds. A baby Capuchin monkey with a wrinkled black Kewpie face and a gray spurt of fluff on top of her head reached her hand out of the cage toward him.

"Aw," he said, and turned to Emily.

The monkey blinked her apple green eyes and squealed, "Woo."

"You know how I'm a sucker for cowlicks," she said, grinning at his, but thinking that another creature to feed other than for profit was self-indulgent extravagance.

Prudence be hanged. She'd been prudent for the whole war. She'd worn prudence like a hair shirt.

"Will you take a sheep dog pup for that monk?" she asked the proprietor, and the deal was struck.

They walked home with Woo on a leash. By the end of the afternoon Woo had unscrewed the salt shaker and sprayed a white rain over the kitchen end of the studio, leapt onto the bullfinch cage on the back porch, and terrorized Susie, huddled in the far corner of her cage, her tail wrapped tightly around her. Woo pinched Tantrum into knowing his place in the scheme of things. Eventually Harold got them to scuffle in play like two kittens, and Woo grew accustomed to the radius of chain in a monkey-proofed corner where the quieter discovery of curiosities close at hand sufficed.

. . .

Lizzie brought over a pan of hot biscuits the next morning, and immediately Woo jumped on her. Lizzie screamed, "Wild beast," and jerked the biscuits away. One fell and Woo snatched it. "A monkey? Honestly, Millie, what next, an elephant?"

"Look. She likes it." Woo ate the biscuit, and her little hands picked up the crumbs. "See? She's a proper monk."

"Fauvism and now Darwinism! This is carrying your modernisms too far."

They laughed. The world, healing itself at last, like new skin after a burn, was too tender for hostility, even a shred.

33: Arbutus

One afternoon Harold arrived hugging to his chest a shoe box bound with yards of dirty string. "Please please come to the beach," he said, his cowlick trembling with urgency. "Now."

"As soon as I finish." She gave the mixture in the bucket one last stir and then poured it into pans to harden into cakes of soap, two years' worth at least, cheap.

He put the box on the mantel and sat on the floor to play with the animals. He loved Woo best, as strange and mysterious a creature as he was. Carefully, he took her tiny hand in his and played "this little piggy" with her thin fingers, speaking it to her softly. Watching all his movements, her eyes close together as if in a perpetual study of something curious, Woo gave Harold more rapt attention than he probably ever got from humans. As a result, he visited more, and in her secret self, Emily knew that was what she'd hoped for.

With Tantrum on one leash and Woo on another, they walked along the Dallas Road cliffs edged with graceful arbutus trees. On the beach, Harold began to gather driftwood. "We have to have a fire."

"But it's July!"

She knew she shouldn't indulge him playing Indian. He screwed up his face and she realized that denying him might push him to some precipice.

"All right. We'll have a fire."

She lit a cigarette and sat leaning against a drift log, loving the slender trunks of arbutus trees, their paper-thin bark in russet and mauve, except where it had peeled away and revealed the tree's raw, saffron and lime green core.

"Are you ready?" Harold shouted. "I've been asking and asking."

In a haze, she turned toward him and was instantly alerted by his air of seriousness, sitting cross-legged near the fire. "I'm sorry. Yes, I'm ready."

With great ceremony he untied the string on the shoe box and wrapped it around his wrist. He pulled out a wrinkled paper and flattened it against his thigh. Woo grabbed for it, and Emily shortened her rope so she couldn't reach.

Harold's cheek twitched. He straightened his back and read.

"*Harold Cook a Canadian. I write myself. Haste on with me. I Harold Cook author of this book was born September 14, 1885. My parents were Mr. Luke Cook and Mrs. Martha Cook. Dead now. They were missionaries. I Harold Cook have one sister Ruth Cook. We lived in villages with Indians. Kispiox Kitwanga Kitsegukla Hagwelget. With Eagle, Bear, Raven who makes strong talk.*"

His story at last. She braced herself. His blue eyes flecked with gold looked up to see if she was listening. For the three and a half years she'd known him he'd only told her scraps of his past and then his face would cloud over and he'd stop. What had boiled or melted inside to let him begin? The death of his parents? The loss of the Kispiox painting? The end of the war?

"I Harold Cook author of this book played with Gitksan boys but my sister Ruth Cook did not. They sent her back to Victoria to live with my aunt Mrs. Flora Cook. I played with boys around the totem poles racing games and hiding games and hunting games. Kitwanga and Kispiox we fished in the Skeena River. Kispiox and Kitsegukla we fished in lakes and heard loons. We climbed trees. We made fires. We made raven calls and owl whooings. We crawl in caves. In Kispiox Tuuns and Muldo and Haaydzims taught me to make bows and arrows for hunting."

He read not like he talked, but like he walked, in fits and starts, conquering rattling fears with every breath. His account told of hunting squirrels with his Gitksan friends.

"He just stops he won't move won't run. Eyes all escaired. My arrow went in. I petted his fur but he doesn't breathe. Haaydzims taught me how to skin it so I saved the fur and tail. I brought it to Mrs. Martha Cook hanging by its feet from a branch the Indian way. If you were there you could see how clean the arrow hole the Indian way. Mrs. Martha Cook screamed and Mr. Luke Cook whipped the Indian out of me."

More trouble hid behind his strangeness than she'd imagined.

He described nightly prayers on bent knees around a Bible from which his father read verses exhorting against savagery and killing. Harold had kept the squirrel skin hidden under his bed and took it out at night to pet. When his mother discovered it by its smell, the screaming began again.

"So I am put on my knees and read to over and over Thou shalt not kill."

He looked up at her, expectant, his leg trembling, his fractured heart bare.

"I want to hear more," she whispered.

Harold searched for another scrap from the box and held it out for her to read. His jerky handwriting dipped down the page.

"No. You read," she said.

He cleared his throat.

"Harold Cook a Canadian. Haste on with me. I Harold Cook author of this book was the only white boy at Lejac Indian Residential School. Boys brought there kicking from far away. Months of cryings little boys big boys for missing

their mamas and fathers and grandparents and uncles and aunties. Mr. Luke Cook and Mrs. Martha Cook worked at the school. They taught Tsimshian boys English and praying. When Muldo and Tuuns say Tsimshian words Mr. Luke Cook beat them with his whip. They still speak Tsimshian so they were tooken gone somewhere. I don't see them for days. When they come back they don't speak anything. They have hurt marks all over. We had to count off in rows but they don't know it so I tell Muldo to say seven and Tuuns to say eleven. Then Muldo call Tuuns eleven. He thought it was his new name. Mrs. Martha Cook cut their hair. They screamed and kicked her. She tied their arms and legs around chairs to cut their hair. Then they looked like me."

Emily felt sick.

He turned over the paper, took a big breath that raised his chest. She passed him the cigarette and he inhaled, bolstering himself.

"Mrs. Martha Cook teach them Onward Christian Soldiers and A Mighty Fortress is Our God. When a bell rang we march in rows to the dining room. They had to sing it before they could lift a fork. When they didn't sing it Mr. Luke Cook made me sing it first. Then they fed me and so then the boys sang. Mrs. Martha Cook fed them but they eat with their hands. They know Mrs. Martha Cook hated that.

"One day I didn't sing it. Mr. Luke Cook told me to sing it. I didn't sing it. He broke a chair and held up the leg of it. Sing it he said. I didn't sing it. He beat me in my face with it. Blood sprayed."

Harold's forehead twisted with the memory. Fear of what he'd revealed shone in his eyes.

"Oh, Harold, no. Your own father?"

Harold hung his head and nodded.

"What a terrible thing. I'm so sorry."

He was a crossover child, an embarrassment to his parents. Not normal. Not loved. Fragile. Rebellious. Brave. A messenger of wounds ignored. Covered up. Across the fire, his eyes possessed a haunted lus-ter. In them she saw some part of herself. Lines squirmed across his forehead. Any second he would crack if she didn't do something. She put Woo in his lap, gathered them both in her arms and cradled his head against her bosom, crooning the comfort sounds she'd heard So-phie use.

She knew now, rocking him. It all became plain to her. Her art did not touch the core, did not illuminate the pain of Harold's friends and hundreds like them. She'd still been seeing with story-book eyes. Her paintings pictured only the glories of the villages, what Harold wanted to remember. That's why he fed on them so, to save himself. But were they true?

She would go to the reserve. She would take her painting things. She would not quail to see what was there. She would see with Harold's eyes. She would paint with the juice of his heart. All this time she'd been waiting for some sign when it was here all along. In Harold.

"Is it all right, what I wrote?" he said against her bosom.

"Yes, Harold. It's brave and beautiful. It makes strong talk."

34 : Salmon

Emily smelled a rank stew of fish offal and human waste as she walked the plank path of the reserve. With people from Kitsilano Point living here now, more garbage lay strewn on the beach waiting for the tide. In all the years she'd been coming here, the conditions of the village hadn't improved. Rusty buckets lying at doorways, rags flapping on bushes, barefoot children, lean, leprous dogs prowling for food—the picture was the same, only it struck her more profoundly now.

Sophie's house leaned drunkenly on its rotting drift log foundation. Emily peeked inside. "Yoo-hoo. Sophie? Anybody here?"

No one answered. She knocked on Mrs. Johnson's door.

"She's probably fishing," Mrs. Johnson said. "It's the first day of the Salmon Moon."

"Do you know where?"

She hesitated, considering. "The river beyond the graveyard. The dog salmon have come."

"Thank you."

The war's end must have mellowed even the Queen of Grump.

Canoes and gas boats bobbed in the inlet. Emily greeted deaf old Charlie Dan, Margaret Dan's father-in-law, and wondered if as a boy he had been beaten for speaking Squamish. Working in a line of people pulling in a net, Margaret Dan gave her a quick nod.

Sophie stood upstream on a boulder surrounded by shallows, gaff pole in hand, sleeves pushed up. Emily walked toward her. Pale fish with wide vertical stripes darted below the water's surface or jumped out entirely. Less fortunate ones caught between rocks lay gashed, their entrails spilling.

On the bank, a girl coiled a rope of rushes into a spiral. Her dark hair shone iridescent—the ghost of Annie Marie. Emily looked for her twin. Nowhere.

"Hello," Emily said. She noticed her crossed eyes. "You're Emmie. Do you remember me—Emily?"

"Ye-es." Her voice started low, then rose.

"You have some big salmon here, Emmie."

"Mama get them."

"They're fine-looking fish."

Actually some of them looked bizarre, their upper lips hooked over the lower like a parrot's beak, and long, pointed teeth stuck out their closed mouths.

The girl swished the rushes in the air to wave away flies. Emily felt an invisible cord connecting her to the child.

Sophie extended the long gaff pole out into the current and held still for a moment. Her arms had grown ropy, which made them interesting. She yanked the pole toward her, impaling a fish on the large barbed hook. In a quick movement she flung it backward onto the rocks, and saw her.

"Em'ly!" Her smile brimmed with gladness. "See? Emmie grew up strong." She raised her voice triumphantly over the rushing water. "Emmie, this is Em'ly come to see us."

Emily stepped onto the boulder to speak quietly. "Where's Molly?"

"Died of life. A year ago."

"Why didn't you write me?"

Sophie shook her head slowly. "Some spirit made it happen. Some spirit doesn't like me." Bewilderment sagged her features.

"Spirit? A Catholic spirit or an animal spirit?"

A brief smile crossed Sophie's face at the question. "Squamish believe in a lot of things."

"Tell me how it happened."

Sophie let a fighting salmon swim by.

"When Molly was sick, I didn't sleep good. No storm that night.

No wind. Nothing. Everything still. Then a big crack like a branch breaking off a tree in a storm, but no storm. In the morning, she was dead."

"What's that have to do with spirits?"

"So I go to the graveyard, and Ancestor was all broke and lying on the ground."

A noisy puff of exasperation escaped Emily's mouth. Sophie's reasoning was illogical, but anything she said would undermine Sophie's slender hold on the cause she'd invented, or accepted. She wondered what it meant when one lost his ancestor—or when a whole community did. She felt trapped by the rigors of native belief.

Emily looked back at the child, her brown legs stretched out beyond the wet hem of her dress, poking bark strands into the coil, absorbed. "She's pretty. I bet you looked like her when you were a little girl. She reminds me of Annie Marie."

"Me too," Sophie said. "She'll be good at making baskets by and by, but not as good as Annie."

The thought of it—Sophie teaching each girl, the sorrow of starting over, yet the hopefulness.

If she had taken Molly, the original Emmie, to live with her as Sophie had offered, would she be alive now? She couldn't have taught her basket making, but she would have gone to Alice's kindergarten, then to school. They would have had happy times, Alice and Lizzie too. Both houses would have been filled with laughter and singing.

But who was she to think that she, Emily Carr, white Canadian, would have been the superior, cleaner, more alert mother, able to prevent what happened? The wrongness of her own thinking slapped her in the face.

"Did you get another Billy dog?" Sophie asked.

"I got two girl dogs to have puppies to sell. They're nice but they're not like Billy, not like an old friend. It's a business."

"Business? You don't paint?"

"A little. But I need to paint deeper. Otherwise I fail."

"Fail?" The word cut the air. "You go with me to the graveyard." Emily's eyes stung and she shrank inside. "I'm sorry."

Years of effort had left Sophie spent. The whites of her eyes were threaded with red, the plum-colored pupils veiled by a misty white film.

Young men wading in the river laid rocks in a row. They were about the age Tommy would be now. How proud Sophie would have been to see her son among them.

"What are they doing?" Emily asked.

"Making a tide wall. When the tide goes out, the fish can't go back out. Easy to catch."

"Easy? They don't have a chance!"

They were tragic creatures, the instinct to leave something behind making them thrash upstream against all odds to unleash their eggs or sperm in one grand moment of fulfillment. She understood that urge. But then, spent with the effort, they died.

"Is Jimmy fishing?"

"No. He's loading wood on ships. A strike is why. Twenty-seven cents an hour. Indian pay. Some days he works eighteen hours. Some days he waits all day and nothing." Sophie poised her gaff and yanked it into another salmon.

"Mama, look!" Emmie ran toward them holding out her coil.

"That's good, Emmie. You're getting better. Don't forget to count." Sophie stepped onto the bank. "Enough fish. We'll get more tomorrow and Emmie will learn how to smoke them."

They put the fish into Sophie's big basket and Emmie's smaller one. Sophie placed the woven cedar tumpline across her forehead to support the basket against the small of her back. Emmie did the same with hers, a miniature of her mother.

On the way home, they picked pink swamp roses to scatter on the children's graves. Emmie lingered at the gate, amused by a spider in a web, but Sophie padded softly to Tommy's new headstone. Emily followed. Brilliant white in the sun, the stone had shiny flecks that caught the light like tiny fish scales. *In loving memory, Tommy Frank 1902–1908.* Sophie knelt and traced the cross with her fingertips.

"I was so happy when I had the money. When the graveman saw I had it, he said the price was more. When I had it again, he said he want to do stones for white people first. I only tell *you* this. Not Margaret Dan." She patted the stone, sat back on her heels, and let some rose petals fall. "No matter. Now Tommy has a Christian headstone and so now I sleep more easy."

It did matter. As much as Harold's friends being prohibited from speaking their language mattered. But if Sophie slept easier, she had to keep her lips fastened with a safety pin.

They paused at Annie Marie's grave, half hidden by a vine snaking across it. Emily pulled it off and scattered her petals.

"Now I show you Molly's grave," Sophie said. "Next to get a stone."

Molly's rough wooden cross bore the inscription, *Molly Frank 1913–1919.* Sophie set down her basket next to it and scattered the rest of her petals. Emily regarded each thing before her—those pathetic dates scratched unevenly, the cross tilted, shriveled lady ferns from Sophie's last visit, fish heads with hooked snouts and jagged teeth spilling out of Sophie's basket, the swamp petals. This was what she should paint if she wanted to paint the truth of native life.

Her hand went to the watercolor pad in her canvas sack, but she could not bring it out. She could not make a painting of Sophie's pain.

"Now that Jimmy is working, it won't be so hard to buy the other stones." Emily hated herself for saying an improbability so cheerfully.

"No. He uses his money for drink. One time I took it for headstones and he beat me. Now I get it by myself."

"Oh, Sophie, no!" It was hard to believe. Jimmy had been so kind to her with Billy.

"Don't think bad, Em'ly. It's just the way."

Emily placed her palm on the earth of Molly's grave. "It's a hard thing being a woman."

"Christian woman," Sophie corrected.

"Squamish Christian woman," Emily said.

They walked past the sunken spot where the ancestor figure used to be, now only a few decayed scraps of wood.

"See? Ancestor's all broke and gone." Sophie walked to the fence and gazed beyond the graves at the sea. "Other Indian babies sometimes live. White women's babies almost always do. I must be bad."

"No, Sophie. You're not bad."

Sophie turned to her with hard, wet eyes. "Then tell me why my babies die."

It would be cruel to say they died because she didn't take them to a white doctor. She imagined Sophie praying to God or Ancestor or Jesus or Mother Mary, or some private spirit, alternating in confusion or desperation, making the rounds, fearing Raven or God or that Kak-woman, stealer of children.

"I can't, Sophie."

As they walked back along the beach, Emmie splashed through ivory foam. "Mama, how does the water know how far to come?"

"It just knows, like trees know when to stop reaching up. A spirit tells each wave. Each tree. Everything."

Sophie studied the ground as they walked.

"What are you looking for?" Emily asked.

"Nice shells. To tell me of sins, so at confession I'll tell Father John every one. If I forget one, I go to hell, he says." She brushed off sand from a shell. "Then I can't see my babies."

"Sarah told me once they go to the sunset."

"She meant heaven. Bad people go to hell." A flicker of playfulness passed her lips. "Father John says."

"Has Father John or the church given you any comfort?"

Sophie squeezed one eye closed and left the other open, as if in hard concentration. "Sometimes."

"Do you know about Dzunukwa?" Emily asked. "A Kwakiutl story woman who lives in the woods and steals children?"

"Like Kaklaitl?"

"Yes, but sometimes she brings treasures too. Good and bad, all part of one thing."

"That's just an Indian story."

She had to be careful. "Maybe church is like that. Good and bad."

Sophie shrugged, watching Emmie slap her feet down in shallow water.

"You talk about spirit. I think we all go where spirits gather," Emily said. "Good or bad, with or without church. Your own spirit in you will naturally lead you to your babies."

Hope lifted Sophie's cheeks. "What about yours?"

"I'm not sure I've found one yet. I keep searching. I hope it's a cedar tree. For a while I thought Killerwhale was my spirit, because I saw whales just as I was deciding to paint all the totem poles. Later I thought so because he dives deep and is gone a long time, but I saw one dead on a beach and it stank, just like any other dead animal."

"Like salmon," Sophie said. "Dying to give birth."

35: Woo

Emily opened the window to the back yard and saw Harold reeling from side to side, stacking driftwood he'd gathered. His voluntary acts of devotion always moved her. His damaged ankle and foot made him stumble and he fell over the handle of the wheelbarrow, upsetting it and spilling the driftwood over him.

"Thank you, Harold. That's thoughtful of you. Come inside."

He fed the breeding griffons, smaller and cheaper to feed than sheep dogs, and then he came upstairs. He looked at the drawing she was working on.

"It's only an imaginary forest. It doesn't have any life." She propped up her old drawing of Lulu and the menstrual hut against a stack of books. Maybe thinking of Lulu saying, *All is one*, might help her to understand forests.

Harold ran through Joseph's repertoire and took Woo off her short chain in her monkey-proof corner for his ritual wiggling of her toes. He promised to watch so she wouldn't get into things.

"Today I am forty years old," he announced.

"Happy birthday, Harold. I didn't know." He seemed without age to her. She put a bowl of custard before him. "We'll have to imagine this as a cake."

"How old are you?"

The question caught her. She'd tried not to notice the onset of tiredness. She glanced at her drawing of Lulu, who probably had children of her own now. "Let's see. It's 1925. Fifty-few, I suppose. Sometimes I feel like an old drift log buffeted about and driven ashore to dry up and rot. I look thick as a log too."

Harold tipped his head, puzzling over that. "I think you look like an Indian." His eyes had all the sincerity of a child.

He was right. Added weight had given her an Indian body.

"Why, thank you. I don't know when I've had a finer compliment."

He smiled in a satisfied way and sucked custard from his spoon.

That was the outer vessel. She still had to work on the inner. "What do you think being an Indian means?" she asked.

"It means you live free. Dance when you want to. Eat and sleep when you want to."

"There was a time when I thought that too, but they're anything but free. Going to jail for potlatching isn't being free. Being beaten for speaking their language isn't either. What else does it mean?"

"It means you see spirits in birds, trees, wind, animals."

"How?"

"The look of things. Muldo said he sees eyes in the forest."

In the forest sketch she was working on, she saw an opening between trees, and drew in it an almond-shaped totem eye with a large black disk as a pupil, lurking. In another place whorls of foliage could be a raven's head if she added a beady eye and shaped the greenery into a beak. She held it up. "Like that?"

Custard plopped off his spoon. "Yes."

She finished the drawing and propped it next to Lulu's.

" 'Walt Whitman, an American'?" he asked.

She opened to a passage they both liked, and read.

"I think I could turn and live with the animals,
  they're so placid and self contained.
I stand and look at them long and long . . .
They do not lie awake in the dark and weep for their sins."

The buzzer startled them. Emily opened the door.

A thin man wearing a rose-colored homespun jacket and wool scarf stood in the doorway, smiling. "I hope you remember me. Marius Barbeau?" He turned his felt hat in his hands. "I visited you—"

"At the turn of the century." Time cut sharp since Harold had made her think about birthdays.

He laughed. "Not that long ago!"

"Well then, during the war."

He didn't look older. His long hair was still brown, bushy above his ears, his ruddy skin textured like an overripe grapefruit. He still had that irrepressible smile. And here she was, in her hair net and waistless homemade dress. Old Mrs. Saggy Socks.

"I bought some paintings," he said.

"Yes, you did." The euphoria sparked again, the hope she'd tried to keep alive by ignoring calendars. Don't be fooled the second time, she warned herself. "And so you came again to stir up some hope I've packed up and basemented."

"The time wasn't ripe before. There weren't any exhibitions during the war. When the Parliament Building burned, the legislature met in the museum. The museum staff barely held on. Have you been painting?"

She let him in. "This is Harold Cook," she said. "Mr. Barbeau. He works for a museum in Ottawa."

"For the National Museum now."

"And that's Woo," she added. "Mr. Barbeau has been to the Skeena, Harold." Harold raised his head and fastened a stare on Barbeau. "He's the man who bought the paintings of Kispiox and Kitsegukla." Harold drew in like a snail. "Harold grew up at Kispiox. At the mission."

"Cook?" Barbeau said. "Luke Cook? Was he your father?"

Harold nodded and snapped his head down toward Woo.

"He had quite a reputation among the Tsimshian."

Harold started "this little piggy" roughly with Woo's toes.

Barbeau's gaze roamed the walls, enthusiasm spreading across his face. "Just as I remembered them." His eyebrows lifted. "What's this? Not aboriginal pottery?"

"No. I made them."

"The designs are—"

"Modeled after Squamish baskets and ethnographic diagrams." She steeled herself for criticism for appropriating the designs.

"They're lively and ingenious. A Dzunukwa feast dish! I can't understand why I didn't notice them before. The power of your paintings, I suppose. Do you sell them?"

"Not anymore. I've stopped making them."

"Why?"

"A question of impurity of purpose. Using native designs. Pots are different than paintings. Painting is for understanding something. Pots were just for income."

"Tremendous! Paintings and pottery, both from native themes."

"And rugs. For me." She pointed to his feet. Eagle from two per-spectives, his head split and laid flat. "I learned rug braiding from a Squamish friend."

"Do you have more?"

"Yes."

"And more paintings?"

"I only paint for myself. Sundays. Some Sundays. For a couple hours." She caught a hint of reprimand in his expression. "There's too much pain in exhibiting. Victoria's an artistic backwater half a century behind the rest of the world."

"Yes. I quite agree. Antiquated ideas about art. If I might say so, you're not painting for the people of Victoria."

"It's taken me years to realize that."

"I don't believe you have. You'd be painting if you understood that." He lowered his voice. "May I see more? I've thought about them all this time."

"Then what took you so long?"

He drew back his chin.

"Forgive me." She waved away her comment. "The basement's bulging with them." She took the key from the fork-and-spoon drawer. "They're not all native subjects. I haven't been back north."

"But you must go. Before it's all gone."

Harold's head popped up, his eyes blazing. He started to ask Barbeau something, but stopped himself.

Barbeau followed her downstairs to the back porch. Out of the corner of her eye, she saw Mr. Pixley's underwear hanging on the line. Rats!

In a few minutes Harold came down and helped her uncover and dust off canvases. He struggled up the stairs with a large one, a potlatch welcome figure, and set it right in front of Barbeau. "It's better to see them outside," Harold said.

One by one he brought up dozens of paintings. He propped the ones from the Queen Charlotte Islands against bushes and between sword ferns so greenery surrounded them like forest, sparkling in after-a-rain brilliance. He leaned the Skeena ones on the brick pottery kiln. All the ones with houses—Tanu, Alert Bay, Mimkwamlis, Guyasdoms—he lined up along the fence to make a panorama of one big healthy village, a mythical place alive with eyes and eyes and eyes.

"Ah! This is how they'd look in a gallery," Barbeau said.

She winked at Harold and he winked back and did a few uncontrollable hops, his face purple as a pansy from his exertions. "Ever noticed how there's always laundry hanging in the villages?" she asked.

Barbeau chuckled and looked at each painting from a distance and up close, fanning himself with his hat.

"What I want to convey is the character of the animal, whether it's menacing or dignified or sprightly or shy, and the character of the man carving it too. I want to go beneath bark or fur or scales to understand the essence of the natural form as the carver did."

"You do, you do. Your interpretations are penetrating."

He chose *Kispiox: Totem of the Bear and the Moon*, and two others. Harold's smile vanished. His eyes took on a look of injured confusion.

What was she to do? She was pulled in both directions. Barbeau talked but his words were a blur of sound. Harold sat cross-legged in front of each of the three paintings in turn, yanking up tufts of grass, and murmuring, "I look at them long and long."

Barbeau regarded him curiously for a moment, then turned to Emily. "With your permission, I'd like to bring your work to the attention of Eric Brown, director of the National Gallery in Ottawa."

"What have you been waiting for?"

"For this nationalist movement to build momentum."

"And is it?"

"Yes, now that the war's over and our men have seen a larger world. The country is beginning to recognize and shape its full identity, unique in the world, and landscape plays a big part in that. Your art makes a fine contribution."

"The Provincial Parliament didn't think so."

"There's talk in Ottawa of an exhibit of West Coast art. I'd like it to combine aboriginal with European-Canadian artists."

"Do you think people will see my paintings as true? As representing illahee?"

Harold perked up again, studying Barbeau, to see if he knew the word.

Barbeau smiled in a fatherly way. "Unquestionably. Every one of them shows the country giving comfort."

Emily and Harold exchanged glances, and Harold let his shoulders drop.

"So, I'll hear from you in another decade?" Emily asked.

"You'll hear from me by—"

"Don't make promises you won't keep. It hurts too much."

"You'll hear by the first of April." He handed her a check.

"The first of April. Spring."

After he left, she and Harold stood quietly looking at the paintings surrounding them. "It's like I'm back home," he said.

"For me too."

It seemed a violation to confine them again to darkness and coal dust, but eventually she said it was time.

"*Swanaskxw, swanaskxw,*" he murmured as he put them away.

"What's that?"

He was quiet until the last trip to the cellar. "Helper of hailat," he whispered.

She smiled. He had an identity now that made him proud.

They climbed the stairs to her apartment and he opened the door. She gasped. Torn newspaper had been flung about the room. Jars of brushes overturned. André's milk spilled. A clay pot broken. A kitchen drawer lying sideways on the floor, all the silverware scattered.

Harold's groan told her they both saw it at once—a canvas smeared with wet cadmium yellow and Prussian blue, a watercolor of a village streaked with alizarin crimson, and little yellow monkey handprints walking across the Eagle rug and spotting Lulu's torn face. And where was the culprit? On the sink counter dipping her yellow hands into the molasses jar.

"You cussed, wicked creature!" she yelled.

"You going to beat her?" Harold wailed in panic.

She grabbed turpentine and a rag and charged toward the sink, salt crunching beneath her feet on the hardwood floor. When she yanked Woo's hand to clean it, Woo shrieked and escaped along the counter. Emily seized her and held on, the little body rigid, both frozen in heat, eye to eye, Woo's green beads lit with terror.

A loud sigh gushed out. "No. That would only teach her hate. There is no good and bad behavior in the jungle."

Stricken, Harold whimpered, his big hands shaking, his part in the disaster dawning on him. "Beat me instead."

While she scrubbed the spidery hands, the tuft of charcoal gray hair sticking up on Woo's head quivered so pathetically it drained her of anger. "She only did what she saw me doing. Whoever senses someone else's creativity is stimulated."

Harold repeated her last sentence. Emily looked at him a moment and finished cleaning Woo's hands and feet and the blue smear across her belly. Then she chained her up. "We can't leave her untied, Harold," she said as gently as she could.

An outbreak of jagged sobbing shook his body and he crumpled onto the floor. "Beat me," he whimpered. "Beat me instead."

Kneeling beside him, she raised his chin and touched her face to his. In all her life, she'd never felt a man's hot tears on her cheek.

"No, Harold. She helped me with more paintings than she destroyed. And you have too." She said it slowly so that it would sink in. "My swanaskxw."

She mispronounced it and felt his smile against her cheek. "When you love, you've got to love through and through."

In a moment she asked, "Don't you wish we could have seen her do it?"

Harold laughed sadly. Her own laughter bubbled up, deep and explosive as Harold leapt up and twirled, pantomiming Woo spilling out salt, chewing off a paint tube cap, squeezing out paint, planting his palms on the floor, on chairs and imaginary paintings, smacking his paws on his monkey cheeks and his furry belly. Woo, free of inhibitions, and Harold too.

36 : Cedar

One Saturday—she'd asked that he never come on Sunday, sisters' day—Harold brought his shoe box again.

"Let's go outside," he said. "Under the maple tree."

"All right."

New leaves were unfurling in a sap green so bright it shocked her. Summer was coming full tilt, and still no letter from Barbeau.

She had tried not to think of him, had tried to go to the mailbox without wanting. Yet she'd kept up Christmas hemlock boughs till February. She hadn't even bent over to smell Alice's spring hyacinths. She'd ignored Lizzie's comments about the blessed season of Christ's

Resurrection. She had her own resurrection to petition for. If Barbeau sent an invitation to exhibit, then she was meant to paint. If April came and went without a peep, then she wasn't, and she might as well never buy another tube of paint, never even think of exhibiting. Squash it dead. It was better dead. Less agony. Lead a normal life. A normal, boring, sterile life.

She yanked out a tall weed and flung it against the tree trunk. A pot of hooey. Deep down, she wanted that show with all the force of a Pacific storm.

Harold brought two chairs from the porch. "Are you ready?" he asked, his cheeks squeezed up to his eyes.

She pulled her thoughts back to him. "Yes."

"*Harold Cook a Canadian. Haste along with me. I Harold Cook author of this book lived at Lejac Indian Residential School near Kispiox. My friends lived there too. The missionaries Mr. Luke Cook and Mrs. Martha Cook made them change their names. Muldo they called Moses and Tuuns they called Thomas and Haaydzims they called Hosea. Me Muldo Haaydzims and Tuuns we dug the potato patch next to the children's graveyard. We learned to march and count and read and write. So now I write myself Harold Cook a Canadian.*

"*Tuuns and Muldo got beat for playing on Sunday so we went to our secret place in the woods where we built a waab out of branches and bark and we play there like it's a bighouse. We don't wear shoes there because Mr. Luke Cook and Mrs. Martha Cook don't like. Tuuns talks and talks about running away back to Kitsegukla but they don't know the way how to go. At night they hear sounds of potlatch in Kispiox singing and drums and yelling and laughing I don't hear but they do and Tuuns rips apart his mattress.*"

Harold stopped and rocked. She felt anxious as his uneven rhythm increased.

"*Muldo carved Wolf on a log long nose slit eyes big teeth all wild looking. I looked at it long and long. I asked him why he carved Wolf and he said because Wolf is free and does what he wants and that's his naxnox that gives him power.*"

He stopped and read ahead silently, then looked up, anguish tightening his scarred forehead. "I don't know. . . ."

"Go on, Harold. I want to hear."

"*One time we found a little squirrel dead and took it out to our waab and we built a fire and spread our faces with ash and Muldo did the Wolf dance his eyes all gleaming and his head tipped back howling way back in his throat jumping around the squirrel and the fire splashing light in his eyes and he held the squir-*

rel in his mouth and shook his head and dragged the squirrel in his dance. I don't have words to say it good how wild he was but he don't eat the squirrel he only pretended and Haaydzims and Tuuns howled and held the squirrel in their teeth and shook it and I howled and held it in my teeth and shook it and we danced and danced and came back late for dinner and Mr. Luke Cook told me to sing it Onward Christian Soldiers and I didn't sing it and he stood over me and he saw blood on my face and blood on Muldo's face and Mr. Luke Cook beat us each one and Mrs. Martha Cook screaming and the next day she packed up my clothes and Mr. Luke Cook made me get in the wagon and she crying and Muldo and Haaydzims and Tuuns kicking and screaming their Tsimshian words and me too and he strapping me in the wagon and Muldo and Haaydzims and Tuuns running behind screaming and in Kitwanga Mr. Luke Cook put me on a riverboat with a mean man to go to Victoria and so I Harold Cook a Canadian lived in Victoria Children's Mental Hospital for six years."

His words sank her into a chasm of pity. "I'm so sorry."

She imagined the boys flinging themselves into their dance, exulting in their few hours of freedom, playing potlatch, and Harold, desperate to be a part of something, imitating in all innocence a sacred dance he'd never seen and didn't understand any more than she did.

He continued to rock, urgently now, staring at the shoe box, unable to look at her.

"How did you get out?"

"I got too old to stay there, so now I live with my sister."

"Good. That's all over now, Harold. And you have the rest of your life to do some happy things."

He raised his head slowly with a look that told her she'd just said something stupid.

"What is the thing you want to do most in your life?"

With his index finger, he touched the lid of the shoe box.

· · ·

On Sunday morning, she lay in bed not fully awake, Harold and his friends dancing in and out of her swirling sleep fog. So that's what happened to whites obsessively drawn by the pull of native drumbeat. They were confined. Labeled as misfits, abnormal, crazy. It was convenient to ignore their cries on behalf of the first people here, the ones tooken gone somewhere who came back mute. And then his finger pointing through the fog to the shoe box.

Her Eagles hovered above her making strong talk, carrying her on their wings above the apartment house, above her sisters, above Victoria and missionary societies and psychiatric wards.

Emily, she asked herself, or Eagle did, what is the thing you want to do most in your life?

She wanted to create one true painting, one painting that people, native or white, would love and say, yes, that's my illahee, the beauty and power and glory of it sweetening the sour.

You don't want to be loved yourself?

She let out a throaty sigh, and thought of Harold, how full he was of feelings desperate for expression, and she, apparently his only outlet. She thought of Alice and Lizzie, how they showed their love for her with elaborate Sunday suppers at two o'clock sharp, and her dogs, how they were always leaping for attention. And Claude, his exuberant and wise love expressed in fish grease and restraint. This love thing had been the slippery fish of her whole life. One thing she knew: It wasn't the incoming of love that mattered, but the outgoing.

No. One pure, true painting was what she wanted, even if it took a hundred almost-true paintings to get it.

She threw on a smock and dashed across the back yard past the kennels without so much as a pause to pet the expectant puppy faces begging for a touch. Sell them all. Simplify. Focus. Point your finger at what you want and do it. Exhibit or no exhibit—paint!

She burst into her sisters' kitchen.

"Have you ever wanted something so wrenchingly that you would throw out everything and risk your life for it?"

Lizzie, up to her elbows in flour, shook her head no.

"Has it ever occurred to you that to clutch at life fearfully, un-willing to spend it, is not a form of gratitude to God for life?"

Lizzie looked at her as if pained by some bright light.

"But to fling one's whole being at a goal of interpreting God's creation—"

"What's all this leading up to?"

"I'm not coming to supper today. I'm going to Goldstream Flats." She turned on her heel. "For the whole summer."

"But I'm making popovers. It's Sunday."

Emily was out the door and across the lane.

· · ·

She got dressed and strode down the block, knowing she had to get away from sisters, tenants, the apartment building. Life was short, and shorter still the number of years a person felt bold enough to face a blank canvas. She sensed the core of her life bubbling up, like liquid electricity coursing through her veins.

She'd seen an old gray caravan trailer in a neighbor's yard bearing a *For Sale Cheap* sign. It was still there! Just an empty wooden box on wheels, it would be dandy fine. She bought it, and had her neighbor haul it to her back yard. She set to work sawing out windows.

In the morning, Monday, she was sawing the wood she'd cut out of the wall in order to use it for a shelf when Lizzie appeared, hands on hips, mouth agape. "What in the world—?"

"I can't go paint for just a couple hours, come back, go again, back and forth. I've got to live where I want to paint, to feel it all around me all the time."

"And so you're going to live like a shameless vagrant? In this gypsy wagon?"

"Look, Lizzie. You might not like to hear me say this, but if Dede had done some of the things she wanted to, she might have died more peacefully. You probably read her letter. She took her bitterness with her to the grave. I refuse to do that."

She thrust the saw forward and the board shifted so her saw stuck. "Hold that steady, will you?"

"But—" Lizzie hesitated, planted her feet wide and grasped the board.

"Watch for splinters."

Emily continued sawing and when Lizzie's section of the board came loose, Lizzie jumped back and dropped it.

"To go to my grave without knowing whether it was lack of talent or lack of perseverance that failed me, without feeling that I'd probed deeply, without sucking out the joy of hearty work, that would be self-inflicted pain I could never forgive myself for."

Lizzie looked at her as if her face, gleaming with sweat and flecked with sawdust, were a stranger's.

"But if I throw my life at art again, like a wild dance, give everything in the search for a deeper seeing, even if none of my family, not a single living being, likes the results, maybe I might feel I'd lived fully. But I'll never find out by staying upstairs and doodling *imaginary* forests."

• • •

On Tuesday, feeling like Dzunukwa putting herself back together again after being dead, she sold the breeding dogs and bought window screening, lumber, and a cot. On Wednesday, she was inside the trailer working on corner bed boxes for Woo, Tantrum, and André, when Lizzie came to the door with a prim look on her face. She was holding some heavy green fabric, folded.

"What's that?"

Lizzie stepped in and thrust it into her hands. Emily unfolded it and held it up. "Curtains! Why—"

"I couldn't stand to think of you out in the woods and some Peeping Tom peering in on you in your nightdress, that's all."

Emily rubbed her palm across the fabric, astonished. "You made these? And green, too." She held one up to a window. "Perfect! How'd you know the size?"

"I measured when you were gone yesterday."

She felt as though the plank floor under them were shifting minutely. Beneath Lizzie's crust ticked a well-meaning heart.

"Thank you."

• • •

"Looks like an elephant," Harold said, seeing the trailer for the first time. "What's it for?"

"For living in."

"Here?"

"No. Goldstream Flats. I'm dreadful hankery for forest."

He walked around it cautiously, peered in the window, stepped inside, and in a few moments hopped out, nearly toppling over. He screwed up his dented forehead in a look sliding from ecstasy to anxiety.

"Can I come? Can I? Can I? I'm your swanaskxw."

"Maybe for a little while, if your sister lets you, but I also need to be alone there. You can use my tent, tell her."

He shook his hands, unable to contain himself. "I'll ask. No. You ask her."

"All right."

Over the next several days, they made ledges for cages for Susie the rat, Joseph, and the bullfinches, rigged a large canvas awning, and fashioned a wood-burning stove from a square pail and a discarded stovepipe, not much different from the one on *La Renarde Rouge*. She stepped back to admire it. *"Formidable, mademoiselle!"*

She packed the trailer with canned food for a month and plenty of art supplies, including a gallon of white housepaint, two gallons of gasoline, and rolls of inexpensive manila paper. She had it towed to a small, out-of-the-way clearing surrounded by moss-sheathed cedars, maples, hemlocks draped with lichen, Douglas-firs, alders spiced with wildflowers. Glorious.

• • •

At breakfast the first morning, she made Harold promise to beat his drum every so often to let her know he was all right. "But not if people are around. If you see anyone, don't dance."

She set off to find a subject, knowing she'd made an intentional decision—to expend her life on painting, wholly and permanently, to remain in the innermost center of her work even though that might be at the periphery of the art world. Barbeau's show wasn't going to make her an artist. Painting was.

She stopped at a likely spot and unfolded her stool and easel, tacked manila paper onto a board, thinned her oil paints with gasoline and mixed them with house paint. It was so cheap she could be free to take wild strokes, but so quick-drying she'd have to work swiftly. The paper wouldn't take studied labor. Now she was ready.

To paint a tree or a totem, she had to look at it long and long, until it resembled no other tree or totem. It was easy with totems, harder with trees. Without a totem pole as a natural center of interest, she had to sort out the chaos of overlapping forms, and select. That density was probably why people thought the forests of the Northwest were unpaintable. She had to shove that aside, get quiet to the bone to let a subject come.

She sat very still, listening to a stream gurgling, the breeze soughing through upper branches, the melodious *kloo-klack* of ravens, the *nyeep-nyeep* of nuthatches—all sounds chokingly beautiful. She felt she could hear the cool clean breath of growing things—fern fronds, maple leaves, white trillium petals, tree trunks, each in its rightful place.

Partly lost to her surroundings, she singled out a cedar, wide at the base, narrowing as it grew. If there was any kind of portrait worth doing, it would be the portrait of a tree. But a portrait had to convey character. The channels in this cedar's raw umber trunk all stretched upward, reaching toward light. It was more than a tree, however noble. It was the manifestation of the attitude that had brought her this far: reaching. Not just the tree, but that idea was her subject. The *things* in a painting were only bits of visible evidence of a still, small voice whispering a truth.

As she began to paint, she saw rhythm in the tree's repeated forms, in the upward reach of the trunk furrows, its bare hanging withes reaching down, its laden boughs tangled with those of other trees. In one sweep she united the branches into a mantle of cedars. Her swinging arm became a swoop of greenery, boughs from adjacent trees breathing into each other, supporting each other, all one.

Loving everything terrifically, humming, half singing "Breathe on Me, Breath of God," she felt unutterably close to the Creator, as though she were an instrument of His presence. Someday, when some God-quality in her was fully in accord with the God surrounding her, she would achieve that one true painting. Maybe it would happen when, like an Indian living in his totem spirit, becoming the thing he held in awe, she saw no difference between herself and the Creator. Right before her eyes she saw something: The more she entered into the life of the tree, as one breath moving, in and out like the tide, one heart-drum beating, the more alive her work became. Oh, the joy of it!

37: Frog

Emily sat on the caravan step studying her work from the week before. There were small private miracles, a successful branch, a patch of open space real and true, but the whole of it, the way to express the forest, was elusive still.

She heard women's voices. Lizzie's and Alice's! Good God! Harold was somewhere off in the woods, apt to burst forth into wild drumming out of pure glee. Which one should she protect from the other?

Lizzie strode toward her and Alice scurried after, nose aimed down to study the path.

"Surprise!" they said together.

"How did you find me?"

"The area attendant pointed the way, and then we heard you singing," Alice said.

"Nobody else could be that off-key and enjoy it so much," Lizzie said.

"We brought supper, Lizzie's corned beef." Alice set her satchel on the picnic table.

"And a cabbage. And tomatoes from your garden, if they're not all squashed," Lizzie said. "We have plates too."

"Family Sunday supper, a tradition still," Emily said.

"And you forgot your cigarette things." Alice reached into her satchel and presented Emily's tin box of cigarette makings.

"Alleluia! Thank you." Emily gave a little bow. "I've turned this place inside out searching for that."

Lizzie set down her bags and looked around, waving away mosquitoes. They set about preparing the meal and inquiring how she was living, curious about every detail of washing and cooking. "But how do you, you know, relieve yourself?" Lizzie asked.

"What do you think they did in Galilee?" She motioned off into the woods.

"Don't you get depressed out here?" Lizzie asked, her voice thin as a pencil line. "It's so—shady."

"No. Everything is growing. Stay out here long enough and you will too. Remember Isaiah? 'The wilderness and the solitary place shall be glad.' The frog song at night rivals any choir."

"You don't get scared? Or lonely?"

"Yes, I do, but I take comfort in knowing I'm not the only one out here." She showed them the drawing she'd done at home of the imaginary forest with eyes.

"That gives me the creeps," Alice said.

"Good. It does me too. The forest is a refuge for a million living things."

"Precisely." Lizzie snickered, then swatted her arm.

Emily handed her the mosquito oil. "Or I can roll you a cigarette if you prefer. That works too." Lizzie wrinkled her nose in disgust, which satisfied Emily immensely. "Think of it as one of nature's paradoxes, that a creature so delicate, just a whisper, can be so wicked."

"What about your painting? How's it going?"

Alice asked! Bless her. Alice asked.

"Better than ever. I think I'm beginning to glimpse how to see ideas instead of mere things."

That seemed to spark genuine interest. She laid out twenty new oils on paper on the picnic table. Her sisters looked at them without so much as one negative comment, though no gushing praise either. What had come over them? Had the Great Popover Refusal convinced them of something?

"It's nice you're not doing Indian things now," Lizzie said.

"Yes. Nice." Let Lizzie have her reason for thinking that. She had her own. "I'm painting life itself, and the spirit of life as I see it."

Thunder growled, swelled, blasted, and Harold's drum imitated it.

"What was that?" Lizzie asked.

Emily rolled a cigarette, and looked around, like Claude had done, looking for spies. "The Apocalypse?"

Chickadees stopped their rippling whistle, and a squirrel scrambled under a log. Lightning crackled close enough to vibrate her collarbone. In the stillness following, frogs sang out their excitement, some in basso profundo, some in falsetto. Big drops made their way through the canopy of foliage. "Isn't it grand, the trees refreshing themselves, one branch offering drink to the one below it?"

"But our picnic," Alice wailed.

"It won't last. It's only a summer shower."

She hoped that was all it was. Then Harold might take shelter somewhere else and only send her a drumbeat to tell her he was all right.

From under the canvas awning they watched the forest darken, the green begin to glow. A diamond drop quivered at the tip of each maple leaf. Rain falling on ferns made them bounce.

"Weather keeps you passionate," Emily said. "No one stuffs the landscape into your eyes here. You have to want it enough to be cold or wet or itchy."

Lizzie's arm shot out to silence her. Only her eyes moved. "Do you hear that?" she whispered.

Harold's drum echoed, followed by a whoop. Emily stifled a laugh. She should probably tell her, but Lizzie's panicked expression was priceless and she wanted to enjoy it a moment longer. Slowly Lizzie turned her head to scan the forest.

Harold whooped again and came reeling between trees, stumbling over ferns, hugging his drum and shoe box. He stopped just short of the awning when he saw her sisters, shoved the shoe box onto dry ground, and tried to hide the drum behind his back. Water dripped from his jaw.

Emily checked Lizzie's reaction—eyebrows knit, mouth agape, hand to her chest. She pulled Harold under the awning and put the shoe box in the trailer.

"Harold, these are my sisters, Alice and Lizzie."

"Your drum!" Alice said.

Emily knew they had assumed, whenever they'd seen him helping in her garden or apartment building, that he was a hired laborer, and she'd done nothing to correct the misconception. "Harold is a dear friend of mine. His parents were missionaries on the Skeena, Lizzie. He's keeping me company for a while."

Lizzie's posture became rigid.

Slowly, enjoying the delicious moment, Emily pointed through the trees to her tent. "His camp is over there. He's working on an important project. He's been a strong influence on my return to serious work, for which I'm mightily grateful. Dry off and come inside, Harold. We're about to eat."

They all crowded into the steamy caravan, and Joseph in his cage sprayed seeds over Alice's food. Rain smacked the tin roof in sharp clicks, trickled down the trailer sides and made gullies around the campsite. "Like Noah's ark, eh?" Emily said.

"Actually quite cozy," Lizzie said, peering out the open door. "Harold, are you also working in the missionary fields?"

In her own way, she was trying.

"No."

"Your parents must have done a world of good bringing the Word of God to the aborigines. Tell us about it, what they did."

"Made them sing church songs and stop dancing."

"Yes, and what else?"

"Mean things. Take boys from families. Whip the Indian out of them. I don't want to talk about it." He stared down at his feet. "You shall not take things from me," he murmured.

Lizzie drew back her chin.

"You are an artist too, then?" Alice said, always the peacemaker.

"Artist. Em'ly zanartist," the parrot muttered. "I'd rather starve."

"To each his own, Joseph," Emily said.

"No. I'm an author," Harold blurted.

Emily felt a sigh skitter through her. That's how it starts, with an urge, an attempt, and a declaration.

"That's wonderful. What do you write about?" Alice asked.

Harold shrank back against the wall. "A song of myself and Indian friends. *Harold Cook a Canadian.*"

Alice leaned toward Harold, her face full of teacherly interest. "Is there anything I could read that you wrote?"

He looked confused. It wasn't likely that anyone had ever asked him. The next step, going public with those dear human pages, was too much for him. He turned to Emily. "You read. Read *Leaves of Grass.*"

"All right." Now wasn't that a change from Lizzie's Sunday scripture reading.

"*Stop this day,*" Harold prompted.

"*And night with me and you shall possess the origin of all poems,*" she said, hoping it would be so.

"*You shall possess the good of the earth and sun,*" Harold went on from memory, rocking to the drone of rain and croaking of frogs.

"*You shall no longer take things at second or third hand, nor look
    through the eyes of the dead . . .
You shall not look through my eyes either, nor take things from me,
You shall listen to all sides and filter them from your self.*"

He smiled, smug in his surprise.

Emily nodded her praise. That ought to gentle them into Whitman. She thumbed through the pages. What to read? *I sing the body electric.* No, no bodies. *I hear and behold God in every object.* No. Better not. It might launch a protest from Lizzie that "God's in Heaven where He belongs. He only *made* trees on the third day. He's not *in* them." Maybe something more subtle since they'd been so congenial. She looked for the passage where Whitman said that a leaf of grass is no less than the journey-work of the stars and that a tree-toad is a *chef d'oeuvre* for the highest, but her glance fell on words appropriate to rain, and she read aloud.

> *"Smile O voluptuous cool-breath'd earth!*
> *Earth of the slumbering and liquid trees!*
> *Earth of the departed sunset—earth of the mountains misty-topt! . . .*
> *Earth of the limpid gray of clouds brighter and clearer for my sake! . . .*
> *Smile, for your lover comes."*

Lizzie leapt up. "Look, the rain stopped," she said crisply. We'd better make a dash to the station." She gathered up her things on the picnic table.

Emily tapped her fingers on her chin. Was it Whitman or Harold that made them anxious to beat a retreat?

"Oh, I almost forgot," Alice said. "I brought your mail."

In the middle of the stack, Emily spotted a letter with *Barbeau* above the return address. A tidal wave slammed against her chest.

"Alice! It's from Marius Barbeau. Why didn't you tell me?"

"I couldn't read the handwriting."

Emily ripped it open. Her eyes raced ahead of her voice.

> *"The National Museum in connection with the National Gallery of Canada would be pleased to have you select sixty paintings from which we would choose a lesser number for a major exhibition, Canadian West Coast Art, Native and Modern, to open at the National Gallery in Ottawa on December 2, 1927. Afterward, it will move to the Art Gallery of Toronto, and the Art Association of Montreal."*

She exploded in a whoop and tossed the letter to Harold, then snatched it back with trembling hands to read the rest.

"A Canadian national art ought to be inclusive. Therefore, the purpose of the exhibition is to mingle for the first time the art of Canadian West Coast tribes with that of modern artists so as to analyze their relationship to one another. We would also appreciate it if you could send a sampling of your hooked rugs and pottery. Mr. Eric Brown, representing the National Gallery, will contact you next month with the details."

She grasped Woo by her hairy arms, swung her onto the picnic table and danced with her. Harold joined in too, stumbling and drumming. Frogs croaked in wild abandon, beside themselves with joy. For her sake, she knew. For her. Lizzie gaped with wide eyes, as if the earth had become dislodged in space. Alice clapped her hands in front of her chin. Emily let Joseph out of his cage. "Artist, artist," she prompted.

"Em'ly zanartist," Joseph squawked.

He shrieked it louder and Harold yelled it with him, twirling. "Emily *is* an artist."

38: Aspen

Emily wedged a hammer claw behind a horizontal board in her back yard fence, and pried. It resisted at first, then came off smoothly, with one long creak. She put it on the stack heaped up beside her. At every squeak, it seemed she was loosening one more plank that had nailed her down.

Lizzie came through the gate carrying a basket of apples. "What in God's name do you think you're doing?"

"Prying. Just like you."

A long satisfying creak loosened another good one.

"Without that fence, Tantrum will run across the lane and tear up Alice's garden."

"I'm only taking off the top ones. It's claustrophobic anyway." She let the hammer fall to the dirt. "Do you have any idea how expensive it is to buy frames for sixty paintings? I have no choice, so thanks for the apples, but let me work."

At first there was Lizzie's typical wincing expression, but when Emily glanced up again, her mouth had softened and she had set down her basket. "I thought I knew all there was to know about my sister and her dreams of being an artist. But I didn't. I didn't know how utterly consuming it is for you."

An hour later, Emily was sanding slats under the maple when Alice and Lizzie marched toward her. Lord help me, she thought.

"We think you should go," Lizzie said.

"Go where?"

"To Ottawa. To the exhibit."

She let out a scoffing laugh. "I'm straightening out nails to re-use them and you think I should take a pleasure trip?"

"Yes, we do." Alice handed her a piece of paper.

She read Alice's shaky schoolmarm printing.

Cancellation of Note
I hereby declare Emily Carr free of debt from the mortgage loan entered into June 1, 1913, and I cancel the remaining balance of $3,138.80.

At the bottom, her signature, *Alice Carr,* in wiggly letters.

Emily had to sit down. "Why?"

"Getting the money back wouldn't mean as much to me as not having the payment once a month would mean to you."

"This isn't just any old art exhibit," Lizzie said. Her mouth, usually held in a tight line, was smiling prettily.

Emily shook her head in amazement. She felt her stony resentment over years of their carping criticism, with hardly a shred of validation, bust with a pop.

Lizzie's smile disappeared into a firm look. "I'll take care of the animals and the tenants. Now will you go?"

She gazed unfocused at utter strangers, women from another land, until Alice waved away a fly and Emily noticed the stub of her finger. "The curtains and now this. Are you sure?"

Their simultaneous energetic nods made her laugh.

"Will they know what's in me by these Indian paintings nobody likes?"

Lizzie hesitated, as though she had that worry too.

"You won't know unless you go," Alice said.

Emily blew her nose. They were so utterly sincere. "I don't know how to thank you. My own sisters and I don't know how."

"Thank us by leaving that fence *alone!*" Lizzie said.

• • •

For the next six months, she rode on sheer momentum, pored over her sketchbooks and watercolor studies from native sites, and painted new oils. She was at her easel by six every morning. It meant a return to painting totem poles, but the trees had been there hundreds of years. They'd wait a hundred more for her. Canvases stacked up so she could barely move around her studio.

"You live in an Indian village," Harold said as he came in after working all morning building a shipping crate with spacers so the new paintings could dry en route. Bewildered by all that was still left to do, he turned slowly in circles and tipped over onto the floor, the task almost too much for him. "I can't—"

"Yes you can, Harold. You're doing fine. Any monkey can paint a picture," she told him, "but it takes real genius to crate."

His body jerked in uncontainable pride. "Swanaskxw."

• • •

Watching a bleak winter sky from the train window, a wide, first class window, since Eric Brown, director of the National Gallery, had sent her the ticket, she ate peanut butter sandwiches and apples from home while her head swam with misgivings. The responsibility of being worthy of her sisters' support was an entirely new feeling, one she imagined a man might have, the obligation to do well at the office or shop in order to fill the plates at home. She smiled, remembering how Alice and Lizzie had waved scarves at the dock as the ferry pulled way, and Harold did a few joy hops, waving madly with both arms. When the train climbed the Rockies, her anxiety eased in the thrill of their snowy peaks, but when it crossed the stubble of endless prairies, nervousness jiggled in the pit of her stomach.

She read a booklet Barbeau had sent her about the other exhibitors, some Group of Seven she'd never heard of, who held that the nation required a new artistic style born of the artist's communion with Canada's vast and varied landscape. These painters had tramped the wilderness together, shared artistic insights around campfires, defended each other against the press, as a brotherhood. All men. All younger. All easterners. All successful. Where did she fit in?

. . .

The evening of the opening reception, she caught sight of herself in the mirror of the seedy hotel room. Holy horrors! Her hair was in a confusion of directions, her body bulging in all the wrong places, her bosoms unwieldy, stuffed into the black crepe dress Alice had made for her. She looked like a potbellied stove, and felt like a damn landlady. Her spunk would dissolve if she didn't leave that instant. Her hands trembled as she locked the door behind her.

She walked into the National Gallery and found Marius Barbeau beating on a drum and singing a Tsimshian song at the top of his lungs. He stopped and hailed her, beat the drum for attention, and announced her arrival. She flushed, tugged down her dress, and took off her gloves to shake hands. Eric Brown, young, dignified, and handsome, with a sweep of brown hair across his forehead, greeted her by holding her hand in both of his.

"Thank you for the rail ticket. It was a glorious ride," she said.

He introduced her to some guests. "She's one of the most interesting painters in all of Canada. We were astounded when we received her work."

His words astounded her, so much that she offered only a muddle-headed response.

"Astounded at the crates too," Marius added. "Built as sturdy as ships with so many nails it took us a day to get into them."

Emily grinned. "Harold Cook made them. You remember, he's the man who hauled up all the paintings from the basement."

Marius slipped her a clipping from the *Ottawa Citizen*. He'd outlined one paragraph in red.

It's a source of keen gratification to everyone interested in the preservation of aboriginal art that Emily Carr of Victoria, BC has, after fifteen years without recognition in her own province, been discovered at last

and her work given the attention it deserves. Hers is the greatest contri-
bution of all time to historic art of the Pacific slopes. Miss Carr is essen-
tially of the Canadian West not by reason of her subject matter alone,
but by her approach to it.

"See?" he said.

She pressed the newspaper to her chest and walked from room to room. To see her paintings displayed among Haida, Kwakiutl, and Tsimshian pole sections, carved feast dishes, ceremonial blankets, baskets, masks—a spasm of joy shot through her. Harold would not have been able to stand still.

But how were these artifacts acquired? Were they lent, like paint-ings, or—? Or the unthinkable. A massive Raven mask with long beak commanded the center of a wall. Kwakiutl, the sign said. A sin-gle hollow drumbeat vibrated in her chest. It looked uncomfortably like the one from the potlatch at Mimkwamlis. Hold your tongue, she told herself. Don't ruin everything by getting riled up. She con-vinced herself she wasn't sure.

The baskets used only traditional designs. Sophie's one-of-a-kind work would have been more spectacular. She could kick herself for not showing it to Marius. She looked for names of the basket mak-ers. None. Only tribal identifications on some of them. Apparently individuals weren't seen as significant. She twisted her gloves like she was wringing out a washrag.

Not finding several of her favorite paintings, she felt herself get-ting worked up in a snit until she counted. There were twenty-six. Her work dominated the show. She shouldn't have counted them. This wasn't about self. It was about seeing.

She walked into another room and it was as if she'd walked into another world. Frozen lakes and waterfalls and craggy rocks and huge, undecorated spaces filled with feeling surrounded her. Here was the room of Lawren Harris, J. E. H. MacDonald, Frederick Var-ley, and others of the Group of Seven. The dark silhouette of a single scraggy pine holding on for dear life to a rock along a wind-tossed lake shore struck her as exquisite, spare and unutterably lonely. She stopped before a Rocky Mountain landscape so clean and simple, so profoundly spiritual that she reeled.

Marius touched her arm. "You look like you've seen a ghost."

"Not a ghost. God maybe. Nothing I ever saw in France moved me like these do. This Lawren Harris is astonishing, the way he eliminates the superfluous. Those dramatic shafts of light." She slapped her cheek. "As if he saw some elemental life force shining in the wilderness. It's what I feel, but he paints it!"

"Would you like to meet him?" He pointed to a man graying at the temples with a widely divided mustache smiling at her boyishly not five feet away.

The age-old gallery trick—an artist pretending to be engaged in conversation while he stands near his work listening to comments of passersby. She should have known.

"Your work expresses the soul of Canada—what I've been striving for all along. If only I could do for my beloved West what you've done for the mountains and the northeastern wilds."

"You have, and you will," Lawren Harris said.

They walked the room together commenting softly on the paintings. "You simplify with such ease, taking liberties that I struggle over," she said. His bare winter aspen trunks and pale cloud layers carried her to a silent, austere world stripped of fussiness so only serenity remained.

"I think if I looked at that aspen long enough and walked into the frame, I could find God," she said.

"That's what I felt too, when I painted it. That's how most of us feel painting Canadian wilderness today. You are one of us. You just didn't know it."

"And here I thought it was only me."

"If you see something that'll improve any of these, tell me, will you?" he asked softly.

"Me? *Me?*"

More than what anyone could ever have said about her own work, that comment—well, she'd ask a blessing for Lawren Harris.

"I see now that my work belongs more to the native people than to me," she said.

"Not at all. Yours are works of art in their own right."

"These don't show what I've begun to work on recently. Just forests. My shapes could be more sculptural. My colors deeper.

Years ago a Squamish woman told me to make the forest darker. I should have gobbled up her advice on the spot."

It wasn't that she wanted to paint like them. She just wanted to capture her western landscape as sparely and purely as they did theirs. She was way behind them in the handling of spaces. Theirs had more rhythm and sweep and poetry than hers, but theirs didn't have the love of native people that hers had.

"You're finding your own way. It's not a question of technique. Technique alone is soulless. You have other resources to draw on. The emotional and spiritual. I see it in the places where you are more expressive than depictive."

"Yes, but I haven't found my way clear to it always."

"It's the seeking and the feeling that's important. Go north again. Go for a different reason this time."

"Yes, I believe I will."

Eric Brown stepped up to them. "Excuse me for interrupting, but there have been some offers on your paintings, Miss Carr. Are they for sale?"

"As if all of this wasn't enough! Yes, they're for sale!"

"And one more thing. Would you be interested in showing your current work at our National Gallery Annual Exhibition next year? We'd be very pleased if you'd consent."

"After twenty-five years working up to this? I'd be a damned fool not to!"

· · ·

She kicked off her shoes in her hotel room and threw herself onto the bed, giddy with gratitude, with love of art and love of country, her mind spinning with Lawren's words—*You are one of us*—his stupendous work—*one of us*—and oh my God.

She scribbled a note to Alice and Lizzie.

Oh, what I've seen! I've found a new self I didn't know existed. How much catching up I have to do. Time is running out. Fifty-six already. Where have I been? Not whole before. From now on, I want the work to break out of me as a river out of mountains, cleanly, unselfconsciously. A million thank you's. Three paintings sold to the National Gallery and there's interest from other people in more. The Group of Seven invited me to exhibit with them next year, and so did the National Gallery. I think, if you had been here, you would have been just a little proud.

She looked through the exhibit catalog, and on the last page, she wrote, *There is something bigger than fact: the underlying spirit, the mood, the vastness, the wildness, the eternal big spaceness of it. Oh West, don't crush me with your bigness. Keep me high and strong for the struggle.*

Part V

39: Raven

"Take me," Harold said when she told him she was going north again. "I can carry your painting things. I can set up the tent. Your swanaskxw."

There'd been a time when she would have welcomed a fellow traveler in love with native culture. It wasn't that he didn't deserve to go, all the help he'd given her, and would give her, especially this time when the trip would be harder on her. She worried that she might not have the resilience.

"Take me take me take me." He dropped to the ground under the maple and rocked, cupping his damaged foot in both palms.

She had begged Father in a similar way to take her with him when he did a circle tour of Vancouver Island. For years afterward she'd thought him mean and selfish for denying her. She knew from her own childhood despair the danger of a wrong move.

"My illahee." He looked on the verge of sobbing. *"You shall possess the good of the earth and sun,"* he murmured, keeping his eyes on the triangle of grass between his legs.

She squatted close to him. "You're my right eye's apple, Harold. You know that. I just can't have you with me. I'd be painting for *you* then, but I can't do that. I have to be quiet and alone there, to paint how the places tell me."

"Are you going to Kispiox?"

"I don't know. The Nass River for sure, and Haida Gwaii."

"You could find Muldo and Tuuns and Haaydzims."

"No, Harold. That's not my purpose. I may not go to Kispiox. I may not even paint native themes."

"My only chance."

He had a sense, then, of his future, the world closing in.

"I'll tell you everything I see. You'll see every painting."

The flare of his nostrils told her he wasn't resigned. She reached into her smock pocket, rolled a cigarette, and passed it to him. He lit it, took a puff, and passed it back. She knew that ritual contributed to his make-believe. Only the excruciating pang of love made her do it. She wouldn't after this.

"The important journeys have to be taken alone. You know that. You've done it. You're doing it now, with your writing. Think how much more you'll have to read to me when I come home."

He looked at the ground and yanked out tufts of grass.

"Look at me," she said.

He raised his head. The corners of his mouth drooped. He opened his palm to her, an offering. "Leaves of grass," he said.

She cupped his hand in hers. "Would you like to borrow my book while I'm gone?"

His eyes opened wide and he fought back a smile, answering her only with a slow nod.

"One other thing. It's not good for you to dance on the beach in plain sight."

"Why not?"

"People don't understand. They might wag their tongues to the wrong person and make it seem that you're a problem."

"To who? I'm nobody's problem."

"Promise me. Dance in your back yard."

"My sister won't let me."

"Then when I come back, you can dance in mine."

· · ·

After battling rain in the Skeena and Nass River villages, she went to the Queen Charlotte Islands. At Skidegate, William and Clara insisted she stay in their new house with glass windows and electricity. William was foreman at a new cannery and couldn't take her to any villages, so she had to hire someone else at $50 for four days. The night before she set out, they ate the fish Clara bought at the company store off English china.

"Did you know, the whole village of Angida on the Nass moved down river away from its poles?" Emily said. "They were full of holes from hunters using them as target practice."

"Awful what's happened," Clara said.

"And Kitwanga's a railway stop now. The poles that faced the river before are planted in cement at the train station now, for beastly tourists. They're coated in thick gray paint. All their carved details, all the faded colors, gone."

"Go back to Tanu," Clara said. "Go to Eagle clan side this time and see Crying Totem. Crying so hard over his dead sons that his eyes dropped out of their holes. Friends had to lift them back in so he could see to eat."

"How did they die?"

"Killed by Boston men from a trading ship."

"I'll look for it," Emily said.

· · ·

On the way south from Skidegate to Tanu a violent storm lashed the hired boat and they were lucky to make it ashore to Cumshewa, where William had held the sail over her so she could paint Raven in the rain. The sculpture was more ominous to her now. Sweeping tongues of foliage had grown in the sixteen years since she'd been here, and were licking at his pedestal, nearly engulfing the brooding bird—Nature reclaiming Raven, taking him to her bosom. It made her see that she wasn't painting just a totem, but the relationship between the totem and the land. She'd paint the scene differently now, more smoothly sculpted, as spare as Lawren's mountains.

Out from under a heavy blue-gray cloud, beams of light shone like layered gauze screens reaching down to earth. She felt a Mighty Being acknowledging her endurance, her return. She realized that she needed to have painted the first version sixteen years earlier in order to let go enough now to pare away detail. She'd had to exercise the traditional out of her so she could get to her own, more authentic personal expression, of Nature outlasting everything.

· · ·

On the Eagle clan side of Tanu she found Crying Totem. His strong, prominent nose, and his lips only a straight groove conveyed great dignity. It was the eyes that were startling. Eyeballs hung down to his waist on wooden sinews stretched in front of a dead frog he was holding. No, they weren't sinews, but rivers of tears pouring out his closed eye sockets. Hanging by streams of water, the eyeballs had been carved into faces.

The opposite of Kitwancool's proud and happy Totem Mother, this Tanu father cried with wrenching formality for his hapless sons. Whatever it meant to the Haida, to her, this Eagle father also cried for the smallpox dead at Raven House in Cumshewa. He cried for the Tsimshian dead of measles in the Skeena. He cried for every father's son sent to war. He cried for Sophie's children, and for Sophie. He cried for Haaydzims and Muldo and Tuuns, some Gitksan fathers' sons, for Harold, and for all the beaten, disfigured, lost. His tears shut no one out.

A heaviness descended on Emily as she began to paint the weeping figure. His streaming tears bleached blue-gray as death, with an advancing army of dark, coned trees in the background, backlit by portentous clouds pressing down to earth, weighted with tears yet unshed—all of it seemed an omen pulling her back home.

40: Sanderling

"You're home!" Harold said at the door when she opened it, handbag and jacket in hand. "I've been waiting and waiting."

"Dear Harold. Here, give me a terrific hug."

Awkwardly, he held his arms out until she stepped into them.

"I've got heaps to tell you, but I was just on my way to the ferry. Come in for a little while."

He went straight to Woo chained in her corner and lifted her onto his shoulder.

"Hey, did you come to see her or me?"

She loved his sheepish laugh.

"Did you go to Kispiox?"

"Two weeks on the Skeena and only one day of good weather, and it was in Kispiox. I felt you tramping beside me." She hunted through new watercolors and found one of Kispiox with tilted poles. "I think there were two dozen still standing. I did a fine one of Frog Woman I missed before. Do you remember that pole?"

He nodded. "Did you see Muldo and—"

"No. They're men now, like you, probably working in a new sawmill."

Better to get it over with. She told him of the gray weatherproofing paint at Kitwanga, the deterioration of poles, the missing ones. His crinkled forehead and eyes that could hardly contain their wetness alarmed her. She had to change directions.

"I made a suit of mosquito armor. Heavy canvas trousers that cinched in under my shoes and a head sack with a pane of glass to see through. Two pair of gloves, one of them leather, and those wicked mites even bit through that!"

His wistful laughter encouraged her.

"I was practically shipwrecked in a storm in Haida Gwaii, rescued by a Norwegian fishing boat in a rambunctious sea. Ooh, was I seasick! Still, I did thirty watercolors plus drawings. I'm thrilled purple. Some of my strongest, cleanest work. That loose work on paper I did at Goldstream liberated me."

"At our camp?"

"Your drumming in the woods helped me too. I'm all het up to paint."

He touched the edge of a Kitwanga watercolor study with Wolf on the midsection of a pole set tightly against a bighouse and filling much of the picture plane. She liked the intensity that this new close-up style gave. Harold's index finger stroked Wolf's snout.

"Will you give it to me?"

What would that do—to have Wolf staring back at him keeping alive those memories?

"I'm sorry, I can't now. I need it for reference for a big oil, but you can see it here whenever you want to. I'll do another just for you." She put on her jacket, feeling pulled in two directions. "Forgive me this skimpy time with you. Come back soon to see all the paintings. We'll have a good, long talk."

Harold trotted along with her as far as the ferry. She gave him a hearty hug. "You'll come soon?" He nodded, and stayed to wave from the dock, small waves, barely holding up his hand.

· · ·

Sophie's gate was nailed shut. The door was closed. There were no piles of basket-making supplies in the yard.

She knocked on Mrs. Johnson's door. "They're gone," Mrs. Johnson said. "Picking hops."

"Where?"

"Go back. Leave her be. For both your sakes." Something covert flickered in her lowered eyes. "I told you before, she's different than you think." The door closed against any more questions.

She walked along the mud flat wondering where she should go. Dozens of sanderlings all faced the water, each one above the shimmery blur of its reflection on the mud. When a wave retreated, they raced toward it in unison to snatch mollusks before the sand covered them up, then darted back on spindle legs at the next frothy onslaught. She loved their defiance of the relentless ocean, their dogged efforts to feed their incessant hunger.

She saw a woman ahead bending down in a few inches of water to pry a clam loose. Her skirt billowed. She was too wide to be Sophie. It was Margaret Dan.

As Emily approached, Margaret shooed away two children. "You come to see Sophie?"

"It's been a long time. She didn't write back after my last two letters."

"Sophie don't want to see you."

"Why? What happened?"

Margaret thrust in a narrow wooden digging spade and loosened some mud. "She lost her history. She was all the time whitelover and then she went to Cordova Street. She's one of those women now."

"What are you trying to tell me?"

Margaret pushed at clumps of mud with her bare toe and then drilled her with a cold stare. "She gone off too. All the time drinks." Blame erupted in Margaret's dark eyes, but also there appeared a satisfaction playing around her mouth that she was the one to tell her this news.

"What about Emmie?"

Margaret leaned back as if to get a better look at the effect of her words. "What you think?" She turned away and jabbed her stick into the mud.

Emily retreated through the frightened sanderlings making their fluty squeaks, ineffectual against the small waves of a passing gas boat. How could it be true—Sophie, barefoot, with dirty feet, standing outside the Cordova Street Cigar Store or Dawson's Tavern, halting and furtive, watching every man for a sign? It must be Margaret's envy of Sophie that made her make false accusations. Sophie's Aunt Sarah would tell her the truth.

At Sarah's doorway, she asked, "What's happened to Sophie?"

Sarah's silver eagle earrings trembled on her stretched earlobes. "Come." She stoked the wood burner and put the kettle on, moving with painful slowness. "She lost her way." Wrinkles waved across her forehead. She eased herself onto the wooden settee piled with quilts, and invited Emily to sit next to her. "She goes away, sometimes three, four days."

"Where?"

Sarah looked at Emily for only an instant. "Vancouver."

"Then it's true? What Margaret Dan said?"

"My own sister's daughter. I been with her when babies came and when they died. Now I don't have nothing to do with her." Sarah rubbed her cheek, digging her fingers into her wrinkles.

"Why?"

"Can't when they go off. Bad for the village. Bad for young girls to see good women turn. Sophie's sick in the belly too."

"If she's suffering then somebody should help her."

"Who? Mrs. Johnson don't talk to her. Mrs. Johnson don't trust her own no more on account of her white husband."

"But he's been dead for years."

"Strange what Mr. Johnson planted in her to make her like that. Margaret Dan goes to her sometimes, but mostly Sophie's alone."

"What if I asked a doctor to come see her?"

Sarah shook her head. "She's afraid of white doctor. She don't want him touch her."

"But . . ." She couldn't say it—white men had already touched her. Emily felt like she was coming apart.

"How long has this been going on? Maybe the twins weren't even Jimmy's."

"No. They his."

"Did Emmie die?"

Sarah nodded.

"She didn't tell me." Sarah's look made her feel foolish for expecting to be told. Emily stared at the glowing orange line around the door of the wood burner where it didn't fit. "She's had more dying than any woman should have to know."

"That's only part of it. She got tired making baskets and people don't buy them. Oh, she wants those Christian headstones. Talks about them till I sick to hear."

"That's why she—?" Numbness slid down her spine.

"Goes to Cordova Street. Money." The words cracked.

"How could she? Is it jealousy of Margaret's headstones?"

"No. She thinks God wants them." Sarah pushed herself up and went to the stove. "You make her into something high. She's only human. Like all of us."

Sophie, who she thought was invincible to pain and loss, as solid as cedar, was cracking, like a slow split down a totem pole.

Sarah put a few shriveled stems into two cups and poured in hot water. "Maybe in the old days, different."

The teacup rattled in the saucer as Sarah handed it to her. Emily watched the little brown shapes twist and sink, darkening the water in plumes. Little brown legs and arms.

"In the old days, families lived together in bighouses. Everything close. Old stories teach things. Now everything's broke up."

The tea tasted bitter and scorched her throat but Emily drank all of it. Out of curiosity, she asked, "What is this?"

"Horsetail. Good for old women," Sarah said. "Now days Indian women don't live long like me."

"How have you managed to?"

With wet eyes, her earrings jiggling, she said softly, "The old ways."

Emily held out her hand, palm up. Sarah was still a moment as if she didn't understand the gesture. Then, slowly, Sarah's hand, the skin like the surface of a walnut shell, came to rest in Emily's.

· · ·

She stumbled out of Sarah's house and followed the muddy path to the cemetery, empty except for the stones. She paused at each one. Maisie's stone, caked with lichen like dull brown lace. Tommy's, already a film of green scum in the indention of the cross. Casamin's, only an upright stick of wood, the crosspiece fallen in the dirt. Was the memory so distant that Sophie had forgotten her first child? And Molly's, still the same wooden cross that probably tortured Sophie with her inadequacy to keep up. Emily passed Annie Marie's before she recognized it and had to come back. A new stone, stark white against the earth, bore the inscription, *Annie Marie Frank In Loving Memory 1903–1911*, with a cross—Sophie's desire fulfilled. Emily knelt and picked off leaves.

She imagined Sophie's small, strong fingers stroking the cross. Annie Marie had watched those fingers, toughened by beargrass as sharp as blades, in order to learn the crossover knot. Would those fingers loosen the men's clothes as they had Annie Marie's dresses? Were the men's hands rough and insistent, or tender beyond all expectation, like Claude's? Or were they like Father's hand reaching between her own clamped-shut legs? The tightening, freezing shock, the instant closing of herself, shutting down all senses, all thoughts— did Sophie ever get over that, or did it happen every time with each new man? Out of love for Sophie, she didn't know which to wish for.

Sophie loved her too, she was sure of it, in a way different from what Margaret Dan meant when she called Sophie a white-lover, as though she, White Woman, had intensified Sophie's pathetic obsession. She gulped air and choked. No! Sophie's need to prove her Christianity was not for her. It was Sophie's own skewed religion, not their love, that drove her.

The church. The church was to blame. And that *nipniit* who preached there.

She strode toward St. Paul's Church with its twin steeples, twice as Christian as one. She passed the door, not wanting to go in and see that dirty red Sacred Heart, a misshapen beet. Ten paces later, she stopped, thinking that Sophie might be inside. Sophie, good and true, kneeling at the altar. She turned back. The heavy door creaked as she entered.

No one was inside. A few wilting asters and phlox drooped on the altar in a glass jar. She did not raise her eyes behind them to the painting, but looked to the side where the wooden Virgin sat serene, the Christ child on her lap. Mary had no wide Kitwancool smile, only a vague dreaminess. There in that figure was Sophie's religion—a worship of mothering.

She heard a tiny scraping noise. Against the wall, a lean rat hurried for a hiding place. She slammed her shoulder against the door on the way out, disgusted with the whole pathetic place.

The rectory next door was a worn box of a house little better than the others, the porch boards warped and loose. She knocked.

Father John answered, pencil in hand, liver spots on his balding head, his jacket coming unstitched at the shoulder.

"You know Sophie Frank," she said.

"Yes."

"Do you know what's happened to her?"

"Come in." He shuffled behind his writing desk and sat down wearily. His calmness infuriated her. "It's a sad case, not unique, though. I've laid six Frank babies in the earth."

"Six? Six, you say? There were half again as many."

"Those have no sanctity of the Holy Spirit."

"So they don't count? They were not brought forth with her blood and nourished from her breast and buried with her tears? They mean nothing?"

"The unbaptized have not been welcomed into God's family."

"God's family?" She clenched the fabric of her skirt in a fist. "Is it a requirement to have a hunk of stone carved with your precious cross in order to be welcomed into God's family?"

He winced. "No."

"How can you let something as beautiful as God become so distorted? Doesn't the Bible say God is not to be worshiped with things made by men's hands?"

"I never told her she had to erect headstones." He tapped the pencil against his thumb. "That's her idea."

"But how could you have allowed her to get such a twisted notion of Christianity?"

"Allow?" He peered over his glasses at her. "Allow?" A noisy puff of breath spewed out.

"Sophie works until her hands are raw to make baskets to turn into headstones, and when the baskets don't sell she sells herself. Is that what you're preaching?"

He glared at her. "Prostitution predated Christianity on this shore. To them, the only disgrace is when a woman doesn't get any business."

She felt the breath knocked out of her. Could Sophie really think that? Could they be that different, she and Sophie? Like Mrs. Johnson said?

"She's been desperate for money for another reason too," Father John said. "Jimmy Frank hasn't been working. Just drinking, both of them."

"Drinking out of despair because she can't keep up. How can you face her every Sunday knowing what you've done to her, making her think she has to sell herself? How can you look Jimmy Frank in the eye, not priest to parishioner but man to man?"

"Jimmy Frank knows," he said with tired boredom, stretching out his legs under the desk so that his slippers brushed her ankles.

"Knows?"

"More than knows. Jimmy Frank finds her the men and waits."

A great claw punctured her heart. "I— I don't believe it."

"Don't be so shocked. In the north, Kwakiutl women have prostituted themselves for generations so their men can afford to give potlatches."

"I don't give a hang about what they do up north. Jimmy Frank's a decent man."

He gave her a condescending look. "It's the way it's done. That's one reason potlatches are illegal."

She put her hands on his desk and leaned toward him. "Then you ought to make crosses and headstones illegal too. You ... you take an innocent people ... and clamp some absurd expectation on them ... something they can't possibly afford. No wonder they've lost their history."

"Innocent? What kind of imaginary Indian have you been believing in?"

She backed away from him, toward the door.

He folded his hands. "Human frailty is universal. Don't expect so much and you won't be disappointed."

"Your prejudice is speaking, not your Christianity."

41: Dogwood

A few days later a letter arrived, folded three times.

September's first day, 1927.

Dear Miss Emily Carr, Hailat.
I am in Wilkinson Road Mental Home in Royal Oak, near Saanich. Please come unless you are all het up painting. I can wait. I've been here before.
Love Mr. Harold Cook Swanaskxw. The end.

Scrawled below it was a disproportionate pencil drawing. Long skinny arms and legs, a tuft of hair, a curved tail. Woo.

What had he done to put him there? On his other hospital stays, he'd just disappear, then reappear without comment. There'd never been a letter. If she hadn't told him of the damaged poles, would this have happened? Or if she had taken him north? Or if she'd given him the Wolf painting?

She took Woo's hand, painted it with cadmium yellow, and pressed it on a small notebook. She gathered pencils, chocolate, and cigarettes, and took the streetcar.

Wilkinson Road Mental Home sat on a ridge in an area of small farms and wooded hillsides. Four octagonal towers and a stone crenelation across the brick façade made it look as imposing as an English castle. The sprawling building was set back beyond a circular drive and a sweep of lawn surrounded by Garry oaks, maples, firs, dogwood, and a spiked iron fence.

"I'd like to visit a patient," she said to the uniformed guard. He opened the iron gate for her to enter.

At the reception desk she asked to see Harold. A woman nodded to an attendant, a large man with a ring of keys on his belt. "A nice fellow, Harold," he said as he opened a padlocked door into a bleak visiting room edged with wooden chairs. "Wait here." His plump face didn't smile, but didn't seem unkind either. He left through another padlocked door.

In a few minutes Harold lurched into the room, stretching out his arms sideways like a crucifix. She held him to her breast. "Are you all right?" He gave a quick jerk of his head, his natural manner.

He swung around to ask the attendant, "Can I show her around? She's my friend."

The attendant led them up iron grated stairs to a locked ward lined with ten narrow iron beds, each with an identical gray blanket and flat pillow. The high barred windows didn't let in much light. The room was clean. That's all she could say for it.

Harold sidestepped between beds, slid his hand under his pillow, and held out *Leaves of Grass* to her, his face a torture of grooves.

"No, dear. You keep it. I'll get another copy."

"But this has your marks."

"That's fine. Then you'll know what I liked."

"Thank you thank you," he said, cuddling the book.

They sat on the bed and she gave him what she'd brought. He hid each thing under his mattress. When he saw Woo's handprint on the notebook, he imitated Woo's squeal.

The attendant looked questioningly at Emily. She explained, and then asked, "Would it be possible for us to go outside?"

"For a little while," he said.

Aspen leaves quaked, showing their silver undersides, and maple leaves rustled in a breeze. "Gorgeous, eh?" Emily said, taking Harold's arm. "Look at those dogwood blossoms!"

His jaw slack, Harold gaped at them as if they would speak.

"Don't they give comfort? How can we think that other things pressing in on our lives excuse us from gratitude?"

"One time here the leaves turned red," he said. "The sun all shining through them. I could see the veins. I thought they were salmon filets hanging in Kispiox."

"I think recognizing good must be the remedy for every woe."

He nodded hopefully.

When the attendant left a distance behind them, Emily asked, "Why are you here?"

A dreamy smile passed over his face. "I was dancing with Muldo and Haaydzims and Tuuns."

"Oh, Harold." She closed her eyes, pained, the image clear, Harold dancing his mad joy dance, beating the drum, leaping and lunging in wild ecstasy with his imaginary Indians.

Hers too. Father John had said as much.

"Where?"

"On the beach. I thought at night it wouldn't matter."

"With a campfire?"

He hung his head. "I tried to send you a smoke sign."

"Then what happened?"

"My sister, Ruth. People told her they saw me. That maybe I'll hurt myself."

She held his hand in both of hers. "How is it here?"

"Like an Indian school." He looked down at his feet.

"Can I do anything for you?"

"They took your tom-tom." Anguish edged his voice.

"Yours, Harold. I'll see if we can get it back."

"They shouldn't have tooken it."

"No, they shouldn't have."

All his features strained with the question of why.

"Sometimes people take what they're afraid of, or what they don't understand. Remember I told you they took the Raven mask at the potlatch? It's like that."

"The boys here are mean. They took some of *Harold Cook, a Canadian* and threw it in the toilet. I hide it now."

"Write it again. Do they let you write here?"

"Yes."

He led her inside to a janitor's closet and knelt in front of a wooden chair, his head down, his large feet turned in behind him, a position of prayer. "The man lets me do it here," he said and lifted the worn shoe box out of a crate of cleaning supplies.

"Your writing is brave and important. Don't ever stop."

He unwound the long string and lifted the lid off the box to show her the torn scraps. The handwriting was nearly illegible.

"Can you take it out of here? To a book-making place? So people will know about Muldo and Haaydzims and Tuuns?" He hugged her knees. "And Kispiox and Indian residential schools?"

"Keep it for now. Read it. It will make you feel better."

"Will you paint it? Kispiox? For me?"

"Of course. I'll bring it the next time I come."

"I was making a Wolf mask. Carving it like Muldo did."

"Where? Here?"

"At Goldstream. Out of a big branch on a tree that fell. The rain came and I didn't want the tom-tom wet and so I ran back to camp and there were your sisters. I looked for it every day after that. I needed to finish and chop it off. I got lost every time."

"Why didn't you tell me?"

"I wanted to surprise you." His voice cracked. His hands shook with urgency. "I wish I had it to scare the mean boys."

The attendant signaled that the time was up—or that he thought Harold's behavior was taking a dangerous turn. All the way to the gate Harold held on to her sleeve. She had to pry his fingers loose. She felt horrible doing it, as if her blood were going cold.

· · ·

Without supper, she climbed the attic stairs and lay under the Eagles. Harold is innocent, she cried. Although he did dance, his nature is innocent. Is Sophie innocent too? She wrestled for a way to make that true, and pulled the quilt over her head.

On the edge of sleep, transparent shapes swirled behind her closed lids. A gray rectangle, Harold's narrow bed. An upright rectangle with a smaller one on top, Harold, crashing through the forest looking for his Wolf carving, with Eagle making strong talk on his shoulder. A ragged brown rectangle, the shoe box tied with a string that trailed off all the way north up the Skeena to Kispiox. A red rectangle, a new Packard Roadster. Harold behind the wheel pulling up the circular drive to a brick house. The Ancestor leaning forward, a hood ornament. A silver rectangle, the grille shaped like a headstone. *In Loving Memory* in garish chrome script.

A woman stepping out from the midnight blue interior of the car, her chiffon dress of burgundy Sacred Hearts, as gossamer as the garment of a ghost. In spite of her high heeled shoes, it was Sophie—her dark hair bobbed, a nosegay of dogwood pinned to her dress. In her hands, an oblong coiled basket covered with a cloth.

Lizzie answering the door. The eagle feather on Sophie's hat trembling when she asks for Em'ly. Lizzie shaking her head no. Sophie saying she'll wait. Alice letting her in.

"So you're Emily's Indian?" Lizzie's voice prissy.

"I'm Em'ly's friend." Whitish bone earrings in the shape of headstones, a cross on each one, quaking like aspen leaves.

Dede gliding in, carrying Mother's silver tea service, asking if she would like a scone or a butterscotch tea cake.

Sophie reaching for one just as Dede pulls back the tray to offer the sweets to Lizzie. "Why do you persist in making baskets no one wants?"

"I have my reasons." Sophie stroking the top basket coil.

"I don't see how you can make a decent living that way."

"No, you don't see." Drawing her shoulders back. "I have something to leave for Em'ly." Sophie placing the basket on the sideboard. The cloth slipping a little to show a loaf of bread, plump and brown. "If Mr. Carr wants me, I'll be at Cordova Street, but tell him I won't take raisins for pay."

Sophie clomping out the door. The sisters crowding around the basket. Alice's left hand, her fingers intact, resting on it. The other raising the bread knife, a sword. Dede lifting the cloth. A naked brown girl baby gurgling up at them from the basket. Lizzie opening her Bible, reading that Mr. Luke Cook and Mrs. Martha Cook took their only begotten son to the sacrifice, and, blind to God's broad embrace, slew him. On his knees at the stone altar, Harold opening *Leaves of Grass,* then writing about his lost Wolf's mask, squeezing out a poem's worth of pain. Man, child, helper, son, lover treading a borderland, passing Sophie going the other way carrying a new headstone away from Cordova Street.

Her own throaty voice saying, My best friends, a white-lover and an Indian-lover, a prostitute and a lunatic. Well, that's just fine.

42: Hemlock

With a saw wrapped in her large canvas sketch sack, Emily scrambled over a tangle of branches on a downed log, and landed on the other side in a muddy muskeg. A raven uttered a hoarse, croaking laugh. She wiped the splash from her cheek and examined every branch, looking for what might have been the beginning of a Wolf carving. She found nothing.

She'd been searching for hours, was dizzy and exhausted from searching, but, out of love, she went on, feeling as though Harold were trotting beside her, desperate to find it. If she envisioned the spokes of a wheel coming out from their campsite, and if she walked every spoke, inspecting every fallen tree for something carved on a limb, she had to find it eventually. But how far from the campsite had Harold gone?

Goldstream wasn't Harold's illahee—quite. No patch of wilderness would serve him as Kispiox and the Skeena had. But for now, it was hers—her land that gives comfort. She liked the sound of the word. Illahee, a lovely chant, sighing like wind in upper branches. *Il-ah-ha-he-ye.* There was comfort here in the high *sweet-sweet* call and then trill of song sparrows. Here she could peel a scent off a cedar, suck it deep and pleasurably into her lungs.

Every direction she looked made her hungry to paint. She was nearing a breakthrough point. She could see cleanly now so many things about forests she wanted her paintings to say, but what if she stopped looking for Harold's Wolf half a dozen steps before she'd find it? She pressed on.

Arches of feathery lichen hanging from hemlocks like shredded veils teased her with phantasmagoric shapes. She heard a rustling, and froze. An indistinct form, possibly four-legged, slunk behind overlapping veils. A wolf? Or only the movement of foliage? Such a brooding forest did things to you, made you see shapes, imagine things, especially on a gray day like today. Still, it was possible that she might come upon a wolf devouring a raccoon that had devoured toads that had devoured mosquitoes. A riot of urges went on here. Why was such a forest called virgin, as if it were untouched? Nothing here was untouched.

Voluptuous curves of foliage coaxed her to enter deeper passages. She felt the pull of a viridian seduction. Lips of leafy drapery seemed shaped in folds and waves leading to purple openings to secret places, a womb in the forest where a fallen hemlock hosted a swarm of insects in its bark. Insects singing their mating songs, larvae, pupae, seeds celebrating their fecundity, cones opening, sap oozing, draped boughs undulating from trunks connecting earth to sky, everything vital, everything expressing a divine Spirit, God filling all space. A single swirl of energy—birth, growth, feeding, breeding, decay—all of it continuous Life, teeming with mystery, and she a part of it. She felt an incoming and an unfurling, a momentary mindlessness, a long-awaited union, a beautiful silent oneness, and she was left with an unutterable calm.

Somewhere near here, Harold's half-finished mask, the art of his impulse nurtured by her, would decay and become humus. A cone would lodge there, drop a seed, and the upward pulse of a slender sapling would squirm up through it, becoming, decades later, after she and Harold were both gone, a mighty thrusting column of live pulp tossing its foliage to the sky.

She leaned against a cedar, feeling that she was resting against the leg of God. She would come back here, to draw deep from the earth, to try to see with her inner eye what quality God was expressing of Himself in all things, including herself, to feel communion. When she could do that, maybe then she could paint. Do you like better to paint or to feel communion? They are the same. Art and Nature and God, all one, indistinguishable.

. . .

When she finished a large oil of Kispiox, she mounted the water-color study from which she'd worked onto a board, and took a frame off another painting for it. She found a plain brown carton with a lid, a little larger than Harold's shoe box, and painted Eagle on it, wings outspread, just as they were over her bed. With her artist's hammer and a nail in her handbag, she took the study and the box to the Wilkinson Road asylum, wishing only that she could bring him news that she'd found his carving.

"I want to give Harold Cook a painting," she told the director, "and I'd like it to hang where he can see it often."

The director's thin upper lip twitched. "We'll see," came the reply. "He's washing dishes from the noon meal now. You'll have to wait." He opened the visiting room for her.

"The act of viewing a painting can heal, you know."

The director cast a blank look at her, apparently unwilling to commit a syllable of response.

"How's he doing?" she asked.

"Fighting against the bars. Not uncommon."

"He wrote me that other patients call him Cookie and have taken to biting him."

"We have placed him separately, but that is only a temporary measure."

"Is he allowed outside?"

"Under supervision."

"And his writing?"

"That is permitted also, but I wouldn't call it writing. Gibberish only."

"Perhaps to those afraid to understand. Will he be allowed to leave?"

"If he drops the Indian."

"I see."

Just like an Indian residential school, as Harold had said. It crept into her craw something awful. If they can't imprison Indians, then they try to lock up Indianness.

In the visiting room she propped the painting at an angle the director couldn't see and sat down. Harold came in, saw it and fell on his knees, his eyes wet the way they got when he looked inward.

"It's for you, Harold. This box too."

Harold's gaze went from the painting to the box, then back again, and on his scarred face that never hid a single emotion, delight alternated with awe at the magnitude of the gift. His head dropped onto her lap and he hugged her legs. "I will look at it long and long."

She threaded her fingers through his blond hair, and they stayed like that for a long time.

· · ·

The director let them hang the painting above Harold's bed. Out of his professional smile leaked more smugness at his own magnanimity than pleasure in the act. Harold immediately remade his bed backward so he could lie in it and see the painting. The director objected.

"Perhaps this can be allowed as a temporary measure," Emily said.

When they were left with the key-toting attendant, Harold pulled out of his pocket her own letters to him and read them aloud. She wished she hadn't been so long-winded. He read about how Woo had peed in Lizzie's shoe, laughing wistfully, as though his joyful play with Woo were irretrievable to him now.

Harold led her to the janitor's closet, and the attendant unlocked it. Harold moved the mops and buckets out of the way, knelt before the chair on the cement, and reached behind the cleaning supplies for the shoe box.

"See how many I have now?" It was stuffed with pages. He handed her a small one. Unlike his note to her, she couldn't make out a single letter in the scratchings. She was losing him. She had found her fullest self through him, and now he was going on where she could not follow.

"Read one to me," she whispered.

"Harold Cook a Canadian. Haste on with me. I Harold Cook author of this book lived all seasons in the Skeena. In fall the river gets thin. Me Muldo Haaydzims and Tuuns we dig our toes into squishy mud on the bank then we dig in our feet and legs and lean back and forth and wave our arms like trees. In winter we don't go to our waab we're not allowed we have to add numbers and recite thou shalt nots. We look long and long out windows at white humps like half moons over children's graves. In spring we see dance laugh sing outside days longer and longer. The gold sun face peeks through green branches we try to climb away to touch it take some in our hands. In summer salmon come up the river shining all silver and smack against rocks. They get so tired but they don't stop they don't stop. We lie real still our hands in pools very still and we lucky catch them in our hands. Haaydzims ask Muldo what the salmon would be for the leaf and Muldo say they are what we are to the salmon but Tuuns say they would be silver spirits."

He had gone to the world of his own making and found his illahee. For him, where he knelt was holy ground.

"Beautiful, Harold. You are a poet."

"Please take it. Keep it safe." He offered her the shoe box.

"All right. Whenever you want it, I'll have it for you. Someday, somehow, memories, yours and mine, will serve. It's not our job to know how. In the meantime, you can use the bigger box."

His whole being, given to her, and lost to her. In his eyes, a flash of holy wildness. She prayed a moment, that it would live.

43: Wolf

After a solid week of exuberant painting for the new National Gallery show, Emily tore herself away from two unfinished canvases and took the evening ferry to Vancouver. She arrived in the morning and walked to Gastown, the Cordova and Water Street area, to look for Sophie. She didn't like being here, but she had to help her somehow. She peered into one saloon after another, Gassy Jack's, The Seven Seas, and Chinaboy's, which she suspected was an opium den. They were wedged between warehouses, hardware stores, tobacco shops, and seedy hotels left over from the gold rush, their window shades drawn down in the middle of the day.

Native women, some shockingly young, leaned in doorways and

murmured to the loggers, seamen, or longshoremen entering or leaving. Did Sophie know these women? Did she have to compete with them? A woman with braided hair wearing a red blouse glowered at her as if to say, What do you think you're looking at?

"Do you know where Sophie Frank might be?" Emily asked.

The woman turned away and went into a rooming house.

Emily caught a glimpse of a plaid skirt with black bands around the bottom, like Sophie's. The woman followed a man around a corner into a narrow mews. Emily hurried after, but when she looked down the lane, no one was there. She'd come here to tell her, as a blood sister would, that she didn't have to do this, to pull her away, stuff money into her pocket, and take her to a stone carver. But what would that do to Sophie, to be discovered like this, coming out of a bawdy house with a man, or standing by a gambling hall, hope brightening her pleading eyes as she offered herself quietly to each man who passed?

She waited on the corner where the mews opened onto Cordova Street, the only way in or out, until she began to feel as though she were trapping her. What was she thinking of! This would not be kind. A blood sister could do it, march right in and yank her away, but she was not blood to Sophie. No matter how close she thought they were, there was that wall. It was a wrongheaded thing to do. She went back to the dock to wait for the next ferry home.

· · ·

She stood on the deck where she always did in good weather. It was cool now in early fall, and the sea was frisky. She buttoned her coat.

Fall was gathering time for Sophie. Basket-making season was just ahead. Did Sophie even make baskets any more? What if she asked her to? Not just one basket, but many? They'd make splendid gifts. They were products of soil and rain, of grasses and roots stitched with her tears to build a vessel for some holy thing like berries or clams or water, these baskets that would buy Sophie's dead children salvation. Certainly Harold and Alice and Lizzie and Jessica should get one. And Marius. Imagine, Sophie's work owned by someone at the National Museum. Dr. Newcombe, Marius, Lawren, and Eric Brown would appreciate them. They might even want to buy more. How many could Sophie make in the next two months if she worked every day? Enough to keep her from Cordova Street?

When she opened the door to her studio late that afternoon, Joseph squawked his outrage at being abandoned, Woo jumped on her when she came close to feed her, and *Totem Mother, Kitwancool* leered at her from the wall, disfigured by a grotesque, wicked grin. It wasn't a wicked grin that she'd meant when she painted her. It was a loving smile that had suggested Sophie's smile to her. Now, *Totem Mother* seemed transformed into a travesty of love debased.

Emily sat down and wrote to Sophie, asking her to make as many as she could, saying that she wanted to buy them all for Christmas gifts, that she'd come for them the second Sunday in December.

• • •

The first gentle snowfall of December had turned unusually foul. On the passage across Burrard Inlet, Arctic wind spiraled into Emily's ears, whistling cold fears that Sophie would be different. She'd find her drunk. She'd find her distant, icy, hardened. Gastown would have scraped her raw and left her scarred. In North Vancouver, granules of snow swirling upward stung her cheeks. She braced herself against the lingering heave of the sea and the unsteadiness of wavering expectations.

Through the snow, houses and derelict boats paled into shades of dirty white and gray. Life seemed to be hibernating. There were no birds, no dogs, no piles of supplies blanketed in white in Sophie's yard. It was as flat as a plate. She saw Sophie sitting at the window where she'd tucked back the gingham curtains to watch for her. Emily let herself in and closed the door behind her. Sophie sat in the pine armchair Jimmy had made, wearing her old wool Cowichan sweater, a blanket over her lap, a just-started basket in her hands.

"Oh, Em'ly. I'm not finished." She lifted the coiled spiral trailing loose ends. "I'm making one more for you now."

"We're never finished."

Sophie struggled to get up, and shook out her leg, motioning for Emily to sit there. She chuckled. "Sometimes my legs go deaf." She pointed to a logging company calendar on the wall with the second Sunday in December marked with an *E*. "See? I knew you'd come today."

Her smile was still as broad as the Kitwancool totem mother's, as loving and pure as it had always been, but the colors had changed. Her skin was yellow ochre, leached of reds, the color of thick phlegm or urine or jaundice. Even her eyes were sallow. The pupils swam in yellow bile.

"Are you all right, Sophie? Have you been sick?"

Sophie shrugged and tipped her head, jiggling her tiny basket earrings, her art diminished to a bauble. "Life isn't always, you know."

"I can take you to a doctor. I'll stay with you and make sure . . ."

Sophie shook her head with such force that her cheeks wiggled. She put more wood in the wood burner and filled the teakettle. "I have baskets for you." She stretched her arm toward the maroon baby carriage filled with them.

There were only a few, not nearly as many as in the past by this time of year. Disappointment bore down on her. Only five. Five wouldn't give Sophie a dog's chance of catching up completely. She looked inside the lidded ones to see if smaller ones were hidden. Sophie had liked to do that whenever she was carrying a child, the outer and inner baskets alike. None. Maybe it was sickness that made her make so few. She picked one up. They were smaller than her usual work, only two hand spans across instead of three.

"They're fine and beautiful, as always."

The one with Eagle would be for Harold. Eagle, who saw far, even into the future, to a time when people would learn from *Harold Cook a Canadian.*

"You have some new designs."

"Margaret says I'm wrong to make them my own way, not the old ways."

"There's no law, Sophie. Make what you like. Let me guess this one." It was a geometric stylization of a beaked head and enlarged feathers. "Raven." She pointed to the back of the basket. "Why is he different here?" The same beaked head was on a different-shaped body on the back.

"You know Raven. Always changing himself so he can steal things from people."

"Ah." Its intricacy made it spectacular. This would be for Marius. "It must have been difficult. You had to plan the two shapes differently but work them coil by coil at the same time." She ran her hand over the bird who stole for sport. "What's it made of? I'm giving it to a man who studies native art. He would be interested."

"Studies? Humph. What's to study? You just use it."

"Sophie, there were baskets at that exhibit in Ottawa, and none of them were nearly as good as yours. I want those men to see yours."

Sophie scowled at the Raven basket, and moved her shoulders in circles, as if she were uncomfortable with the idea.

"You're an artist, Sophie. That's what you've always been, and what you'll always be."

Sophie's face became lined with doubt. Her grape-colored mouth was incapable of stopping the quivers that passed over it.

"Vancouver isn't the only place to sell baskets," Emily said.

Sophie's gaze went from basket to basket.

"Tell him beargrass and cherry bark over cedar root. The beargrass is all black because I buried it once and then forgot about it for a year." She laughed. "But it was still there."

The old Sophie, amused by her own foibles.

Emily picked up another basket. Animals with pointed snouts and tails chased each other around the surface. "What's this?"

"Wolf. Made out of horsetail root. We've had wolves on the reserve come down from the mountains."

"Then I'll give it to a Toronto artist who paints the north. Lawren Harris is his name. He'll love it."

One flared basket had a reddish horizontal line running around it with half circles resting on it at intervals. She picked it up and looked at Sophie for an explanation.

"Sunsets, where dead babies go. Mothers too, if they're good. It's like heaven."

If Sophie still had hopes for heaven, then she didn't feel the disgrace of sin, just as Father John had said. And if that was so, the casualness of her prostitution was distressing and made her feel a heartsickening gulf of difference between them.

Sophie hadn't mentioned Emmie. Maybe she'd worn herself out with mourning. Emily turned the basket in her hands, counting ten sunsets, nine for her babies, one for her, the basket hopeful of a reunion. Summoning hope from some deep wellspring after each baby's loss had been the amazing thing about Sophie. It still was. Sophie's face glowed golden, her smile momentarily young.

"I want to give one to you," Sophie said.

"Which one?"

Sophie pulled her mouth to one side and thought, then held up the unfinished one. "This one. Now you have to come back."

They were silenced by a wolf's howl, a hollow yawp tearing the air that made the world stop for a moment.

"We hear them all the time now. Not much rain this fall until snow today. Deer come down from the mountains to drink from the puddle by our tap. Now wolves come too."

The howl cut the air again, a chill keening that brought the wilderness close, just outside the door.

"Last week Margaret Dan's daughter Shaula had a baby, and a wolf ate the afterbirth that fell out of a tree."

Emily remembered Shaula as a little girl who had played with Annie Marie. For an instant, she imagined Annie Marie a young woman now, a mother herself.

"That's horrible, Sophie."

"Wolves have to eat too."

"How do you know for sure it was a wolf?"

"Frank saw it, and the cloth all torn and wet."

"Did he do that with your babies? Put it in a tree?"

"Some of them. Casamin and Maisie and Tommy. I don't know which ones afterwards."

She shouldn't have asked. A slackness passed over Sophie's face.

"It's so when the tree grows, so will the baby. Strong and straight." Sophie paused to consider something, and shot a look at Emily. "That's not why they died—him not doing it for every baby."

Emily sensed a mounting danger in that subject.

"It wasn't anything Indian. I never looked at anyone sick when I was carrying. Never looked at a dead person or a rabbit. I never cried out when a baby was coming."

Sophie was relentless in charging down that road of thought. With every coil worked on these baskets she must have been working up to tell her something.

"It's not an Indian reason."

Sophie wrapped a rag around the kettle handle and poured warm water into a basin to wash her hands, as if clean hands were necessary for what she had to say. She moistened her lips.

"They died because the first twins came before we were married in the church." Anguish tightened Sophie's face in a way Emily had never seen before, a fear of judgment conquered when the words were said.

Sophie dried her hands on her skirt and glanced at her collection of shells on the window ledge. Her eyes were shiny dark stones of yearning in an arsenic yellow wash.

"Father John said we're punished for our sins. We had our Squamish marriage, but Father John doesn't believe in that because he say God wasn't there."

Margaret Dan had judged Sophie and made that condemnation public. Even Aunt Sarah had judged her, abandoned her, in fact. If Sophie saw her, Emily, as disapproving right now, it would crack the solidness they shared. For Sophie not to see judgment in her eyes, there had to be none in her heart, not a speck. She searched, and found only ache.

"The marriage you had is all you need. The blessing of Father John can't make your babies live or die."

A wolf howled again, a stretched rope of a sound.

She realized with a pang—she had just wiped away Sophie's reason for the children's deaths. The question of Why, then? gaped before them both. A hunk of wood shifting in the wood burner startled them.

"Margaret Dan said you came and I wasn't here."

Emily wasn't going to bring it up. She didn't want to hear how Sophie would explain where she'd been. Sophie wouldn't lie to her, would she? She didn't want Sophie to lie, but she didn't want her to tell the truth either.

"I missed you," Emily said.

"I missed you too." Sophie crouched to open the wood burner and put in another wedge of wood.

Sophie turned toward her, kneeling. "I know you know about what I do. Margaret said she told you." Emily shook her head and Sophie held out a chafed, sallow hand to silence her. "It's worth it, Em'ly. For the babies."

With the orange glow of the fire silhouetting Sophie's face, Emily saw in her eyes glazed with moisture how she must have suffered in giving the ultimate of love for each child, how she'd sacrificed her own soul for her children's. It hadn't been a casual decision. Emily knelt with her by the wood burner and enfolded her, and for once, Sophie didn't pull away. Emily felt a tightness in her stomach letting go, a sloughing off, like a cramp releasing. She understood obsession. She accepted all.

They drank mint tea and Emily told her of her trailer at Goldstream and of painting only the forest now, in darker shades. "Like you told me the first time we met. I should have listened. Some things it takes me a long time to learn," she said.

"Me too."

She knew it would insult Sophie to give her all the money she'd brought, regardless of there being only five baskets, so she lined them up on the floor and asked how much.

With her foot, Sophie moved them from right to left, adding. "Fourteen dollars." While Emily counted out the bills, Sophie watched, eagle-eyed, as if knowing she wished to slip her more.

Emily looked down at the bills still in her hand. "May I pay for Emmie's stone?" The question quiet, unable to be held. "I feel like her auntie."

Both of Sophie's hands went up to press against her mouth, and she uttered a sweet soft cry in one high note. She nodded. "Emmie's Love Ancestor."

Emily slid the rest of the money she'd brought under the bills she'd already laid on the table.

"You want some salmonberry cake? I made some for you to take to your sisters. I bet they never ate it before."

Emily smiled at the thought. She liked the chewy substance like dried jam that she'd eaten with Sophie many times. "No, I'm sure they haven't."

"Salmonberries good this year. No worms."

"Thank you, Sophie. We'll have it for Christmas. Indian fruitcake. It's a good share."

Emily noticed the unfinished coil of roots on the floor. "Get that basket done, Sophie. I'm coming back."

44: Alder

"There's a *Colonist* review of the Women's Canadian Club exhibit if you want to see what they think of your kid sister in this town," Emily said, pointing with her paring knife as she peeled a potato. It was Lizzie's birthday and she was fixing supper for them in her studio.

Alice picked up the clipping. "You read it, Lizzie. The print's too small for me."

"*Nationally Recognized Local Artist's Work Bewildering,*" Lizzie said. "The same old story."

"I want you to read every word," Alice said.

Emily heard Lizzie's labored intake of breath above the faucet running.

"*Emily Carr's work at the National Gallery in Ottawa last March prompted Director Eric Brown to declare her conception of art as big as Canada itself, adding that if she lived in Europe she would be acclaimed among the greatest artists of her day.*"

"Wonderful, Millie. What good luck," Alice said.

"Luck? Luck?" She shaved the potato with quick swipes. "Funny how the more I practice, the luckier I get."

"*Nevertheless, Miss Carr's saturation with the barbaric efforts of the aborigine, as seen in several paintings in the Women's Canadian Club show here, makes us wonder what would have been her artistic career had she remained in England where she was born.*"

Alice pushed out an exasperated grunt. "Well, you can't trust a reviewer who doesn't even get his facts straight."

Lizzie continued.

"*Residence among aboriginal races, whether in Africa or India or Australia, has tended to make the English resemble those with whom they have been in contact.*"

"Why, that's horrid," Alice said. "Aren't you angry?"

"No! This one said something more intelligent than he realized." Emily waited for a reaction. Nothing. "On that pile of papers on the mantel is a review of the *new* National Gallery show from the *Ottawa Citizen*. Read the fourth paragraph."

Alice looked at the photograph of *Indian Church* printed in the article and handed it to Lizzie. Emily turned to face her. She knew it would spark a reaction, and she didn't want to miss one twitch of it.

"Emily Carr from British Columbia is at her best when working on a big scale. Her inspiration is derived from the forest which she opens to us with the intimacy of a lover to probe its inner recesses. Her trees are menacing phallic giants, their foliage dark feminine openings.

"Millie, how could you want us to read this . . . this trash?" Lizzie's voice rose to a squeak.

Lizzie's moral brown eyes darted from Alice to her, and the thin blue skin under them tightened. Poor, dear Lizzie, Emily thought. Even if she explained, Lizzie could never understand how she had experienced a sort of consummation in the wilderness, or how she could make love to the universe by painting. It would mystify her because her God had not blessed her with an imaginative mind.

"Frubbish. One man's opinion. My trees aren't menacing. Go on." She turned back and smiled into the sink.

"Her totems celebrate native spirituality and her strikingly vivid Indian Church *is one of the most interesting paintings in the exhibition. She is as possessed with the creative urge as that powerful and tragic figure of the last century, Vincent van Gogh."*

"Pish and splutter," Emily said. "Poor van Gogh."

"I hope this won't make you unbearable," Lizzie said.

She pared more recklessly. "When that plumber came to fix this sink and saw the paintings, he said they made him love Canada more. That meant heaps more than a review."

"Well, I like *Indian Church*," Alice said. "It looks so thin and lonely out there under the trees."

"Lawren Harris of the Group of Seven bought it. Now didn't that send me into a drunken spin."

She wondered if Lawren ever yearned for compliments. Maybe it was the nature of artists to crave praise. *Something* had to feed the inner person for the lifetime labor of bringing a person's work to maturity. The trick was to keep praise from hurting that work, and to keep on seeking.

"Well, it's all yammering anyway. It's your own reckoning you have to go to bed with. You can't make a shroud out of reviews."

. . .

Emily stretched and primed eight canvases for the Toronto Society of Artists Annual Exhibition. The submission date was only a month away. Every day had to count. She took a load of paint rags downstairs to wash, and heard the mailman whistling.

"Only one today," he said, and handed her a letter.

Her fingers trembled, ripping the flap. It was from Jimmy Frank.

Dear Emily,

I have to tell you the sad news that Sophie died a few weeks ago. I'm sorry I didn't write you sooner. Margaret and Sarah tried to help her toward the end but she got sicker and sicker coughing up all the time and not wanting to eat because her stomach was all blowed up. As for me, I'm going up to Squamish to live with my brother. It's too sad for me here. Only memories and hard to keep away from drink. I hope you are well. Sophie loved you like a sister.

Jimmy Frank

A scream boiled up in her tight, bruised throat and lodged there, clotted. She dragged herself upstairs and looked at Sophie's portrait, her Fauve skin raw sienna, red earth, Prussian green, violet—every color but the jaundiced yellow she'd seen the last time. She imagined Sophie swirling in some pale sunset, welcomed by her children, all of them unnoticed by the world. Not a ripple.

What could she do? Send money for a headstone? And what should it say? In Loving Memory of Sophie Frank—Mother, Basketmaker, Christian—Worn Away by Dogma?

Like a sister. Yet she hadn't written to ask her to be with her at the end.

. . .

Alice stood at Emily's doorway holding a picnic hamper. "You haven't painted a dab for two weeks since you got that letter," she said with a touch of judgment. "It's Saturday. I'll go wherever you want, just so you paint."

Listless, Emily looked at her brushes, alien things, and then at Alice, standing resolutely. "Does it mean a bean to you if I paint or not?"

"Of course it does. I'll pay for the streetcar. Get your paints."

Emily chose a logged-off hillside near Langford. They stepped between stalks of dark pink fireweed, their capsules releasing seeds with tufts of hairs that made them airborne. She blew them away from her face, opened her camp stool, and sat absolutely still, waiting. Alice sat a ways off, crocheting.

The sweep of hillside had been mutilated. In a day, virgin forest had been ravished, five-, six-hundred-year old trees hacked off indecently, their stumps horrific headstones. Some splinters were left upright where the trunks had wrenched and come apart. Screamers, she called them, imagining the gunshot crack of the great trees splitting, that awful final sway, the thunderous groan, the crashing down, the executioners with saws and axes stepping back to brace themselves for the answering tremble of the ground. It was a graveyard left exposed to heal itself with the help of seeds and wind and rain and time, daring to grow just to be ravaged again in some dim future. The short new alders, the first trees to come alive again, spread their toothed leaves above Juneberry shrubs and mangled stumps, preparing the way for cedars and firs to follow. Whitman's words came ringing: *The smallest sprout shows there is really no death.*

One spindly virgin fir, bare of branches for most of its height, a hundred times taller than the new growth fringing its base, had been spared. Forsaken rather. It would yield no income. It stood alone, its brothers and sisters maimed and felled. Its far feathery top danced in the wind, as mad and joyful as any of Harold's dancing.

That's what she would paint—pure Spirit frolicking alone in wind song. The far-flung branches, the clouds, her loaded brush, her arm, all swaying as one. Movement the primal, healing thing.

She painted, hardly speaking to Alice all afternoon, but feeling her quiet solicitude. She came to a stopping point, and showed her the painting. "I'm going to call it *Scorned as Timber, Beloved of the Sky.*"

Alice's eyes shone. "Perfect."

When they finished their picnic, Emily said, "Let's stop at Ross Bay on the way home."

Alice straightened up suddenly. "The cemetery?"

. . .

They walked down wide avenues of pines and maples past obelisks, headstones, and plaques, to the Carr graves in a rectangular plot. No tangled vines crept across the single plaque, no stray ferns, no wild camas. Only pine needles and some cones.

"Why did you want to come here after all these years?"

"To see what I'd feel at a sister's grave. I think I understand now how you felt in France. Helpless and bewildered. Thinking that if you'd been here, or done this or that, it wouldn't have happened."

"It took Sophie's death for you to figure that out?"

"Yes." She set down her painting things. "Dede would probably hate to recognize this, but she had something in common with an Indian. In different ways, she and Sophie both played the parent to their last dying breath. Both of them suffered awful loneliness at the end. It's that lonesomeness of death that's killing, even before the final moment."

"Final? Is that what you think?"

"No. I meant the final moment here."

"You're grieving more about Sophie's death than you ever did about your own sister's."

"Dede and I had no similar loves or aims, like Sophie and I shared." She sighed. "*A good share,* Sophie used to say."

"We all have to make do with what we're given," Alice said, an edge to her voice.

"Yes, that's what you did, make do—even with your younger sister and all her orneriness."

"And the more ornery you got in doing what you wanted, the more rigidly Dede became a model of uprightness."

"Righteousness, you mean. Petrified in self-righteousness."

"That's uncharitable of you. You've never been able to forgive her?"

"I guess not. I know it's peevish. I've felt compassion though."

"Well, that's a start. Stubbornness is a bitter herb, Millie."

"I know," she said softly. "I used to think it was an accident that we were all born into the same family, but no. Nothing is accidental. Maybe rubbing our sandpaper selves against each other has been good, has worn down some rough spots to make us smoother."

"One would hope."

"Maybe in later lives we'll all be sorted out not in physical families, but in soul families."

She stepped back, leaving the needles and cones as they had fallen.

· · ·

Still needing peace, a few days later she strolled among red alders and cottonwoods and cedars, touching their trunks, smelling their aromatic fibers. She followed Goldstream River all the way through the forest to the narrow muskeg by the sea's deep inlet. The arrow grass in the mud bent over in curves, Whitman's *beautiful uncut hair of graves.* Sophie would have understood him.

Emily took off her shoes and paddled her feet in the soft mud at the water's edge. She dug her toes down into shiny raw umber ooze, cool and smooth, until her feet were buried. It was a sort of earth salve, like Sophie's *tamalth.* The stillness in the air settled her. She wiggled her feet down farther, watching wavelets lap at her ankles, feeling anchored like that tall, lone tree at Langford.

Looking back at the forest edge, she noticed a cedar elevated with its exposed roots wrapped around nothing but air, as if standing on its toes. A century ago a seed must have lodged in a fallen log and sprouted. Nourished by that fallen tree, its roots had grown around the nurse log, now decayed and gone. How silently the forest tells stories. How deeply she had grown from Sophie's nourishment.

It wasn't only disease-prone Indian children who died. No one was spared the sharpness of being cut off right when the very next thing one was going to do was what one had intended all along. The old fear that skill and wisdom come too late hammered at her temples. Her own time was running out. She might learn her spirit song too late to sing it.

Whenever it came, she would sing it in paint. She would paint Sophie's life as burnt sienna tree stumps against waves of new growth. Paint her as a white Indian church against towering, dark emerald trees. Paint Harold as an eagle soaring, not needing feet. Paint Dede's sense of duty as a crow cawing, Lizzie's moral life as a single, straight-ribbed fir, Alice's effort to understand as the soft, embracing arm of a hemlock, lichen-draped as a familiar shawl. Paint herself as a sea-tossed drift log beached in an unknown cove, a solid, corsetless mountain, a solitary tree doing a mad joy dance.

She lifted her skirt and squirmed down farther, the incoming tide loosening the earth for her. Mud up to her calves, she leaned forward and back, the earth securing her as it always had. She tied up her skirt around her hips and leaned farther, the movement planting her deeper, the danger enticing, her body reeling like a sapling in a storm. She raised her arms and let them sway like feathered boughs.

A hermit thrush spilled one long crystalline note, stilling all the earth to listen, and then poured out an ethereal flute song, over too soon. She closed her eyes, waited. Again, that purest of tones, long-held, chillingly beautiful, and then the cascade of melody like a tumbling stream. A spirit song. For her.

If she could sing like that thrush, what would she sing?

She would sing the forest eternal. She would place her body in the womb of trees. She would bleed into the earth. She would place her bare feet onto moss and spiced pine needles, peat and mud, and up between her toes and through her pores would ooze the rich dark syrup of Mother Earth, and over her ankles would swarm tiny insects, and around her shoulders would float the exquisite flowing drapery of her green hemlock cape. She would take great gulps from slender bars of silver light, forest-filtered, like incandescent strands of old women's hair. She would bow to the sturdy white pine, the brave, pioneering alder, the cooling Sitka spruce, the mighty Douglas-fir, the sorrowing hemlock, the sheltering maple, her beloved cedar. She would bow to the Wild Cedar Woman who dwells in the forest. She would hold her wooden hand, sing her wild *huu, huu,* and put herself back together again and again. She would drink the forest liquids and drench herself in possibility.

Author's Afterword

In paint and words, Emily Carr casts a tall shadow, one which has accompanied me in western forests ever since I made her acquaintance in 1981 in the Emily Carr Gallery, once her father's warehouse in Victoria. After years of research and ruminations, she is a mix to me now of what I've read about her, what she has written, both private and public, and what I have written of her. In reaching for the essence of her painting subjects, she wrote, "There is something bigger than fact: the underlying spirit." As she wanted to paint the spirit of a thing, so have I wanted to offer the spirit of her courageous and extraordinary life.

When reading a novel treating a real life, it is wise to consider it speculative fiction presenting what could have happened. That Emily altered facts and chronology of her life to suit a story and to formulate a myth of herself permitted me to take certain liberties for the sake of the narrative.

Some of the characters are inventions, or derivations of actual people. Sophie Frank is not. However, in truth she did not lose nine children. She lost twenty-one. Children's graves bearing the Frank name are still scattered in the Mission Reserve cemetery in North Vancouver. I've walked through brambles in the drizzle to find them. Her first child was born in 1892 when Sophie was thirteen. A boy named Casimir lived the longest, ten years. One baby named Emily was born and died in 1914. Sophie's grave is marked 1879–1939. Jimmy's is 1873–1952.

Though one might wish for Emily to have had an experience like the one I invented with Claude du Bois, there is no evidence for such a one. Jessica represents friendships Emily surely had with women, although she frequently complained of loneliness. The real New Zealand painter Frances Hodgkins does not appear in Carr's journals. Biographers report that Emily mentioned a nameless woman with whom she studied at Concarneau, mistaking her nationality for Australian. Though Hodgkins kept a more-than-weekly correspondence with her relatives, not a single letter appears during the six weeks that Emily was studying with her. André Laffont is an invention; Harry Phelan Gibb and John Duncan Fergusson were her actual teachers in France. Little is known of Harold Cook, who is an extension of a real missionary's son whom Emily met in Kispiox and visited in an asylum, and who was writing an autobiography. No records of it remain. The chronology of her trips, paintings, reviews, and Dede's and Sophie's deaths is approximated to fit the needs of pacing the narrative.

Current practice demands different terms than what I've used in some places: First Nations people for Indians, Kwakwaka'wakw for Kwakiutl, Nuu'chah'nulth for Nootka. With apologies to those who may object, I have used the terms reflective of Emily's language, time, and perspective as one of the settler society. Emily was painfully conscious of the thin line between appreciation and appropriation. Like her, I hope I have come down on the right side of this line.

This book is not a life; it is a story. I like to imagine the real Emily Carr peering through dense foliage at us, secretly satisfied yet amused by all the spit and sputter.

• • •

Although my experiences with Emily started in that warehouse gallery on Wharf Street in Victoria, my fascination with her soon led me to the Emily Carr House on Government Street where she was born, and to her beloved Beacon Hill Park. After years of reading works by and about her, I realized that my feelings for her ran too deep to go unexpressed, so I set out with my husband to trace her footsteps in preparation to write a novel.

In 1989, after seeing her astonishing paintings at the Vancouver Art Gallery, we sailed through the Queen Charlotte Islands where we walked among ruins in Tanu, Skedans, Cumshewa, and Ninstiints, a UNESCO World Cultural Heritage Site with two dozen poles, erect, leaning, and fallen. They would have thrilled Emily had she been able to go to Ninstiints on the extreme southern point of the archipelago. At Tanu, two Haida women, mother and daughter, kept watch over the single remaining totem pole, fallen and encrusted with lichen. Serving us tea and bannock bread with jam, they related the sad tale of the decline of their ancestral home.

In 1992, we paddled our way in a kayak to Mimkwamlis on Village Island, where a few beams of a longhouse spoke of the fine potlatches there. Pieces of two rotting poles covered with moss remained from those Emily had seen. Thomas Sewid, the Mamalilikala watchman, invited us to visit his grandmother, the late Flora Sewid, wife of the Kwakwaka'wakw Chief Jimmy Sewid. Graciously, she recalled for us her memories of Emily at potlatches, played her drum, and sang. At the U'mista Cultural Centre in Alert Bay, we listened to a young Kwakwaka'wakw girl spin the story of Dzunukwa.

In the British Columbia Archives, I held in my hands Emily's worn copies of *Leaves of Grass* with her penciled underlinings, and felt ineffably close to her. To skeptical minds in the twenty-first century, some of her thinking might seem rhapsodically romantic, and her pantheism a late bloom from the nineteenth century tree of Transcendentalism. Nevertheless, both have appealed to me, and sent me to forests in her spiritual wake. Even now, discovering some new fact about her, or imagining her, after two heart attacks and a stroke, pushing herself around on the butter crate scoot box she'd made in order to have the mobility to keep painting, I'm deeply moved.

A few years before her death in 1945 at age seventy-four, she was asked what had been the outstanding events of her life. She responded, "Work and more work! . . . loving everything terrifically. . . . The outstanding event to me is the doing—which I am still at. Don't pickle me away as a done."

Illustration Credits

Part I
Emily Carr, *Indian Village,* Sechelt, British Columbia, watercolor. British Columbia Archives, PDP 00648

Part II
Emily Carr, *Crécy-en-Brie,* watercolor, 1911, British Columbia Archives, PDP 04682

Part III
Emily Carr, *Totem Mother, Kitwancool,* oil on canvas, 1928, 109.5 × 60.0 cm, Vancouver Art Gallery, Emily Carr Trust, VAG 42.3.20 (Photo: Trevor Mills)

Part IV
Emily Carr, *Big Raven,* oil on canvas, 1931, 87.0 × 114.0 cm, Vancouver Art Gallery, Emily Carr Trust, VAG 42.3.11 (Photo: Trevor Mills)

Part V
Emily Carr, *Tree Trunk,* oil on canvas, 1930, 129.1 × 56.3 cm, Vancouver Art Gallery, Emily Carr Trust, VAG 42.3.2 (Photo: Trevor Mills)

TRIBES
of
BRITISH
COLUMBIA
and
SOUTHERN
ALASKA

YUKON

BRITISH COLUMBIA

Kispiox
Kitsegukla
Kitwancool
Kitwanga
GITKSAN
Angidah
Nass River
Skeena River

NISGA'A

Ketchikan

Prince
Rupert

COAST TSIMSHIAN

Yan Masset

COAST MOUNTAINS
CANADA
U.S.A.

PRINCE OF WALES
ISLAND

ALASKA

Juneau

Sitka

TLINGIT

Skagway